The Myth of Quetzalcoatl

# THE Myth OF Quetzalcoatl

Religion, Rulership, and History in the Nahua World

Alfredo López Austin

Translated by Russ Davidson
with Guilhem Olivier

UNIVERSITY PRESS OF COLORADO
*Boulder*

© 2015 by University Press of Colorado

Published by University Press of Colorado
5589 Arapahoe Avenue, Suite 206C
Boulder, Colorado 80303

All rights reserved

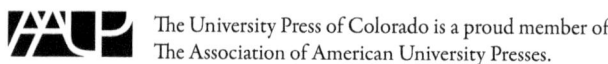 The University Press of Colorado is a proud member of
The Association of American University Presses.

The University Press of Colorado is a cooperative publishing enterprise supported, in part, by Adams State University, Colorado State University, Fort Lewis College, Metropolitan State University of Denver, Regis University, University of Colorado, University of Northern Colorado, Utah State University, and Western State Colorado University.

ISBN: 978-1-60732-390-7 (paper)
ISBN: 978-1-60732-399-0 (ebook)

Library of Congress Cataloging-in-Publication Data

López Austin, Alfredo.
 [Hombre-dios. English]
 The myth of Quetzalcoatl : religion, rulership, and history in the Nahua world / Alfredo López Austin ; translated by Russ Davidson with Guilhem Olivier.
    pages cm
  Summary: "The Myth of Quetzalcoatl is a translation of Alfredo López Austin's 1973 book Hombre-Dios: Religión y política en el mundo náhuatl. Despite its pervasive and lasting influence on the study of Mesoamerican history, religion in general, and the Quetzalcoatl myth in particular, this is the first English translation of the work"— Provided by publisher.
  ISBN 978-1-60732-390-7 (cloth) — ISBN 978-1-60732-399-0 (ebook)
 1. Aztec mythology. 2. Aztecs—Social life and customs. 3. Quetzalcoatl (Aztec deity) I. Title.
  F1219.3.R38L5913 2015
  972—dc23

2014048160

# Contents

*List of Figures* — vii

*List of Tables* — ix

*Foreword: Return to Quetzalcoatl*
*David Carrasco* — xi

*Introduction*
*Alfredo López Austin* — xv

*Translator's Note*
*Russ Davidson* — xix

1  1 REED — 3

2  THE INITIAL FOCUS OF FOREIGN ORIGIN — 7

3  THE SKEPTICAL FOCUS — 23

4  THE CRITICAL FOCUS — 27

5  THE END OF A TRUNCATED HISTORY AND ITS CONSEQUENCES — 41

| | |
|---|---:|
| 6 Men and Gods | 43 |
| 7 Space and Time | 77 |
| 8 The Nature of the Man-God | 107 |
| 9 The Life of the Man-God | 147 |
| 10 The History of the Man-God | 167 |
| *Epilogue* | 195 |
| *Bibliography* | 197 |
| *Index* | 217 |

# Figures

| | |
|---|---|
| 6.1. Códice Azcatitlan, plate vi | 57 |
| 6.2. Códice Azcatitlan, plate vii | 57 |
| 7.1. Códice Azcatitlan, plate xii | 85 |
| 7.2. Códice Azcatitlan, plate iv | 90 |
| 7.3. Códice Boturini, plate iv | 91 |
| 7.4. Hypothetical relationships between occurrences related to the beginning and the end of the Mexica migration | 101 |
| 9.1. Myth, legend, and history: Three possible relationships | 149 |
| 9.2. Pathways taken by myth in helping shape historical narrative | 162 |

# Tables

6.1. Examples of protector gods of different peoples and cities — 45

6.2. Correlations between districts-*calpullis*, temples-*calpullis*, occupations or offices, and deities in Tenochtitlan — 61

6.3. Correlation between crafts and the protection granted by specific patron gods — 67

8.1. Examples of gods and ruling leaders mentioned in the sources as guides — 110

8.2. Examples of names of peoples or cities bearing the names of gods or human eponyms — 112

9.1. Progenitors and their male offspring — 151

# Foreword
## Return to Quetzalcoatl

DAVÍD CARRASCO

> It is the capacity for rising to a clear perception of structures of thought and knowledge, of their similarities and criteria of truth and validity; above all a grasp of their central principles—and therefore of what is the nerve and muscle and what the surrounding tissue in any human construction, what is novel and revolutionary in a discovery and what is development of existing knowledge—that lifts men intellectually. It is this that elevates them to that power of contemplating patterns, whether permanent or changing, buried in, or imposed on, the welter of experience, which philosophers have regarded as man's highest attribute; but even if they are mistaken in this, it is surely not an unworthy goal for what we like to call higher education.
>
> ISAIAH BERLIN, *THE POWER OF IDEAS*[1]

In the last ten years I have worked on one of Mexico's most beautiful and revealing early colonial pictorial "maps," the Mapa de Cuauhtinchan No. 2.[2] One challenging question when facing the historical puzzle of the labyrinthine story of the Chichimecas is, when did the narrative show major changes or turning points? Asking this same question about major turning points in Mesoamerican studies leads us to this new publication and the sustained innovative achievements and "clear perception of structures of thought and knowledge" by the Mexican anthropologist Alfredo López Austin.

Did his profound impact on Mesoamerican studies begin with his two-volume *Cuerpo humano e ideologia: Las concepciones de los antiguos nahuas* (1987), published in English as *Human Body and Ideology: Concepts among the Ancient Nahuas* (1988)? Some may argue that the Spanish and English versions of his synthetic *The Myths of the Opossum: Pathways in Mesoamerican Mythology* (1993) or his *Tamoanchan/Tlalocan: Places of Mist* (2000) were the game changers. An argument can be made that it all began as far back in his succinct 1975 article "Algunas ideas acerca del tiempo mitico entre los antiguos nahuas" and took a new turn with his *Oxford Encyclopedia of Mesoamerican Cultures* article "Cosmovision" (2000). In Mesoamerican archaeology, perhaps Proyecto Templo Mayor, directed by Eduardo Matos Moctezuma was the greatest turning point in the last fifty years. For Maya linguistic studies, we can pin the prize for game changing on the cracking of the Maya code over several decades with some credit to Linda Schele as the pioneer. In written scholarship, my answer to the question, where and when did a superior Mesoamerican "turning point" in interpretation begin—where did a *new* "grasp of central principles" show forth—is López Austin's Spanish edition of *Hombre-Dios: Religión y Política en el Mundo Náhuatl*, first published in 1973. With the University Press of Colorado's smart move to publish Russ Davidson's meticulous translation of this book under the title *The Myth of Quetzalcoatl: Religion, Rulership, and History in the Nahua World*, we discover where and how López Austin elevated the discourse through his "power of contemplating" unseen patterns, permanent and changing, that were "buried in, or imposed on, the welter of experience" in Mesoamerica.

To begin to grasp López Austin's significance and influence in Mesoamerican studies just peruse the articles of the recent publication *The Art of Urbanism: How Mesoamerican Kingdoms Represented Themselves in Architecture and Imagery*, edited by William Fash and Leonardo López Luján. You see traces of López Austin's vision, language, categories, writings, insights, and arguments throughout the fifteen essays, often acknowledged by individual authors and present without acknowledgment. His writings about *hombre dios*, divine possession, *tamoanchan*, *cuerpo humanos*, myths of the opossums, the *altepetl*, *monte sagrados*, and cosmovision have come to permeate Mesoamerican scholarship as those of no other thinker in recent memory. This influence and new interpretive language all started with this book's publication in Spanish—and now this book has a new birth in English.

This return to Quetzalcoatl is appropriate, for in his new introduction to this book, Alfredo writes about the "cyclical character" of his work. As though describing the serpentine and circular pathways of the Mapa de Cuauhtinchan he writes, "One constantly returns to the causes that underlay and inspired the resolve to write; the roads we face, and take, become circular." For him his "obsession" with the complexity and richness of the "mysterious nature" of the history of Quetzalcoatl and the city of Tollan led him to write *Hombre-Dios*, wherein he identified the bedrock questions that led his prodigious, amazing career to move forward *and backward*.

I believe the present publication in English will reveal the book to be what the great Italian essayist Italo Calvino calls a "classic." In his free-flowing essay "Why Read the Classics," Calvino gives fourteen "suggested definitions" of a classic, including a "book that has never finished saying what it has to say."[3] For Spanish-speaking readers this book is already a classic, still saying much and well over forty years after it first appeared. Now the classic is reborn in English, and soon many more students and colleagues at a growing number of universities will gain access to the author's deeply engaged work on the religious imagination of the long and continuing history of Mesoamerican societies.

I express my gratitude to the University Press of Colorado for the contributions this book will make to future scholarship and understandings of Mesoamerica's long history of Quetzalcoatl, "other" Tollans, *hombre dioses*, and politics. In the end the best comparison is between Alfredo's achievement and what Isaiah Berlin says at the beginning of this preface. If anyone among us can be said to demonstrate the capacity for grasping the central principles and showing us what has been the nerve and muscle *and heart* in the human constructions of Mesoamerica, it is Alfredo López Austin, who began that journey in this publication that helped lift us intellectually into a new era of understanding.

## NOTES

1. Berlin, *The Power of Ideas*, 223.
2. Carrasco and Sessions, *Cave, City, and Eagle's Nest*.
3. Calvino, "Why Read the Classics."

# Introduction

ALFREDO LÓPEZ AUSTIN
MEXICO CITY, DECEMBER 2013

Broadly speaking, our life unfolds and develops amidst the confluence of two types of time: time that is linear, unidirectional, and irreversible and time that is circular, cyclical, and repetitive. The difference between them has proved to be grist for the history mill, leading many who study the past down a wayward path; they have used this difference, and the supposed opposition that it sets up, to ground and subordinate history and its meanings in and to the conceptions of time that the major cultures have evolved. I believe that this scheme of categorical opposites, while attractive, is false. As peoples and individuals alike, we live simultaneously in the consciousness of both types of time, something that the older among us can appreciate more vividly.

Whenever the possibility of a reedition or a translation of one my books presents itself, and a certain obligatory question is put to me, I tend to reflect on this problem. Reeditions and translations constitute turns, whether large or small, in the cycle that began with the original publication. In their own way, they are a return to the starting point of the editorial part of a work. In the case at hand, the translator, Russ Davidson, asked me the familiar question: Would I like to take advantage of the occasion to revise, or modify, or amplify what I had written some four decades earlier? I answered as I had on previous occasions, that I did not think it opportune. In general, such changes as I have made involve only truly glaring problems: a wrong fact or datum, an unfortunate misprint, a rash proposition; oversights that, once recognized, have led to many a restless night. As for any remaining problems, they are entries in the ledger of unsuccessful experiences that help one acquire the understanding that, while no work is perfect, it nonetheless demands maximum care. Hard lessons, these, but they prepare the way for future work and for aiming at the chimera of perfection. For the researcher and his labor of investigation and writing, it is the reality and the imprint of linear time.

Yet the cyclical character of the researcher's work is likewise present and calls for recognition. In all this work, one constantly returns to the causes that underlay and inspired the resolve to write; the roads we face, and take, become circular. The cycle manifests itself in the form of permanent obsessions. The researcher is again animated by themes that, in the passage of time, have taken on new semblances and configurations; the questions that are never wholly answered strike us once again, and we find ourselves swimming in what seem to be the same waters as before.

All of the foregoing fully applies to *Hombre-Dios*. From an early age, and throughout my younger years, the history of Quetzalcoatl—its mysterious nature—captivated me, to the extent that I submerged myself in the historical sources that spoke of this strange personage. Subsequently, with the greater fund of information that only time can bring, I ventured to formulate the set of ideas that took shape in *Hombre-Dios*. Since these, however, were anything but orthodox, they sparked a debate that I carried on with myself for years. Only by slow degrees did I reach the point of accepting these ideas. Yet the cycle—the obsessive cycle—had taken wing, so that time and again, in subsequent works, all of the bedrock questions reasserted themselves. One of these was the emergence on earth of a host of terrestrial cities that aspired to be copies, extensions, the living inheritance of those rising up in the heavenly spheres, such as Paradise reflected in Jerusalem, or the cosmic Tollan projected in the Tula of Quetzalcoatl—a transposition to the world of men that was repeated down the centuries in Chichén Itzá, in Xicocotitlan, in Cholula, even in Mexico-Tenochtitlan. In due course, this phenomenon appeared in the studies I carried out on other cities, in particular, the mythical Tamoanchan, to which I devoted the book *Tamoanchan y Tlalocan*.[1] Elsewhere, in still another turn of the wheel, I examined—jointly with my son, Leonardo López Luján—the complex political dynamic that produced the tangled confusion of multiple Quetzalcoatls: the Quetzalcoatl of myth, of legend, and of history. Thus, our book *Mito y realidad de Zuyuá*.[2] For decades now, the obsession has also caused me to return to the theme of divine possession, or to what can be seen as a *nahualización* of the gods,[3] who manifest themselves in the bodies of human beings so that the latter can carry out and fulfill their whims, desires, purposes, and functions. Similarly, the figure of Quetzalcoatl as a mythical personage is another theme to which I constantly return—for example, in his manifestation as Ehecatl, the god of the winds, when he makes the musicians of the Sun the victims of his deceptions; or in his role as the maker, with his own blood, of the first men; or how later he divides himself into multiple gods so they, in turn, can become the patron gods who, in mimicry of Quetzalcoatl, will create different groups of humans out of their own substance. Thus has the obsessive return of Tollan and Quetzalcoatl recurred in my life. In the future, when my own being will have dissolved into nothingness, Tollan and Quetzalcoatl will mock my obsession with them and, indifferent to it, will go on rising up as great mysteries in the stream of history.

But again, I return to linear time. The book should remain unchanged. Like all individual works, it is a social product that corresponds to a particular era. As such, it reflects the scholarly questions and preoccupations of its time—the historiographical and ideological currents then in vogue; the difficulties imposed by the scant range of documentary sources; the echo of the dialogue, now free-flowing, now abbreviated, with one's colleagues; and the teachings of our academic mentors and guides, among them the unforgettable H. B. Nicholson, whose work *Topiltzin Quetzalcoatl* circulated among us, though it was not published until many years later. In sum, *Hombre-Dios* is firmly anchored in linear time. It was, with all its errors, a small piece of the enormous puzzle of the Mesoamerican historiography of its day.

We are a product of the dialectic of our conceptions of time: that of linear time, that of cyclical time. In rebellion, I attempt to evade both forms of time in the smooth folds of continuity. On its first appearance, I dedicated *Hombre-Dios* to Martha Rosario. I go on doing so today, as always, with my love.

**NOTES**

1. Alfredo López Austin, *Tamoanchan y Tlalocan*, Mexico City: Fondo de Cultura Económica, 1994; trans. Bernard R. Ortiz de Montellano and Thelma Ortiz de Montellano as *Tamoanchan, Tlalocan: Places of Mist* (Niwot: University Press of Colorado, 1997).

2. Alfredo López Austin and Leonardo López Austin, *Mito y realidad de Zuyuá. Serpiente Emplumada y las transformaciones mesoamericanas del Clásico al Posclásico*, Mexico City: El Colegio de México, Fideicomiso Historia de las Américas y Fondo de Cultura Económica, 1999; abridged version trans. Scott Sessions as "The Myth and Reality of Zuyuá: The Feathered Serpent and Mesoamerican Transformations from the Classic to the Postclassic," in *Mesoamerica's Classic Heritage: From Teotihuacan to the Aztecs*, ed. Davíd Carrasco, Lindsay Jones, and Scott Sessions (Boulder: University Press of Colorado, 2000), 21–84.

3. Translator's note: See chapter 7, page 82, for a definition of this concept.

# Translator's Note

Russ Davidson

The translation, and there have been many, of any of Alfredo López Austin's books and essays is always a welcome occurrence for those who want deeper insight into the wellsprings of Mesoamerican religious beliefs and cultural practices. Yet the publication of an English-language edition of *Hombre-Dios: Religión y política en el mundo náhuatl* carries particular significance, for this book occupies a special place in the López Austin canon. Submitted in 1972 as the author's master's thesis and revised for publication the following year by Mexico's National Autonomous University, *Hombre-Dios* is the keystone and starting point for all his subsequent work. Its examination of the Quetzalcoatl myth and, most strikingly, how that myth operated in everyday life, affecting the actions and comportment of commoners and rulers alike, opened the way to a deeper and more nuanced understanding of the Mesoamerican worldview, or *cosmovisión*, to use López Austin's useful term. Despite its importance, however, *Hombre-Dios* somehow escaped translation. With its appearance in an English-language edition, this landmark book can now find a wider audience and readership.

Several people played a key part in helping bring this translation to fruition, and I would like to acknowledge each of them: Ethelia Ruiz Medrano, who first proposed that I undertake the project, and subsequently helped in a number of ways, not least as a voice of constant encouragement; Davíd Carrasco, who immediately endorsed the idea and has capped his support by writing a critical preface; William L. Fash and Elizabeth Hill Boone, who likewise strongly supported the project at an early stage; Guilhem Olivier, whose assistance in helping me comprehend and translate various Nahuatl terms and usage was such that I felt duty bound to count him as a virtual co-translator with the provision, of course, that any errors of translation are mine and mine alone; and López Austin himself, who similarly read the translation and provided needed clarifications and explanations. My thanks also to the staff of the University Press of Colorado, who have guided the manuscript through to publication.

On the matter of orthography, the spelling of Nahuatl terms and names, and of those in other indigenous languages, is that employed by López Austin. Following his practice, these terms (but not personal or place names or the names of gods and goddesses) as well as numerous Nahuatl expressions and passages found throughout the text have been italicized. Spanish words with no common English equivalents also appear in italics on first use in each chapter. In several cases, where standard English language translations already exist of passages quoted by López Austin, I have chosen to use them and have referenced this fact in the corresponding endnote.

A final note concerns the author's introduction. When initially published in 1973, and again in subsequent printings, of 1989 and 1998, respectively, the book bore no introduction or prefatory statement. This new accompaniment is a definite enhancement, for through it we learn what originally inspired and motivated Alfredo López Austin to research the subject of Quetzalcoatl, how his ideas toward it have shifted and evolved over time, and why—though the book is now more than four decades old—he rejects the notion of amplifying or revising it.

The Myth of Quetzalcoatl

# 1

## 1 Reed

The protagonist of this investigation, Ce Acatl Topiltzin Quetzalcoatl, the son of Iztacmixcoatl and Chimalma, was born—for the well-being and great good of men—in the high plateau of central Mexico in the year 843 or 895 or 935 or 1156 . . . but then again, was he ever really born? The truth of the matter eludes us, for on the basis of a scrupulous examination of the sources, it is possible on the one hand to deny that he actually existed while affirming on the other that he died in Uxmal, on the *Pirámide del Adivino* (Pyramid of the Magician, or Soothsayer), on the fourth day of April, 1208, at six o'clock in the afternoon, Yucatán time.[1]

Moreover, the problem does not date, as might be conjectured, to when the Spanish conquerors—commanding not just the battlefield of war but of historical narrative as well—added fragments of the indigenous tradition to the histories they wrote of the people they had defeated and subdued. Add such fragments, to a greater or lesser degree, they certainly did; yet the elusive nature of Mesoamerica's most compelling historical personage had proclaimed itself centuries before the fateful encounter between America and Europe. Those writing later, during the post-conquest period, were also influenced—in some cases, powerfully so—by the tales and legends surrounding this bearded priest-king. As he oscillated in the telling between the credible and the imaginary, Ce Acatl edged dangerously close to the brink where distortions and inaccuracies tend to cause historians to lose interest.

The indigenous sources—and here, if one insists on using the term precisely, is where the first taxonomic problem will be encountered—seemingly were contrived out of a perverse pleasure in the prospect of confusing future historians: many of these sources not only make reference to Ce Acatl but do so in a way that is richly detailed; and again, not only are they numerous and filled with details, they are also shot through with contradictions. The name by which he is known changes, variously, from Ce Acatl to Nacxitl, Tepeuhqui,[2] Meconetzin, Ahpop,[3] Guatezuma,[4] Kukulcan,[5] Ru Ralcan . . .[6] His life is split into two, so that we come upon him twice, under two names, the protagonist of two histories, in two separate epochs and in different *pueblos*, within the pages of a single author's work.[7] Elsewhere he is mistaken for another, being given the name Topiltzin, while his mortal enemy is assigned another of his names, Quetzalcoatl.[8] By turns, he is identified as being tolteca, chichimeca, or tenochca. In Spanish sources, he is mentioned as early as 1526,[9] and different versions of his miraculous life have been pieced together—for example, in the indigenous communities of Coatepec de los Costales, in the present-day state of Guerrero, by Pedro Carrasco Pizana (1943) and in Jáltipan, in the state of Veracruz, by Antonio García de León (1966).[10] Surprisingly, in the historical source where his appearance as a king or priest would be most expected, no such reference to him is made.[11] On the other hand, the beautiful verses that tell of the destruction of Tollan contain commentaries on his life,[12] as do glosses on the proverbial sayings of the ancient Nahua.[13]

In light of this situation, we can readily grasp that a simple statement of the content of the indigenous sources would equal the length of this book, or more. The need for any such review of the literature has been obviated, however, by the stellar doctoral thesis of H. B. Nicholson.[14] What is needed now is an investigation of the possible causes of this apparent confusion, a state of affairs that cannot, obviously, be ascribed to any deliberate, perverse intent to confuse and misdirect. If historian after historian, for more than four and a half centuries, has confronted the same problem, then providing a brief overview of the history of this biography would seem to be a useful starting point.

It was Alfonso Caso who logically divided the problem of Tollan and the Toltecs into three phases, the first of which he labeled "naïve" because it tried to explain miracles on the basis of miracles themselves.[15] The second phase was termed "the skeptical" because it denied the existence of Quetzalcoatl. And the third he called "the critical" because—across the full complex of material—it sought to isolate and distinguish the mythical from the historical. Alfred Tozzer identified and added a fourth phase to this scheme, which he denoted as "the perplexing," or "the elusive," in that it maintained an unsatisfactory separation between the figures of the priest-king and the culture hero.[16] For my part, I have found it helpful to use the classification adopted by Caso but to alter it slightly in two ways. First, by replacing the term *phase* with *focus* since, although a distinct temporal sequence is discernible, the lines separating these phases blend into each other; and second, by substituting the category "initial and of foreign origin" in place of "naïve." As for the characterization of perplexing, or baffling, that Tozzer adds, it really applies more to the entire history of the biography than to a particular phase or stage within that history.

In treating the history of the biography of Quetzalcoatl, my approach within each focus is chronological, and while all of the opinions and ideas I discuss have their place in the story, some are important because they have empirical value, some because of the influence they have exercised, others because they represent the thinking of a large cadre of scholars, and still others—a not insignificant number—because they are patently nonsensical or outrageous.

Finally, in setting the framework for this study, I cannot think of a comment more to the point than one made by Paul Kirchhoff to us, his students, when there seemed to be no way to clarify or sort out some confusing and conflicting information in the sources. "I failed to understand Mexico's pre-Hispanic history," he remarked, "until I discovered that each figure was his own grandmother." Kirchhoff said this in jest, yet I have had to recall his words all too often.

## NOTES

1. As specified by Spinden, "New Light on Quetzalcoatl," 507–8, 511.
2. Heinrich Berlin and Silva Rendón, *Historia tolteca-chichimeca*, 76. Unless otherwise noted, citations to this source are from the 1947 edition.
3. This name is little known. It is mentioned by Fuentes y Guzman, *Recordación florida*, 2:389.
4. Fernández de Oviedo, *Historia general y natural*, 10:103–5.
5. Landa, *Relación de la cosas de Yucatán*, 12–13.
6. *Relaciones de Yucatán*, 1:121.
7. Alva Ixtlilxóchitl, *Obras*, 1:44–56, 470–71.
8. Durán, *Historia de las Indias*, 2:73–78
9. I found this reference to him in Bandelier, *Report*, 171n2. The document in question is titled "Real ejecutoria de S.M. sobre tierras y reservas de pechos y paga, pertenecientes a los caciques de Axapusco, de la jurisdicción de Otumba," in García Icazbalceta, *Colección de documentos*, 2:9–10.
10. Carrasco, "Quetzalcoatl," 89–91; and García de León, "El dueño del maíz," 349–57.
11. Heinrich Berlin and Silva Rendón, *Historia tolteca-chichimeca*, passim.
12. Garibay K., *Poesía náhuatl*, 3:1–2; and Lehmann, *Una elegía tolteca*, 13–14.
13. Sahagún, *Historia general*, 2:217–18.
14. Translator's note: In the intervening years, Nicholson's dissertation was turned into the book *Topiltzin Quetzalcoatl: The Once and Future Lord of the Toltecs* (Boulder: University Press of Colorado, 2001).

15. Caso, "El complejo arqueológico," 85–96.

16. Tozzer's actual name for it was the "baffling period." See his *Chichén Itzá*, 1:27. I am grateful to Nicholson's *Topiltzin-Quetzalcoatl* (page 39) for directing me to this reference.

# 2

## The Initial Focus of Foreign Origin

According to the early fifteenth-century chronicler Peter Martyr, the first instance in which the Spanish learned of Quetzalcoatl occurred in March 1517, when the conquistador Francisco Hernández de Córdoba led an expedition into Yucatán. In Martyr's words, "[The Spaniards] saw that they [the indigenous inhabitants of Yucatán] had crosses, and in asking—through an interpreter—about their origins, were told by some that as he passed through those places, a man—endowed with great beauty—had left the aforementioned relic as a remembrance. Others explained that a man more resplendent than the sun had died on it. Nothing for certain is known."[1] What *is* clearly known, however, is that Martyr was wrong in having conjured the presence of interpreters during that time. The report of the crosses, confirmed by other sources, nonetheless remains a starting point for a notion that would later interweave with the idea of a voyaging Quetzalcoatl. The cross is the first indication that Europeans believed they had discovered evidence of previous contact between the Old World and the New. A similar conjunction—in respect to the sacraments of baptism, confession, and Holy Communion, and to the ideas of the flood, of a Tower of Babel, of the confusion of tongues, of the trinity, or of a virgin who conceives a child—would soon come to be of profound concern to Christians. There are two ways to contextualize these associations: still distanced from the tradition of the redemption and from the intercession of divine truth and institutions, the Indies became a renewed scene of contact with supernatural, evil forces; or, unbeknownst to the Old World and to its historical-religious consciousness, the Indies were blessed with the redemptive presence of an apostolic current. Many years later, Fray Juan de Torquemada would take the first of these interpretations, that Satan was present in the Indies, to its logical extreme. The second explanation would have a strong impact on the life story of Ce Acatl.

Fray Pedro de los Ríos, about whose life we know little but who, in his commentaries, has provided extremely useful information about the religious thought of the indigenous population, is among those who find, in the very history of Quetzalcoatl, a basis for conjecturing that the Indies suffered contact with satanic forces. This way of thinking suited those who, like the good monk, entertained a medieval vision that transferred the Christian concept of the struggle between the powers of good and evil to the new lands across the ocean. If the native inhabitants believed that a heavenly god (Citlallatonac) dispatched an ambassador to inform a virgin (Chimalma) of her conception of a son (Quetzalcoatl) without any contact with a man, and if this story is accompanied by falsities and absurdities, then here is proof (for Ríos and his kind) that the Devil had preceded the arrival of the Spanish evangelists so that he could attribute to himself the glory of being the god in heaven who sent down the message.[2] Quetzalcoatl, if we continue to follow Ríos's reasoning, is not a true person but a fictitious being employed by the Devil to poke fun at the naïveté of the unseeing natives.

The history of Quetzalcoatl is at its most disconcerting during this initial period of contact. New Spain's first viceroy, Antonio de Mendoza, collected elements of it and sent them, in 1540, to his brother Diego, then serving as the Spanish ambassador to Venice.[3] The viceroy does not seem to have harbored any thoughts of engaging in a critical analysis of the history; he merely relates the story of Orchilobos, the miracle-working father of Guatezuma, without inferring the presence of any demonic or apostolic contact. Between Huitzilopochtli—Orchilobos—and this Guatezuma, who appears to owe his name to a convergence of Cuauhtemoc and Motecuhzoma, Mendoza parcels out the most outstanding actions and events that other sources attribute to Ce Acatl. The viceroy's historical account takes place in Tenochtitlan. Moreover, despite the apparent string of confusions, it has a ring of authenticity, such as might derive from the specific traditional stories related by an indigenous informant.

It was perhaps Motolinía who took the first step toward sanctifying the life of our protagonist. He at least finds him honest and chaste, the first in practicing the sacrifice of bleeding his own ears and tongue against the evil corruptions of speech and hearing. All the same, he considers the teachings of the penitent Quetzalcoatl to be of little benefit, since it was Satan who subsequently applied this form of sacrifice to his worship and service.[4] Motolinía also speaks of the prophecy of the return of Ce Acatl and states that the Indians had taken him for their god.[5]

An anonymous work, the *Historia de México* bases its negative view of Quetzalcoatl on the great amount of mythical content provided by its informants. The son of two gods, Camaxtli and Chimalma, Quetzalcoatl, in this telling, begins a life punctuated by miracles and tales that defy simple understanding: his brothers place him on a mountain of fire to destroy him, but he squeezes himself into the crevice of a rock; upon emerging, armed, he hunts an animal that he delivers to his father; he later kills all his brothers and fabricates goblets out of their skulls; he ventures to Tollan, where he lives for 160 years; Tezcatlipoca arrives to persecute him and, taking flight, Quetzalcoatl spends 290 years in Cuauhquechollan, followed by a stay of 260 years in Cempoallan; and finally, perceiving that he is cornered, he shoots an arrow into a tree, works himself into the crack it has produced, and dies.[6] How does the author of this history explain Tezcatlipoca's defeat of the wondrous Quetzalcoatl? To begin with, he believes in a life suffused with miracles. In addition, he ascribes a demonic nature to both of them; and since demons are fallen angels and angels are divided into the higher and the lower, Quetzalcoatl's status is deemed inferior to that of his adversary.

The picture sketched in 1552 by the humanist historian López de Gómara was diametrically opposed to this stream of thought, and I include it in this section principally for its role as a progenitor and not because it falls into the group that Caso labels naïve. In López de Gómara's voice we hear the influence of Renaissance thinking. Furthermore, if my sequence did not posit the interplay of contradictions among the three foci, and the great influence that time acquires in this process, I would not hesitate in giving López de Gómara his place among the authors of the third focus: those historians who labored to distinguish the mythical from the historical. From the outset, and despite the presence of the cross among the Indians of Acuzamil, he rejected the already-floated argument that the gospel had been preached in the Indies before the arrival of the Spanish.[7] Subsequently, in referring to Quetzalcoatl, López de Gómara aligned himself with the euhemeristic tradition against any and all who would not see myth for what it was, but instead took it for the real and thus conflated or confused miracles and natural events. Theirs was the Quetzalcoatl as the virgin man—honest, penitent and temperate, religious and saintly—the preacher of natural law who served it by example. The native people believed he was a god and that he disappeared at the seashore, unknowing or concealing the truth of his death, and they took him as a numen of the wind.[8] In short, López de Gómara strictly divided his information. On one side was the history of the actual person; on the other, indigenous beliefs grounded either in a simple-minded naiveté or in the sly desire to deceive. And through it all, the pellucid personality of Quetzalcoatl emerges intact, unchanged.

López de Gómara composed his history in the calm of Spain, his interpretation of events thus far removed from the immediate scene of action. In the New World, by contrast, Fray Bartolomé de las Casas felt the searing emotions produced by first-hand reports emanating from his own bishopric, reports whose findings he sanctioned by including them in his *Apologética historia sumaria*. Regarding the life of Quetzalcoatl, las Casas added little to what Motolinía had said: he was a man with white skin, tall, with a broad forehead, large eyes, long black hair, and a long, bushy beard. He preached that his people would return one day, and the native inhabitants took the Spaniards to be the heavenly descendants of this voyager, although their conduct soon blotted out that first impression.[9] With respect to the other thread of the story, las Casas enthusiastically reiterated what Francisco Hernández, a priest in his bishopric who understood the native language, had managed to extract from an Indian notable. The priest discovered that the Indians believed in a celestial god with a three-person incarnation—the Father, the Son, and the Holy Spirit (Izona, Bacab, and Echuac, respectively)—the second of whom was born of the maiden Chibirias, who dwelled with God in heaven. Bacab was slain by Eopuco, who flogged him and placed a crown of thorns around his head; afterwards, he was lashed to a piece of timber, on which he died. He remained dead for three days, and on the third day he came back to life and ascended to heaven, where he dwells with God the Father. Later, Echuac furnished and filled the land with all that was necessary for the benefit of men. This tradition had been transmitted to Hernández's informant from what his community knew, which in turn was based on the preachings of twenty men who had arrived sporting great beards and long robes but no headdress. One of them was called Cocolcan.[10]

Exactly what it was that the Indian notable recounted to Hernández is difficult to know. From what can be deduced based on the names of the gods he mentioned, he seems greatly to have wanted to understand things as he was prone to, converting the indigenous narrative into full-blown Christian history. What is certain is that in las Casas's work one encounters within the same person, who is called by two names—Quetzalcoatl and Cocolcan—the bearded white man and the preacher of the new gospel, two ideas that some years in the future would converge and intermingle.

The impetuous bishop of Chiapas, however, was not prepared to draw this conclusion openly. He placed the responsibility for the report squarely on the shoulders of Francisco Hernández and made an anonymous Franciscan a witness to it, then further mentioned—by way of analogy—that, according to other contemporaneous reports, the apostle Saint Thomas had once preached in Brazil. He did not go so far, however, as to endorse all these claims categorically. "In the end," wrote las Casas, "these are secrets known only to God."[11]

One of the most beautifully rendered Quetzalcoatl stories, in which miraculous happenings feature prominently, was recorded by Fray Bernardino de Sahagún. The Franciscan friar, overly conscious on the one hand of his evangelizing role and too disposed on the other to give credence to the tales of indigenous informants, speaks of Quetzalcoatl as a real person, mortal and corruptible, an intimate associate of demons, and now consigned to burn in hell by the dictates of divine justice.[12] The solution, the alternative, is easily grasped, and perhaps Sahagún was only finding a way to preach, in the simple language of fire and brimstone, to the newly converted who might still be awaiting the true return of Ce Acatl. In any case, Sahagún says nothing further about Quetzalcoatl.

At last, between 1570 and 1579,[13] the writing was completed on the work that brought together the linkage that had been gestating since the first crosses were encountered. Its author, Fray Diego Durán, is one of the giants of Mexican historiography. The venerable man, whom Durán alternately calls Topiltzin, Hueimac, or Papa was, according to indigenous traditions, a chaste and penitent priest who stirs memories of episodes that seem miraculous. Indeed, so miraculous do they seem that the devoted friar preferred not to describe and record them in their totality, to avoid falling into errors for which the church might later reprehend him. All the same, he fixed upon the words of Saint Mark, which refer to how the apostles were sent to preach the gospel to all creatures throughout the world. Were the Indians not also God's creatures? Did traditions not hold that Topiltzin had come from faraway lands? Was Topiltzin not the creator of beautiful sculptures and Saint Thomas, a flowerbed? The evidence was sufficiently persuasive for this Dominican that, setting caution aside, he states that "we can probably take it that this holy man was an apostle whom God deployed to this land."[14]

Yet he only arrives at this conclusion after a prolonged investigation. Nor was he content to rely on translating the textual meaning of indigenous documents into Spanish, as was the case throughout much of his work. On this point, Durán decided to go straight to the source; he traveled to three pueblos—Ocuituco, Chiauhtla, and Coatépec—and spoke with an elder in each one. He described one of these encounters as follows: "Wanting to satisfy myself to a greater extent and obtain some detail from the Indian, in order to fill in the picture and finish my writing, I again asked of him what prompted that saintly man to take leave of this land." Durán implored his interlocutors, "with all the humility in the world," to show him the book that they said Topiltzin had left behind. And when he found out that they had burned it, he was distressed and scolded those responsible for the fiasco. He assumed that the book "could have been the Sacred Scriptures in the Hebrew language." Durán thought past the crosses, past the memory that the native inhabitants guarded of Topiltzin, past the traces he had left, and found that the presumed apostle—whose followers covered their heads with conch shells—had been depicted in the codices: he appears as a bearded man, with a red, graying beard and a large nose, seated with an air of great restraint. Durán was doubtless looking at the image of the wind god represented with his half-bird mask.[15]

The story that he compiled about Topiltzin is full of curious and unusual elements. Apparently, Durán did not want a single sin to have stained the life of the presumed apostle and, in service of this wish, tells the story of how two necromancers harangue Topiltzin to get married, how they introduce him to the harlot Xochiquetzal in her chambers and give false testimony about his incontinence. Topiltzin goes off, leaving his two malefactors momentarily triumphant. Durán gives the name Tezcatlipoca to one and to the other—curiously—he gives the name Quetzalcoatl. Durán's motive in doing so may have been exculpatory—to relieve our hero of the errors that the sources, in his judgment, had wrongly ascribed to him. The author of the Códice Ramírez continued the history of this evangelist. Topiltzin-Quetzalcoatl-Papa was a man of great holiness, given to fasting, undertaking penances and vigils, and issuing warnings against all vices. He spoke out against idolatry and the pagan rites practiced by the native inhabitants. He had to depart but, to those who would avenge the evil doings of his enemies, promised to return. He was a great sculptor who carved a crucifix. He bequeathed a book, by way of a missal, to the indigenous people that the missionaries and clerics, despite their diligent efforts, were unable to find but which was understood to be the Bible. He performed so many miracles that he was considered to be more than human.[16] The image, then, quickly took shape, and the Christian colonizers took satisfaction in having discovered the causes underlying the presence of crosses in the New World.

Fray Gerónimo de Mendieta repeats the assertions of Motolinía and las Casas, though he does not appear to grasp the problem of the relationship between our protagonist and the spreading of the gospel.[17] Fray Jerónimo Román y Zamora follows exactly the same line as Mendieta.[18] Diego Muñoz Camargo, on the other hand, returns to the idea that Quetzalcoatl's miraculous life, which led him to be taken as a god, was due to his connivance with Satan, adding to this part of the story that Topiltzin himself could have been fathered by an incubus.[19] At the start of the seventeenth century, Fray Juan de Torquemada provides another version of a foreign Quetzalcoatl. Coming from the direction of Pánuco, strange men asking to be domiciled arrived in Tollan from unknown lands. Although according to Torquemada the opinion of some was that these men were Romans or Carthaginians, the fact that they ate human flesh and marked their faces with stripes inclined him to think they came from Ireland. Ultimately beset by strong doubts, he concluded that "as far as this is concerned, so as not to talk nonsense, it can only be left to God." Unable to maintain themselves in Tollan, the strange travelers went on to

Cholollan, where they intermingled with the native inhabitants. Their chieftain, Quetzalcoatl, a blond and bearded white man possessed of magic and the power of necromancy, was taken as a god because of the tales he told. Affronted in Tollan by Huemac and Tezcatlipoca, who engaged in adultery against him, the incensed ruler abandoned Cholollan to live among his own. From there, he launched a campaign to expand into distant lands until Huemac pursued him, forcing him to flee toward the territory of the Maya.[20]

Torquemada could not countenance the idea than a Christian evangelist had been present in the New World before the arrival of the Spanish. The merit of his work lies in its overarching conception: the attempt it makes to integrate the history of the Old World and that of the New into a single universal narrative, reducing the latter into a complement, or appendage, of all that was already known about the former. The Indies thus stand, in large measure, as the territory of Satan, where demonic worship has taken root as a crude copy of true worship and where the similarity in ritual practices, institutions, and beliefs stems from the powers of evil, not those of good.

Gregorio García was a Dominican friar from Toledo who traveled through both the northern and southern parts of the Indies and later wrote *Predicación del Santo Evangelio en el Nuevo Mundo, viviendo los apóstoles*, printed in Baeza in 1625. Unfortunately, I have not been able to consult this work, which—as affirmed by Ignacio Borunda—was difficult to obtain even as far back as the eighteenth century.[21] In another work, García appears to adhere closely to Torquemada's thesis, though we now realize that his parroting of Torquemada was something added by the book's editor.[22] Both Manuel Orozco y Berra and Alfredo Chavero cite García as one of the defenders of the theory that Saint Thomas had been present in America.[23]

Another figure who takes his place among the historians of the first half of the seventeenth century is Fernando de Alva Ixtlilxóchitl, who, unquestionably drawing on indigenous traditions, provides two versions of the history of Quetzalcoatl. In the first version, the protagonist is Quetzalcoatl Huemac, chieftain of the Toltecas, a just and holy man who preaches goodness and worships the cross. This ruler counseled his people to install a monarchy whose lordly class would be drawn from among the Chichimecas, which indeed came to pass. Disillusioned by the little that came from his moral preaching, he departed to the east and there he disappeared, but not before warning that a curly-haired man would emerge from the Chichimeca dynasty to rule, a man who at the outset would be wise and discrete but at the end of his reign would bring about the downfall of the Toltecas in a year *ce ácatl*, or within 512 years, and that he—Quetzalcoatl Huemac—would then return to preach once again. In the second version, the protagonist is Topiltzin

Meconetzin, the curly-haired man, who upon fulfilling the prophecy of the year *ce ácatl* is deposed and, as he flees, claims that he will return within 512 years, in a year *ce ácatl*, to punish his enemies.²⁴ If we take the period of 512 years as 520, we will grasp that Alva Ixtlilxóchitl has perfectly interwoven two parallel histories.

The intriguing part of Alva Ixtlilxóchitl's narrations lies in how he tailors the tradition of his Chichimeca ancestors such that they turn out to have been Spaniards. Consider the assertions that he makes, in a disconnected, apparently random way, in different parts of his work. The Toltecs—from whom, at the time of the conquest, the Mexica lords claim descent—arrive not with a king but merely with a chieftain, Huemac, upon whose advice a line of rulers is sought from among the Chichimecas.²⁵ The Chichimeca kings were tall and bearded, with white skin like the Spanish.²⁶ Xolotl, lord of the Chichimecas, was a white bearded man, "though his beard was sparse."²⁷ Topiltzin Meconetzin was a Chichimeca king and therefore also white and bearded. The prince Nopaltzin married Axcaxochitzin, the legitimate daughter of Pochotl and the niece of Topiltzin Meconetzin.²⁸ For this reason, Nezahualcoyotl can claim to be descended from Meconetzin.²⁹ Topiltzin journeys to the land of his ancestors, giving notice that his people will return to punish the descendants of the enemy kings.³⁰ In short, if the Spanish—bearded white men, worshipers of the good and the cross—come out of the east in a year *ce ácatl* and wreak havoc upon the indigenous rulers, they are unquestionably the men who were foretold by both Huemac Quetzalcoatl and Topiltzin Meconetzin—that is, the latter's own people. The Spanish have thus returned to the New World.

From another angle, the tradition of Quetzalcoatl-Saint Thomas also gets reinforced. When referring to the *mixe* people of Cempoaltépec, Francisco de Burgoa reports that Fray Juan de Ojedo found, as though they had been carved into the rock, the traces of human footprints on an outcropping of the mountainside. Burgoa's statements correspond to testimonies, in the indigenous tradition, about the passage of Ce Acatl through these parts. This information, buttressed by similar accounts emerging ever more frequently from South America, caused Burgoa to suspect that Saint Thomas had been present in New Spain.³¹ Fuentes y Guzmán refers to the same sort of footprint traces in Guatemala and is convinced they accord with those of an apostolic evangelist, without concerning himself if that person was Saint Thomas or Saint Bartholomew.³² In a similar vein, the posthumous work of Luis Becerra Tanco, published in 1685 in Seville under the title *Felicidad de México en el principio y milagroso origen que tuvo el Santuario de la Virgen María nuestra Señora de Guadalupe*, argues insistently for Saint Thomas's appearance in the New World, proof of which he finds in the resemblance between the Greek word *didimus* (or *didimo*) the saint's sobriquet, and the Nahuatl suffix *-coatl*, which forms part of the name Quetzalcoatl—both of which mean "twin."³³

In 1680, Manuel Duarte, a Jesuit, apparently born in Portugal in 1624, who for fourteen years was the *procurador* (ecclesiastical judge) for the Mexican province, handed over a manuscript to the viceroy Carlos de Sigüenza y Góngora so that the latter could edit it. The title of Duarte's collection of writings seems to have been *Historia de Quetzalcoatl*, which the nineteenth-century Mexican historian José Fernando Ramírez affirmed was the same work that he published under the title *Pluma rica, nuevo fénix de América*.³⁴ According to Ramírez, this document, which tries to show that Saint Thomas preached in the New World, was the basis for a work whose authorship, around 1690, has been attributed to Sigüenza y Góngora.³⁵ This work of Sigüenza, today lost, was said by Sebastián de Guzmán y Córdova to bear the title *Fénix de Occidente. Santo Tomás apóstol hallado con el nombre de Quetzalcóatl entre las cenizas de antiguas tradiciones conservadas en piedra, teoamoxtles tultecos y en cantares teochichimecos y mexicanos* to "show that the apostles had preached everywhere in the world, and therefore [had done so] in America, which was not completely unknown to the ancients. It also shows Quetzalcoatl to have been the glorious apostle Saint Thomas, this being proved in the meaning of one and the other name, in his vestments, his doctrine, the prophecies that he makes; he [Sigüenza y Góngora, as the manuscript's putative author] relates the miracles he performed, described the sites where and the signs through which the holy apostle left traces of himself, when he enlightened these parts where at the very least he had four disciples."³⁶

Still other authors make similar assertions. For example, the seventeenth-century monk, Fray Agustín de Vetancurt, insists, like Becerra Tanco, on the parallelism between *didimo* and *coatl*.³⁷ Lorenzo Boturini maintains that he has found enough evidence to affirm that Saint Thomas preached in New Spain, as he had in the viceroyalty of Peru, the distinction being that in the former he was known as Quetzalcoatl.³⁸ The eighteenth-century historian and man of letters, Mariano Veytia, brings together a majority of the proofs adduced by many preceding authors and concludes that, if one can sidestep the confusions between Quetzalcoatl—Huemac, the divinatory founder of Tollan, and Topiltzin—the true figure behind them is undoubtedly Saint Thomas. As additional proof, Veytia cites the bird sculpted on the apostle's tomb in Meliapor, which is the same *quetzalli*, or quetzal bird, that serves as allegory in the New World.³⁹

The only author to question the powerful current of opinion that identified the priest-king with the apostle was the Jesuit historian Francisco Javier Clavijero, who argued, rationally, that the few credible reports should be separated from the childish, mythical accounts offered by other historians.⁴⁰

During the last decade of the eighteenth century, the tide of such foolish proofs as the quetzal of Meliapor or the pairing of *didimo* and *coatl* overran itself in the unbridled imagination of Ignacio Borunda, who made a remarkable series of misguided arguments. To his critics, Borunda was

> a man of very good practices, hard-working, full of talent, but on the other hand of a rather brooding, recondite genius and gloomy disposition, who from his youth in the Real Colegio of San Ildefonso frequently manifested an imagination capable of going off half-cocked. Devoted in recent years to [studying] the Mexican language, and—through his profession as a lawyer—taking on some commissions related to Indians and dealing with them and making visits to several of their pueblos, he now believed himself capable of executing his first stroke and of setting right the wrongs committed, in the literary sphere, by a bevy of historians in the Indies who had written up to the present time.[41]

This judgment will seem tame to anyone who delves into the book, a veritable compendium of ridiculous, confused, and entangled reflections sustained by the astonishing filological pirouettes of someone dealing with a language—in this case, Nahuatl—about which he lacks the slightest knowledge; someone who, by latching onto some supposed etymology, manages to reach the conclusion he wants. But at least in Borunda's case the work remained in manuscript form,[42] unlike some contemporary writings—equally given to fantasizing but of distinctly lesser quality—that ramble on about the civilizing effect that the Maya had on the world. Unpublished, yes, but not entirely unedited, since Borunda's manuscript was presented to Fray Servando Teresa de Mier, who, on December 12, 1794, inspired by the document and in the presence of New Spain's viceroy, assured the faithful gathered in the Basilica of Guadalupe to hear his sermon that the image of the Virgin Mary had been impressed not onto the cloak of a humble Indian but, miraculously, onto the cape of Saint Thomas. Saint Thomas, who had journeyed to the New World, had, in Mier's rendering, deposited it in the Tenayuca Mountains so that it might be venerated. Although initially convinced of its authenticity, the Indians soon turned apostate and abused the image, which they were not able to erase. The saint proceeded to hide the cape, which remained hidden until, ten years after the conquest, the Virgin appeared before Juan Diego, bringing forth the piece of fabric and requesting the construction of a temple.[43] It was a memorable day for the biography of Quetzalcoatl, as it was for that of Fray Servando. As punishment for his wayward sermon, the monk was condemned to ten years exile and confinement, a sentence that launched him on a succession of adventures, arrests, escapes, and rearrests across distant European lands.

Borunda's ideas, given expression by Mier, provoked a backlash of criticism against the identification of Saint Thomas with Quetzalcoatl. The Mexican savant Antonio León y Gama argued that the sources spoke of a striving warrior Quetzalcoatl who tried to extend his dominion as far as Oaxaca and Yucatán. If Quetzalcoatl had died in Cholollan, how could his tomb reside in Meliapor, a city in South India; and, by the same token, how could the tradition that maintains he was martyred there stand up to scrutiny? León y Gama also disputed that a superstitious man, a necromancer, who was worshipped as a god and ruled over people who consumed human flesh, could be a preacher of the Catholic faith. He reasoned that the crosses and other found signs were insufficient proof that Christian preaching had occurred before the arrival of the Spanish; that, while granting that the indigenous population might have been capable of receiving the gospel, not even the faintest reasons existed to speculate that Saint Thomas or any other saint had journeyed through the New World; and finally, that the proposition that the image of the Virgin was painted on Saint Thomas's cape, not on the *ayate* (a cape made of maguey fiber), was rash and impious.[44] Following León y Gama, Alexander von Humboldt formulated a new approach—that of considering a non-Christian foreign origin for Quetzalcoatl. In his mind, the clues were manifold. First, bearded men, more light-skinned than the indigenous inhabitants, were present in different parts of America, although it was impossible to trace their exact origin. Second, they all displayed certain qualities; they were priestly in character, lawgivers, peace loving, promoters of the arts, and, in general, a force for civilization. Given these factors, as well as the time frame of their appearance, the monastic institutions they founded, the symbols of worship that accompanied them, the calendars that existed, and the type of documents they created, Humboldt postulated that Quetzalcoatl, Bochica, and Manco Capac appeared to hail from East Asia, perhaps from among one of three peoples: the Tartars, the Tibetans, or the Ainu.[45]

The French archaeologist and historian, Charles-Étienne Brasseur de Bourbourg, continued this general line of speculation, purporting to find in the figure of Quetzalcoatl—whom he studied along with the counterpart figure of Votan—a pilgrim led by the hand of providence to liberate men from savagery. These charismatic leaders had come to America to instruct people in the law, religion, government, agriculture, and the arts. In the mind of their beneficiaries, however, they stood and were recalled as figures in whom the culture hero became confused with the creator of man and the universe. Upon appearing in the lands that they would civilize, these heroes immediately searched for seeds, to get agriculture started. For reasons unknown, our protagonist of foreign origin, Quetzalcoatl, returned to the East, designating some of his comrades to lead his new community. The myths in which this bearer of civilization takes part are but symbols of his beneficent actions. Considerably later, the lives of other men—Quetzalcoatl Chalchihuitl and Topiltzin Aacxitl Quetzalcoatl, who received their names in memory of the civilizing hero—would serve to confuse massively, as though all the stories were one, the history of the latter, thus giving rise to the historical problems over which every researcher has stumbled.⁴⁶

In 1868, Manuel Herrera y Pérez was still upholding the thesis of Quetzalcoatl-Saint Thomas,⁴⁷ and "The Necromancer" strikes at the possibility that the saint or any other primitive Christian Jew could have preached his religion in ancient Mexico.⁴⁸

According to Orozco y Berra, if Saint Thomas the Apostle, who lived in the first century, and Saint Thomas of Meliapor, who lived in the fifth or sixth century, cannot be identified with our protagonist, one can nevertheless posit that some Catholic Icelandic missionary, bearded and white-skinned, preached the gospel in Mexico and, as testimonies, left the crosses that later so bedeviled the Spanish. But then, what does one make of the much more ancient Mayan crosses? A thesis similar to Brasseur de Bourbourg's allowed Orozco y Berra to conclude that Votan, who assuredly left very differently styled crosses, could also have been a missionary, but of Buddhist persuasion. He further states, regarding the miraculous nature of his life, that subsequent centuries performed the task of deifying the figure of the preacher, identified as he was with the planet Venus, and that his struggle with Tezcatlipoca, defender of the ancient cult that forced Quetzalcoatl to abandon the city of Tollan, was represented in the movements of Venus and the Moon. Or, alternatively, that the movements of the two celestial bodies themselves spurred the antagonism between the two men; on this point, Orozco y Berra's explanation was not very clear.⁴⁹

In 1892, Othón de Brackel-Welda offered still another theory—pompous, precious, and anachronistically providentialist—that Quetzalcoatl could have been none other than the sixth-century Irish seafaring monk, Saint Brendan.⁵⁰ Four years later, Eugène Beauvois wrote about the Christian influence in the religious life of pre-Hispanic Mexico, and he was followed, in 1898 and 1912, by Charles Félix Hyacinthe Gouhier, the Comte de Charency, who peddled his ideas about possible Buddhist or Nestorian preaching having crossed over to Mexico via the Pacific Ocean.⁵¹ By this time, however, the theories about Quetzalcoatl's life that placed his origins outside the New World had been largely cast aside by a new line of interpretation: the skeptical. All the same, the well of old interpretation had not run dry, and it continued to generate new, unanticipated examples. It stands to reason that the life of Quetzalcoatl should remain a favored theme across the full spectrum of present-day diffusionist theories, and it is a wide spectrum, even when restricted to the scientifically serious. We can use Thor Heyerdahl as an exemplar of the authors, among the diffusionist party, who have a keen interest in our protagonist. Preoccupied by the long-held belief in the bearded, white-skinned man—the foreign, civilizing man who is covered by a great cloak and who enters into the mythology of America bearing the names Con-Tici Viracocha, Bochica,

Itzamna, Kukulcan, Votan, Condoy, Gucumatz, and Quetzalcoatl—and likewise concerned by the presence of an iconography in which he believed he could perceive traces of the Semitic, Heyerdahl underscored his opinion that ancient contacts had taken place between the Old World and the New.[52] In a work published in 1971, B. C. Hedrick argued against opinions of this sort, such as those proffered by Lucile Taylor Hansen, who in 1949 identified Quetzalcoatl with Jesus Christ.[53] The year 1971, the very year in which Hedrick assailed these authors, saw the publication, by Jacques Lafaye, of *Quetzalcoatl et Guadalupe: Eschatologie et histoire au Mexique (1521–1821)*, in which Lafaye argued for a possible relationship among the German god Nerthus, the Norse god Njordr, and Quetzalcoatl, based on the similarity—not a very strong one, in my judgment—that all are numens of the wind, bestowers of riches, and protectors of voyagers; and that Njordr had possessed an earthly existence.[54]

**NOTES**

1. Mártir de Anglería, *Décadas*, 1:399.
2. *Códice Vaticano Latino*, plate viii.
3. Fernández de Oviedo, *Historia general y natural*, 10:103–5.
4. Motolinía, *Historia*, 7.
5. Motolinía, *Memoriales*, 60, 83; and Ibid., 51.
6. Motolinía, *Historia*, 112–16.
7. López de Gómara, *Historia general de las Indias*, 2:29.
8. Ibid., 117–18, 377.
9. Las Casas, *Apologética historia*, 1:645–46.
10. Ibid., 648–49.
11. Ibid., 649.
12. Sahagún, *Historia general de las cosas*, 1:90.
13. Garibay K., *Historia de la literatura*, 2:51–52.
14. Durán, *Historia de las Indias*, 2:73–78.
15. Ibid.
16. *Códice Ramírez*, 105–6.
17. Mendieta, *Historia eclesiástica*, 1:99–100.
18. Román y Zamora, *Repúblicas de Indias*, 1:57–58, 170.
19. Muñoz Camargo, *Historia de Tlaxcala*, 39–41.
20. Torquemada, *Los veinte*, 1:254–56, 2:20.
21. Borunda, "Clave general," 3:325.
22. García, *Origen*, 262. This trickery on the part of the editor, Andrés González de Barcia Carballido y Zúñiga, was pointed out by Lee Eldridge Huddleston in his *Origins of the*

*American Indians: European Concepts, 1492–1729*, Latin American Monographs 11 (Austin: Institute of Latin American Studies/University of Texas Press, 1967): 106–9. The first edition of García's *Origen de los indios* appeared six years before the publication of Torquemada's work.

23. Orozco y Berra, *Historia antigua*, 1:71; and Chavero, *Mexico a través de los siglos* volume 1, 304.

24. Alva Ixtlilxóchitl, *Obras históricas*, 1:20–21, 32–37, 50–55.

25. Ibid., 30.

26. Ibid., 33.

27. Ibid., 101.

28. Ibid., 2:42–43.

29. Ibid., 1:55.

30. Ibid.

31. Burgoa, *Geográfica descripción*, 2:201–2.

32. Ibid., 3:399.

33. Borunda, *Clave general*, 242; and Veytia, *Historia Antigua de México*, 1:136.

34. Ramírez, *El apóstol*, 356–67.

35. Ibid., 355–56.

36. Sebastián de Guzmán y Córdoba, in the "Prólogo a quien leyere" (prologue to the reader) that he wrote as the editor of the first edition of the *Libra astronómica* and reproduced in Sigüenza y Góngora, *Libra astronómica*, (16).

37. Ventancurt, *Teatro mexicano*, 1:373.

38. Boturini, *Idea de una nueva historia*, 158, 217.

39. Veytia, *Historia Antigua de México*, 1:112–44.

40. Clavijero, *Historia antigua*, 52, 151–53.

41. So wrote José de Uribe and Manuel de Omaña in the opinion they rendered against the sermon delivered by Mier. See Nicolás León, "Causa formada al doctor Fray Servando Teresa de Mier . . . ," 81.

42. Two published versions currently exist—the one listed in the bibliography and another, brought out in Rome in 1898, under the guidance of the Duke de Loubat and published by the Casa de Jean Pascal Scotti.

43. On this point, see Nicolás León, "Causa formada al doctor Fray Servando Teresa de Mier . . ."; Alonso Núñez de Haro y Peralta, "Edicto de 25 de marzo de 1795," in Nicolás León, *Bibliografía mexicana del siglo XVIII*, 1, part 3: 182–87; and Mier, *Historia de la revolución*, [1:]xiv–xxiii.

44. León y Gama, "De la existencia de los gigantes . . . ," vols. 8–12. I am indebted to Roberto Moreno for providing me a photocopy of this document.

45. Humboldt, *Sitios de las cordilleras*, 36.

46. Brasseur de Bourbourg, *Histoire des nations*, 1:42–61, 108–9, 111, 114–16, 120–21, 217, 237, 240, 253–80, 288–311.

47. Orozco y Berra, *Historia Antigua*, 1:72n83.
48. Ramírez, "El apóstol."
49. Orozco y Berra, *Historia Antigua*, 1:53–89.
50. Brackel-Welda, "Apuntes para un estudio," 606–32.
51. Both Beauvois and Charency are mentioned by Lafaye, *Quetzalcoatl*, 229.
52. Heyerdahl, "The Bearded Gods Speak," 199–238.
53. Hedrick, "Quetzalcoatl," 255–65.
54. Lafaye, *Quetzalcoatl*, 229.

# 3

## The Skeptical Focus

More than a century has now passed since one of ancient Mexico's most eminent students, Daniel G. Brinton, refused to accept the history of Quetzalcoatl as describing the life of a human being. What had centuries before served to underpin the thesis that Saint Thomas had visited the New World—the ubiquity of testimonies spread across a large part of the continent—led Brinton, whose field of interest reached well beyond the limits of what we today call Mesoamerica, to discover the existence of a series of religious concepts that displayed a striking similarity. They spoke of a national hero—a mythical, master civilizer, who at the same time was identified with the supreme deity and the creator of the world. Frequently represented as having a twin or as being one of four brothers, he is born of a virgin mother, or at least does not need to be conceived through sexual contact. This hero comes into conflict with his twin or his brothers and emerges triumphant in the end. His birthplace is associated with the East. He does not die, but instead, miraculously disappears. Moreover, it is believed that he dwells in the place of his origin, from where he must one day return. He is portrayed as being white-skinned and bearded, with an abundance of hair and attired in full, loose-fitting cloaks.

To construe Itzamna the Maya, or Quetzalcoatl, or Michabo the Algonquin, or Viracocha as human beings would be to accept (their) lives as virtual carbon copies of each other and filled with mythical doings and happenings. According to Brinton, these four, along with many others, are simply figures who, properly understood, should be identified with the deities of light. Their incessant struggle—such as that which Quetzalcoatl maintains with Tezcatlipoca—is simply the succession of day and night, of light and darkness. If in some versions Topiltzin appears as the son of Tezcatlipoca-Camaxtli, this relationship should be taken as metaphor, in the sense that day comes out of night. As for his abundant head of hair and great beard of reddish color, they are characteristics of the gods of dawn, rays of light that arise from his body. The Spanish explorers and conquerors, white-skinned and bearded as they were, thus became confused with the people of the divine voyager not only by the native inhabitants of central Mexico but also by the Maya of Yucatán, the Muiscas of Bogotá, and the Quechua of Peru. Quetzalcoatl has *ce ácatl* as a birth date, a sign that also serves to designate the lands that lie in the East. His men are called "children of the sun," "children of the clouds," and "those who run all day without resting" and disappear together with their god of light. Tollan is none other than the Place of the Sun—a syncopated name—and therefore a mythical place. It is the expression of the tendency to glorify an older, better time, a lost golden age, and—for the Toltecs—to convert their ancestors into divinities or men who possess an extraordinary nature.[1]

Despite the various etymological distortions to which Brinton resorted to make his interpretation hang together, his work was unquestionably pathbreaking. Not only does it mark an important moment in the historiography of pre-Hispanic Mexico, it also sets forth a series of problems—many of them still with us—as well as the methodological bases for their solution. There is still much to learn, one and a third centuries on, from Brinton's attempts at piecing together the puzzle. Indeed, we seem to have been too hasty in turning in other directions before availing ourselves of much that this scholar taught us.

According to Konrad Theodor von Preuss, Tollan is the city situated on the sea where dawn breaks, in the country where the Sun comes up, on the great site of sacrifice.[2] As such, it is a mythical place, and mythical too, is Quetzalcoatl—the Morning Star who loses the opportunity to turn himself into a sun because of his fallen chastity. Huemac Tezcatlipoca, who succeeds in transforming himself into a sun deity, is also mythical. Both this supposed history and the myth of "The Morning and Evening Star" should be interpreted thusly, as von Preuss learned during the fieldwork that he carried out among the Nahuas of Durango in 1907. His central thesis, that at bottom the story told of a cosmic event, was based on the explicit statements of his informant, Matilde Jesús, who, before launching into the supposed legend of the two brothers—both hunters of deer—told von Preuss that it involved a tale about the two stars.[3]

The skeptical focus also framed the thinking of another great scholar of ancient Mexico, Eduard Seler, although it is difficult to pinpoint the moment in which this German philologist broke through to gain his deepest insight, since, meticulous researcher that he was, Seler maintained a constant dialogue not only with other scholars of the period but also with himself. In his writings, however, one can easily perceive the ebb and flow, the flexibility of his theories, as they bend and give way under the weight of new arguments and, perhaps in some instances, new inclinations.[4]

The most interesting position that Seler takes, I believe, centers on the problem of Quetzalcoatl's journey toward the East. If the myth of Tollan, which Seler takes to be the theoretical placement of the center of the world, is to be interpreted as an account of natural phenomena, then a movement of the heavenly bodies in a direction contrary to the movement of the sun can only be understood as the apparent backward movement, or retreat, of the Moon between the stars on the parallel 13° 10′ 36″. In its quarter phase, moreover, the Moon arrives at the Sun and thus disappears in Tlapallan (the Country of the Red) in Tlapco (the Place of the Dawn, the East) and Tlatlayan (the Site of the Great Fire)—all these names designate the point where the night star disappears, blotted out by the Sun.[5]

In his 1923 monograph, *The Gods of Mexico*, Lewis Spence likewise adopted the skeptical view about the life of Topiltzin. For Spence, Topiltzin is the protector god and god of culture who has been humanized. Kings and political rulers have been called by his name, a name that harkens good fortune in the dealings of men, and the illusion of his existence has created a putative history, that of the founder of the Toltec civilization. The prevailing winds that blow during the rainy and dry seasons produce the mythical struggle between Quetzalcoatl and Tezcatlipoca; the favorable winds are linked to the Toltecs, civilized farmers and workers of the land who benefit from them. The regenerating power of the rains and Quetzalcoatl's recapturing of youthful energy explain another part of the myth: the idea of god is humanized and, as such, gives birth to the idea of his existence as a priest-king, culminating in the establishment of a dynasty of rulers who carry his name. In addition, he is associated with the *tonalámatl* (a divinatory almanac used in pre-Hispanic central Mexico), with the Moon, with Venus, with wisdom, with the breath of life, with the performance of penances, and with the four cardinal points.[6]

Spence was followed by George C. Vaillant, who some two decades later situated the Toltecs in two capitals: Teotihuacan, on the eastern shore of Lake Texcoco, and the other on the lake's western shore, near Azcapotzalco. They worshipped Quetzalcoatl, the god of civilization, and gave his name to their priests as a title. For Vaillant, the supposed life of Quetzalcoatl is a myth, signifying within it the struggle between the defeated god of civilization and the later gods of war and heaven in the Aztec religion.[7]

Finally, based on the myths found among five indigenous peoples—the Hopi, the Cora, the Huichol, the Pápago, and the Luiseño—that invoke a carnivorous figure, a seducer and source of goods for human beings, David H. Kelly identifies

Quetzalcoatl as a product of the Yutoazteca contribution to the Mesoamerican cultural world, with the figure of a zoomorphic divinity.[8]

## NOTES

1. Brinton, *American Hero-Myths*; and Brinton, "The Toltecs and their Fabulous Empire."
2. Preuss, "El concepto de la Estrella Matutina según textos recogidos entre los mexicanos Del Estado de Durango, México" (paper, special session of the Geographical Society of Berlin, December 12, 1904) cited by Seler, "Algo sobre los fundamentos naturales," 288–311.
3. Preuss, "El concepto de la estrella," 375–96.
4. Some of Seler's opinions about Quetzalcoatl, Tollan, and the Toltecs will be found in his monograph *Comentarios al Códice Borgia*, 1:67–73; and in his shorter pieces: "Quetzalcoatl-KuKulcán en Yucatán"; "Periodo de Venus en los escritos hieroglíficos," 117–18; "Algo sobre los fundamentos naturales," 307–18; and "Aztlán, patria de los aztecas," 40–43.
5. Seler, "Algo sobre los fundamentos naturales," 312–13.
6. Spence, *Gods of Mexico*, 139–44.
7. Vaillant, *La civilización azteca*, 51.
8. Kelly, "Quetzalcoatl," 397–416.

# 4

## The Critical Focus

The skepticism directed toward those who saw in Quetzalcoatl the evangelizing preacher of the gospels had scarcely taken hold when a new school of thought emerged, one that postulated the existence of a true historical figure and, parallel to that, discarded all of the providentialist ideas, the tales of the miraculous, and the naïve acceptance of sources remote in time. In 1884, Adolph Bandelier expressed the opinion that one could clearly distinguish between a god on the one hand and a historical figure on the other, both of whom had the name Quetzalcoatl; and beyond these two, he also identified a new figure, created after the conquest, in whom the influence of such Christian traditions as the performance of desert penances and the four-day descent into hell was evident. This figure, the son of one named Camaxtli, was the political and religious leader of the Toltecs, whose community was of recent founding. Moreover, Camaxtli, a local ruler born in remote lands, had originally been taken for a man, pure and simple. According to Bandelier, the lack of knowledge that later existed regarding the life of Ce Acatl very likely contributed to his deification as the wind god. Worshipped in Cholollan, a city dedicated to commerce and rich in a variety of goods, he was viewed as both the patron of merchants and a prosperous figure himself.[1] Once again, the god, and the very conspicuous economic characteristics of his worshippers, are born out of the euhemeristic impulse.

While Bandelier confined himself to a logical, dispassionate analysis of a historiographical problem, the French traveler and archaeologist Désiré Charnay adopted a

DOI: 10.5876/9781607323990.c004

more combative posture, beginning with his emphatic repudiation of the argument that Tollan was an imaginary city and that the Toltecs had never existed. According to Charnay, they not only had existed but also were the constituent members of a highly civilized community that had, as its ancient political leader, warrior, or lawgiver, a man whom tradition subsequently made into a god of both the wind and wisdom, the companion of Tlaloc.[2] Charnay's broadside was directed at Daniel G. Brinton, who only a short time before had denied that Tollan was anything more than a city of legend or the life of its king anything other than an enchanting myth spun out of ideas about the heavenly bodies. Brinton, however, was not in the least dissuaded. Rather than enter into a full-blown refutation of Charnay, he simply stated that the latter had wandered off track when, in his *Les anciennes villes du Nouveau Monde*, he went so far as to sketch a map of the Toltecs' migrations. Charnay's entire theory, Brinton asserted, was unfounded.[3]

Mexican intellectual and political figure and early archaeologist Alfredo Chavero extended the analysis into deeper terrain and cast a more penetrating eye on the problem. While also attacking the argument that Quetzalcoatl had not actually existed, Chavero avoided any point-by-point refutation. His thinking had doubtless been influenced in some measure by the opinions of the opposing school since, though he believed that Quetzalcoatl was a historical figure—a priest and religious reformer who fought against the practice of human sacrifice—he also agreed that Quetzalcoatl's life became confused with an assemblage of astral symbols that subsequent generations then accepted as true, miraculous episodes. Quetzalcoatl the historical figure was a beautiful, chaste man who, as a youth, lived an austerely penitent life in Tollantzinco. His religious beliefs led him to establish a beneficent government, characterized by moderate ritual customs and practices, that coincided with the period of greatest Toltec prosperity, for which reason all of the inventions of the arts, agriculture, mining, and even the discovery of the sweet liquid of the maguey plant (used by the Nahuas to make pulque) were attributed, metaphorically, to him. The hand of resistance was never raised against the magnanimous rule of this wise king-priest. And when he died still exercising power, his successor, who as a priest of the same god, Quetzalcoatl, carried the same name, experienced the severe reaction of the bloody followers of Tezcatlipoca. As a consequence, new successors and new conflicts built up a cascade of events that injected complexity and contradiction into a supposedly singular life. The confluence of the episodes of multiple existences with the mythical motives of the heavenly bodies completed the picture of the legend: Quetzalcoatl is Venus and Tezcatlipoca the Moon, the round mirror that terrifies the elderly king-priest with the image of his own reflected face. Quetzalpetlatl—the priestly caste, the precious mat—is the surface of the sea waves of the Pacific below which the Evening Star sinks, in such fashion that it was seen by the Toltecs when they dwelled on the coast. The priest remains in his tomb, in a disappeared state, for four days, to emerge again as the Morning Star. The Sun approaches in an aurora of red clouds, like a bonfire, and the star melts in the fire, disappearing amid the singing of birds of great beauty whose trilling heralds the new day.[4]

Five individuals—the Mayanist Juan Martínez Hernández, Bishop Francisco Plancarte y Navarrete, Manuel Gamio, Miguel Othón de Mendizábal, and Enrique Juan Palacios—initiated a new stage in this age-old, ongoing controversy: for them, the traditional Tollan ceases to serve as an adequate homeland for the priest; instead, only the monumental urban center of Teotihuacan is deemed worthy of having housed ancient Mexico's most notable figure.[5] The region of Tula in the state of Hidalgo, Gamio informs us, has yet to be explored in depth (he was writing in 1922); but given the nature of the terrain and its topography, one can deduce that a great city, such as the famed urban complex described by the early chroniclers, was never erected there. Teotihuacan's imposing size, on the other hand, brought into relief (for Gamio et al.) the serious error—whether it lies in a name or an idea—of considering Hidalgo to have been the ancestral home of the Toltecs, of Ce Acatl.[6] Nonetheless, the controversy lived on, reaching a crisis point two decades later; and it continues down to the present, albeit with less fervor, pitting the partisans of Tollan-Xicocotitlan in the state of Hidalgo against those of Tollan-Teotihuacan in the state of Mexico.

The picture of the purely historical Quetzalcoatl continued to be sketched ever more precisely. Teotihuacan had already been sanctioned as the proper cultural and spatial framework for Quetzalcoatl, but Herbert J. Spinden now furnished the specific calendrical confirmation. The question of when—that is, in which century particular events had unfolded—was laid to rest: according to Spinden, the day on which Quetzalcoatl established the Toltec era was 6 August, in the year 1168. The lighting of the new fire, a ceremony (of Mayan origin, in Spinden's view) repeated every fifty-two years, occurred on 16 February 1195. And on 4 April 1208, Quetzalcoatl expired. He had conquered Chichén Itzá, in Yucatán, in 1191 and, aided by Huetzin and Ihuitimal, extended his domain from Durango in the north to Nicaragua in the south, making three principal cities the seats of government: Teotihuacan in the Valley of Mexico, Chichén Itzá on the Yucatán Peninsula, and Iximché in present-day Guatemala. Having spent his youth in Yucatán, he returned to his native land, the high plateau country of central Mexico, armed with novel social ideas and a new religion, and there constructed the serpentine columns of Tollan, on the model of their counterparts in far-off Chichén Itzá.[7] By relating the circumstances of his life based on the documentary sources, Spinden set aside the mythological attributes and recovered Quetzalcoatl as a historical personage, an individual who had lived in a particular time and place.

The euhemeristic interpretative line was carried forward by R. J. Ceballos Novelo, for whom the central problem in the biography of Ce Acatl was to isolate the city in which the king-priest had lived.[8] Not surprisingly, the pursuit of archaeological excavation intensified the debate around this issue. In 1873, the geographer Antonio García Cubas had identified the ruins of Tula, in the state of Hidalgo, and some time afterward, Charnay explored, excavated, and made discoveries on this same site. Unfortunately, because of his careless and unscientific practice, he also destroyed much of the archaeological context of what he excavated. In 1935, Francisco Mújica Diez de Bonilla found and handed over four stela on which the figures of elegant persons had been sculpted. The systematic investigation of the zone, however, got underway in 1940, led by Jorge R. Acosta, Hugo Mohedano, Alberto Ruz, Ramón Galí, and Jorge Obregón. From another angle, if one sets aside several other developments—the map made in 1864 by Ramón Almaraz, Charnay's explorations of 1885, the reports submitted by William Henry Holmes in 1897, and the excavations carried out first in 1884–1886 and later, in 1905, by Leopoldo Batres—then the opening for a full-fledged debate occurred in 1917, with the start of the rigorously scientific explorations of the monumental site of Teotihuacan, directed by Manuel Gamio and his team. Work on the site continued, and by 1940 had yielded enough data to greatly enliven the debate, which encompassed more than one discipline. The archaeological findings had spurred the interest of historians, and their engagement in turn inspired continued archaeological investigation. Between 1935 and 1938, the discussion began to heat up noticeably. In the lattermost year, Alfonso Caso, Ignacio Marquina, Wigberto Jiménez Moreno, Paul Kirchhoff, and Mario Mariscal brought the discussion to a new level by selecting the research sites that seemed most likely to lead to a resolution of the problem.[9] Two years later, as noted above, systematic exploration began on the Tula site, and in 1941, a special meeting of the Mexican Anthropology Society was convened, dubbed the "Primera reunión de Mesa Redonda sobre problemas antropológicos de México y Centroamérica," in which, as the story has it, the discussion between those who defended Tollan Xicocotitlan as the site where Quetzalcoatl lived, versus those who granted that honor to Tollan Teotihuacan, became so intense as to reach a boiling point.

One of the partisans of the Teotihuacan-Tollan thesis was Enrique Juan Palacios, who had started the argument many years earlier. Palacios did not deny the possibility that there may have been persons in Tula de Hidalgo who bore the same name as the great priest, or that this—in his judgment—small city might have carried the title of Tollan, which was common to many important urban centers. Rather, he felt that reasons of chronology (the influence that Kukulcan had during the tenth century within the territory of the Maya, a time period when Tula lacked any comparable colonizing strength) or archaeology (the presence of common architectural elements in Teotihuacan and Chichén Itzá versus their absence in Tula) or simply ground-level comparisons between the large, ancient, strong metropolis and the weak Tula-Xicocotitlan, forced him to conclude that the Toltecs, whom the sources describe as famous artisans and craftsmen, were the builders of Teotihuacan.[10]

Details gleaned from historical sources are more evident in the arguments advanced by Jiménez Moreno, arguments that he based primarily on the identification of geographic features that match up with what is recounted in the ancient legends of Tula Xicocotitlan, where the same or similar place names are still preserved.[11] Jiménez Moreno's studies concerning the figure of Quetzalcoatl, however, go well beyond the problem of determining the location of the Toltec capital.[12] On the basis of wide and deep reading, he tried to integrate data from historical sources, the contributions of archaeology, and the myths collected by modern ethnologists to elaborate a highly detailed history of Quetzalcoatl, which begins with the arrival of Cazcana tribes led by the father of our protagonist. His father, who is known as Mixcoatl and later is taken for a god, impregnates Chimalma with Topiltzin, then dies before his son is born. Educated by his grandparents in lands that today form part of the state of Morelos, the young man absorbed teachings that spoke of a god, Quetzalcoatl. These teachings inspired him to become a priest, and he adopted the god's name. Subsequently, he recovered the throne of the empire that his father had founded, introduced the new religion that countered the ideas of the Toltec-Chichimec population—Nahuas, bearing the traces of Otomí influence, who worshipped Tezcatlipoca—founded the city of Tollan, was driven out of it either in 897 or in 999, withdrew from the region, and later died in Mayan territory. Huemac, one of his later successors as ruler of Tollan, again abandoned the city in 1156 or 1168. Another group that featured prominently in this historical narrative was the Nonoalcos. Descendants of the Teotihuacanos and neighbors of the Toltec-Chichimecas, they were Pipil people from Coatzacoalco and also worshiped Quetzalcoatl. This story about Quetzalcoatl can be considered one of the great efforts to bring together, as a logical whole, a great mass of material that by its nature resists falling into a coherent unity.

Alfred Tozzer and J. Eric Thompson expressed an opinion that seems entirely reasonable if one knows the Mayan sources in depth. The unquestionable relationship among Quetzalcoatl, Ehecatl, Ah Nacxitl, Xuchit, Topiltzin, Tlamacazqui, Ce Acatl, Tlalhuizcalpantecuhtli, Huemac, Kulkulcan, Hunac Ceel Cauich, Gucumatz, and Tohil, and the impossibility that a single figure to whom these names were given could, over his life alone, have been at the center of so many episodes and chapters in Mayan history, covering both space and time, lead to the conclusion that we are dealing with different men who are perhaps united by a title or a surname.[13] It is simply inadmissible that the life of the journeying Toltec in the Mayan zone could have lasted long enough that it permitted him to achieve all of the heroic feats of which the sources speak.

The supporters of Tula-Xicocotitlan as the Toltec capital continued to uphold their argument. Based on archaeological comparisons, and against Palacios's claims, Ruz found that a verifiable relationship had existed between Tula-Xicocotitlan and Chichén Itzá, but not between Teotihuacan and Chichén Itzá.[14] Pedro Armillas similarly agrees with the connection—validated by their common place names—of Tula-Xicocotitlan,[15] taking as his reference point Jiménez Moreno's historical reconstruction, which he then enriched with new components. At the core of Armillas's thinking was the dissimilarity and apparent lack of any relationship among the diverse attributes of the god Quetzalcoatl: creator and also bestower of the vital force, Venusian deity and also wind god. For him, the matter clearly involved the merging of three different gods under a single name; a dead chieftain, later to be deified, became identified with one of them. This process occurred in a cultural environment in which the transformation of heroes into gods was an all-too-common phenomenon. The deified lord and leader, who apparently dates to after the ninth or tenth century, gave rise to a series of men who carried his title, as is clearly shown in the sources of Maya origin. The struggle between Quetzalcoatl and Tezcatlipoca can be interpreted as a political-religious conflict. And more particularly, as possibly the bellicose action of the son of Mixcoatl who, as the priest—*Quetzalcoatl*—of a god who is not the god of his pueblo but rather of the group with whom he coexists and who descends from the cult of worship that had lost power, wants to impose under the god that bears his name a theocratic organization against the barbarous god, Tezcatlipoca, of his father's pueblo.[16]

As the archaeological investigations went forward, the problems—far from disappearing—became more complicated, in part at least because the process was skewed. Neither the interpretations of researchers nor the information revealed in the sources were properly calibrated or reconciled with the discoveries in the field. For example, Jorge R. Acosta found it mysterious that there was no evidence or record whatsoever of the rivalry that existed between the worshippers of Quetzalcoatl and the worshippers of Tezcatlipoca; no image of this god of the night (Tezcatlipoca) had been found in Tula-Xicocotitlan and Toltec-constructed buildings of the most recent vintage were decorated with representations of Tlahuizcalpantecuhtli, one of the forms taken by Quetzalcoatl. Acosta's supposition, after he had made this illuminating observation, was that the struggle could have been between Quetzalcoatl, the Morning Star, and Tlahuizcalpantecuhtli, the Evening Star.[17] Unfortunately, this line of reasoning, or hypothesis, was much weaker than the observation that preceded it. Better that Acosta would not have sought such a simplistic solution to a problem that was so difficult.

Alfonso Caso, supported by Thompson's observation regarding the absence of metal in Teotihuacan—something hardly compatible with the high reputation of Toltec goldsmiths and silversmiths—also aligned himself with the identification of Tula-Xicocotitlan as the homeland of Quetzalcoatl.[18] With respect to the life of the priest, however, Caso did not see things in an equally clear light. He discussed a myth of opposition between saintliness and wickedness, which in the realm of cosmic struggle is represented by the astral gods Quetzalcoatl and Tezcatlipoca. During the Toltec era, this myth attains not only mythical but historical characteristics. The cosmic struggle is transformed into a moral struggle, in which the king is obliged to abandon Tula, persecuted by the faithful adherents of Tezcatlipoca.[19] Are we dealing here with the interpretation of a historical event, which some time after its occurrence is raised to the level of a myth? Or are we, perhaps, dealing with the historical coincidence of an earlier myth that is, by chance, matched by an actual similar occurrence—the cosmic and the human drama converging, as it were? There is no adequate explanation.

In the face of these opinions, Laurette Séjourné entered into the argument, defending the identification of Tollan with Teotihuacan and offering an idealized interpretation of the life of our protagonist. In her judgment, Tula-Xicocotitlan could not possibly have served as the priest's home, since the rise of this city coincided in time—the tenth century—with the brutal clash caused by the arrival of nomadic hunters, a clash that had released the Mesoamerican pueblos from the mysticism that gripped them in preceding eras.[20] If Sahagún provided place names that seem to identify Tollan with the city in present-day Hidalgo, it only means that Sahagún was in error.[21] The images of Quetzalcoatl had existed in a city of a thousand years greater antiquity.[22] Teotihuacan, on its merits—ancient and monumental—was the homeland of the priest turned into a god,[23] the first king of Tollan, Tollan-Teotihuacan,[24] a wondrous man who preaches a doctrine such as those who throughout the history of humankind postulate the pain and torment of sin and the need for purification:[25] a doctrine that invokes the exalted revelation of the eternal unity of the spirit and liberation from the prison of the self;[26] a doctrine in which action is the force that liberates the spirituality that encloses every earthly particle and saves matter from obliteration and the weight that impedes the ascendant course of the soul.[27] All of the foregoing can be known through the myth, since Quetzalcoatl himself elects Venus to represent his parabola; the course of the Evening Star is the same as that followed by the soul, since the soul "descends from heavenly dwelling, enters into the darkness of matter to raise itself up once again, glorious, in the moment of the body's dissolution."[28] The episodes in the life of the priest express, metaphorically, the message revealed in the heavenly origin of man: the demons are vexed by his purity and invent the subterfuge of "giving a body" to he who is spirit.[29] The priest's city, Teotihuacan, literally means "the city of the gods," thereby designating the place in which man is transformed into a god and the serpent—matter—acquires the wings that enable it to reach the upper regions.[30] Down to the very level of symbolic expression in the plastic arts, every theological fundament is verified, and the curved figure that appears frequently in ceramics, the *xicalcoliuhqui*, represents the internal movement that translates into the source of liberating energy.[31]

Moreover, while the man of genius, the glorious man, the visionary saint, dwells upon the land, endowing his people with the seed that bears the fruit of civilization, which spreads across all of Mesoamerica,[32] this tremendous dynamism arises and flows spontaneously, until the Mexicas—the villains of the story in this supposed paradise of happiness, revelation, and holy life—burst upon the scene and, deploying their bloody "reason of state," poison and corrupt the laws of internal human perfection taught by Quetzalcoatl.[33] Yet the inheritance was such that, even into the ceramic arts, it permitted different communities—equally and by common agreement—to parcel out and share its legacy. "Each ethnic group would limit itself, so as to make its own what essentially amounted to just one [skill or technique]: the Zapotec, etching or carving lightly on stone; the Maya, bas-relief; the totonacas, cutting and working precious stones; and the Mixtec, painting."[34] If history tells of events that seem to sully the life of the saint, it is solely because the grandness of his name caused it to be repeated and given to other figures, among them the Topiltzin of bloody memory who lived in Tollan—the other Tollan—during the tenth century.[35]

It hardly seems necessary to expend time and energy in a lengthy, well-founded critique of this brand of thinking and the orientation underlying it. The image of the wise-redeemer-visionary saint, who through his towering spiritual powers leads people, creates civilizations, and saves men from sin, should be cast aside for what is: worthless, demeaning, justifying the oppressive binding of men, and manifestly false. It suffices to note that another thesis like Séjourné's—idealistic beyond all reason—would be hard put to carry our protagonist any further into the realms of perfection, since in her telling he has already attained an unsurpassable point of false glory.

Rather, let us return to the man in whom we began to glimpse the blood, flesh, bones, and sweat of a human being. Quetzalcoatl, the ruler of Tollan, had to have lived at a certain point in time. On this key question, Paul Kirchhoff saw but two logical possibilities: they indicated either the first king of Tollan—or at least one of the first—whose departure took place 159 or 169 years before the downfall of the Toltec empire (which occurred under the rule of Huemac) or a king who was contemporary to Huemac. In the latter case, each could have occupied their posts simultaneously or one could have followed immediately upon the other, and the departure of Topiltzin prompted the collapse of the capital and its satellite communities. Both possibilities may be considered valid and set either at the beginning or the end of Tollan. Based on the *Anales de Cuauhtitlán*, Jiménez Moreno opted for the first, whereas Kirchhoff, relying on the remaining sources, believed the second to be correct. The contemporaneity of Quetzalcoatl and Huemac is sufficiently documented in the history, which contains references to persecutions, wars, rivalries, and periods of joint rule. A priest, who bore the name of the god to whom he was devoted, was the recipient of attacks by other religious persons who also harassed his partner in rule, Huemac, when the rebels tried to install the practice of human sacrifice. Quetzalcoatl refused to bow to the entreaties made by the partisans of this bloody ritual, but Huemac did, and the unity between the two was broken. Defeated and shamed because his enemies succeeded in tempting him to lose his chastity, Quetzalcoatl fled, while Huemac, succumbing to the same temptation, lost the priesthood through his sexual transgression but obtained civil ruling authority as a reward for his defection.[36]

Kirchhoff's study, published in 1955 as the prelude to another work that remained in the project stage,[37] clearly delineated the evolution and major lines of the argument. He was correct in stating that a strict reading of the sources placed the lord of Tollan either at the start or the end of the Toltec empire, and that there was no room for arguments that put him elsewhere on the continuum or that posited even more radical alternatives. He had settled on his interpretation on the basis of a meticulous, objective analysis of the sources. Unquestionably, however, Jiménez Moreno had also examined the problem with historiographical rigor. Thus, the only way to achieve final clarity seemed to lie in totally denying the worthiness of particular groups of primary texts. By this means, one or the other school of thought, resting on a discrete body of primary source material, could be validated. Predictably, this strategy simply created a host of new questions and promoted a precarious middle ground of uncertainty. But the stakes were planted, and there they have remained.

The biography of Quetzalcoatl has been modified since then and he has been the subject of extremely interesting research, but as far as clarifying the time period of Topiltzin's life in Tollan, we have come no further.

Walter Krickeberg states that if all of the legendary and mythical elements in Quetzalcoatl's life are eliminated, one can perceive a Toltec history that is divided into two periods: the theocratic, represented by Ce Acatl, worshipper of the god Quetzalcoatl; and that of the warrior princes, of Huemac, worshipper of Tezcatlipoca. Two migrations, composed of two different types of Toltecs, promoted the confused image of these people, believed by some sources to have been the agents of a peaceful life, while reproached by others for their bellicose, conquering character and their blood-soaked religion.[38]

H. B. Nicholson, after an extended review of the sources that speak of Quetzalcoatl the man, concludes that Topiltzin is unquestionably a historical personage, albeit one whose life has been modified down through time and tradition by patterns of myth, legend, and folkore.[39] The son of Mixcoatl, he lived during the early days of Tollan, to whose throne he ascended in a way that is still unclear. Once in power, he is merged on the one hand and confused on the other with one or more of the deities who bridge the attributes of fertility, rain, wind, and creation. He was a religious innovator and introduced the rites of self-sacrifice. Because of ill-defined opposition to his religious doctrine, he was forced to emigrate, probably at the head of a considerable number of followers, and disappeared on the eastern horizon, out of sight of his former vassals on the high central plateau. It is possible that several rulers bearing his name set out for and reached Yucatán.[40]

Ignacio Bernal focused on the complexity of the history of the celebrated Ce Acatl, king of Tollan. According to Bernal, this complex history derived from the custom of giving the name Quetzalcoatl to all of the god's priests, whose lives were later fused together in the chronicles.[41] This idea, which as we have seen did not originate with Bernal, would acquire new importance some years later, under the urgings of Román Piña Chan.

Miguel León-Portilla contends that even more important than establishing the existence of Quetzalcoatl as a living man—which in itself still entails complex, unresolved problems, especially for his life in the Mayan world—is the recognition that he was viewed as a central figure in the spiritualism of pre-conquest Mexico, to the extent that the philosophical thinking ascribed to him came to dominate an entire cultural epoch.[42] According to the sages of antiquity, Quetzalcoatl conceived of a universe threatened with destruction, a universe created and controlled by a supreme, dual god, and that many other gods had perhaps been no more than manifestations of this prime god. It was incumbent upon mankind to stay attuned to this god by attending to the task of artistic creation, mimicking that of the universe. The idea of the fatal destruction of the world impelled this native philosopher to conceive of a world beyond, in which human thought reached new heights—a place of knowledge called Tlillan Tlapallan, the site of that which was red and black.[43] The journey to Tlillan Tlapallan is the end point, the culmination that signifies the overcoming of present reality as the true aim of wisdom, the highest ideal set forth by this culture hero.[44]

In 1962, César Sáenz published a book devoted to Quetzalcoatl in which he placed the focus on archaeological evidence. Regarding the historical personage, he mentions somewhat off-handedly that various men had lived who bore the name Quetzalcoatl and in this context cites the opposed arguments of Jiménez Moreno and Kirchhoff.[45]

In 1963 and 1964, Enrique Florescano followed Jiménez Moreno's line, upholding the view that the religion that Ce Acatl adopted in Xochicalco—the land of his grandparents—flowered as a reaction to the lustful, disordered life that members of the theocracy led in Teotihuacan, a state of affairs that brought about the ruin of civilization from top to bottom. Consequently, the new religion stressed austerity, meditation, and the constant performance of religious duties. The worship of this religion was shared by the Nonohualcos. It was they who lent support to the Toltec Ce Acatl as lord of Tollan, where they coexisted with the Toltecs. A religious conflict ensued only later, and this community—less civilized but victorious in battle—allotted to itself the glories and wisdom of its former partner city, turning *Toltec* into a synonym of great artist. Florescano also rebutted Séjourné's claim that Teotihuacan was the Tollan of Quetzalcoatl. Her claim rested, at least in part, on the discovery she made of a ceramic piece on which a bearded person appears and at whose side appears a feathered serpent on a mat. For Florescano, this evidence carried very little weight when compared to the picture, carved on stone, of Ce Acatl Topiltzin Quetzalcoatl that existed in Tula-Xicocotitlan. Séjourné's Plumed Serpent in Teotihuacan was, in Florescano's view, the image not of the priest-king but of an older cult, organized around the worship of a deity of vegetation.[46]

For Piña Chan, the overriding interpretive problem surrounding the life of Quetzalcoatl is the plurality of personages who bear the name and exercise the power as doubles of the god. Over time, Topiltzin Quetzalcoatl comes to be associated with the ruler and political figure, the civilizing hero, the inventor of the calendar and of the game of *pelota*, the discoverer of corn and of the bounty of the land, and the creator of the Sun of the Toltecs and of the planet Venus: "Ce Acatl Topiltzin Quetzalcoatl, Kukulcan, Cuchulcan, Gucumatz, Tohil, Nacxitl, Votan, etc., are the same deity; they are later converted into mythological figures born of the god and raised to the level of culture or civilizing heroes, from whom various groups come to descend (Toltecs, Xiues, Tzeltales, Quichés); but the deity was the precious plumed serpent, the planet Venus and its vital cycle, the worship of which was enriched by priestly ideals."[47]

According to Piña Chan, Quetzalcoatl is a concept resulting from a religious symbolism that becomes integrated over time and draws upon contributions from different cultures. Toward the end of the Classic period, the many ideas of which it is composed are synthesized into a true philosophy. It was not born of a real person. Rather, the god gave his name to certain rulers, whom the sources confused with the deity. Thus, as Piña Chan's intriguing thesis has it, it is the god that arises first, then later the myth, and then ultimately the man.[48]

Finally, Robert Chadwick expounds the unsettling thesis that Toltec history was copied from the Mixtec codices and that the life of Quetzalcoatl and Huemac in Tollan, according to the Códice Chimalpopoca, amounts to no more than the first and second dynasties of Tilantongo, in the Mixteca Alta. Throughout his essay, Chadwick correlates dates, place names, and personages and concludes that the Tollan of Quetzalcoatl must be the monumental Teotihuacan, not the city in present-day Hidalgo. The conflict between our protagonist and Tezcatlipoca began in Teotihuacan. The struggle between dynasties continued, with the final battles recorded as having taken place in the region of the Mixtecs.[49]

## NOTES

1. Bandelier, *Report of an Archaeological Tour*, 169–215.
2. Charnay, "La civilisation toltèque," 281–305.
3. Brinton, "Toltecs," 83.
4. Chavero, *México a través de los siglos volume 1*, 303–11; and "Explicación del códice geroglífico de Mr. Aubin," 76–90.
5. Mendizábal and Palacios, "El templo de Quetzalcoatl," 2:343–54.
6. Gamio, introduction to *La población del Valle de Teotihuacan*, 1:lxi–lxii.
7. Spinden, *Ancient Civilizations*, 172–75; and Spinden, "New Light on Quetzalcoatl," 506–11.
8. Ceballos Novelo, "Quetzalcoatl," 257–65.
9. Ruz Lhuillier, *Guía arqueológica de Tula*, 27–28.
10. Palacios, "Teotihuacan, los toltecas y Tula," 113–34.
11. Jiménez Moreno, "Tula y los toltecas," 80; and Ruz, introduction to *Guía arqueológica de Tula*, 10–11.
12. In addition to the two items just cited, see the following by Jiménez Moreno: "Síntesis de la historia pretolteca," 1094; "Síntesis de la historia precolonial," 222–25; "El enigma de los olmecas," 125–26, 136–37, 139; "'Advertencia' a la obra de Lehmann," in *Una elegía tolteca*, 4–5; and *Notas sobre historia antigua*, 22–34.
13. Tozzer, *Landa's Relación*, 22n124; Tozzer, *Chichén Itzá*, 1:28; and Thompson, *Grandeza y decadencia*, 123.
14. Ruz Lhuillier, *Guía arqueológica de Tula*, 47.
15. Armillas, "Teotihuacan, Tula," 65.
16. Armillas, "La serpiente emplumada," 162–78; and Armillas, "Tecnología, formaciones," 28–29.
17. Acosta, "Interpretación de algunos," 107–08.
18. Caso, "El complejo arqueológico," 90, supported by Thompson, in the latter's *Excavations at San José, British Honduras*, J. Eric Thompson (Washington, DC: Carnegie Institution of Washington, 1939), 90.
19. Caso, *El Pueblo del Sol*, 39–41; and Caso, "Quetzalcóatl," 33–34.

20. Séjourné, *Pensamiento y religión*, 94–95.
21. Séjourné, "Teotihuacán, la ciudad sagrada," 201–2.
22. Séjourné, *Pensamiento y religión*, 95.
23. Séjourné, "El mensaje," 159.
24. Séjourné, "Teotihuacán, la ciudad sagrada," 183.
25. Séjourné, *Pensamiento y religión*, 64.
26. Ibid., 35.
27. Séjourné, *Un palacio en la Ciudad de los Dioses*, 12.
28. Séjourné, *Pensamiento y religión*, 69.
29. Ibid., 67.
30. Séjourné, *Un palacio en la Ciudad de los Dioses*, 12.
31. Séjourné, *El universo de Quetzalcoatl*, 56.
32. Séjourné, *Un palacio en la Ciudad de los Dioses*, 12.
33. Séjourné, *Pensamiento y religión*, 35 and Séjourné, "El mensaje," 163–64.
34. Séjourné, *Un palacio en la Ciudad de los Dioses*, 12.
35. Séjourné, "Tula, la supuesta," 157–60.
36. Kirchhoff, "Quetzalcoatl, Huemac."
37. It was to have been titled *El fin de Tula: Quetzalcoatl y Huemac, los colhua y los mexica*.
38. Krickeberg, *Las antiguas culturas*, 209–13.
39. Nicholson, "Pre-Hispanic Central Mexico," 22.
40. Nicholson, "Topiltzin Quetzalcoatl," 314–27, 360–61.
41. Bernal, "Huitzilopochtli vivo," 150.
42. León-Portilla, "Quetzalcóatl: Espiritualismo," 127.
43. León-Portilla, "El pensamiento prehispánico," 29, 34.
44. León-Portilla, *Quetzalcoatl*, 33.
45. Sáenz, *Quetzalcoatl*, 10–14, 17.
46. Florescano, "Tula-Teotihuacán"; and Florescano, "La serpiente emplumada."
47. Piña Chan, *Arqueología y tradición*, 80.
48. Ibid., 80–81.
49. Chadwick, "Native Pre-Aztec History."

# 5

## The End of a Truncated History and Its Consequences

Much could have been added to this history of a biography, in which I collapsed entire treatises into a few lines and omitted many others completely. My intention, however, was simply to provide the backdrop for studying a political-religious problem. As we have seen, the sources are at loggerheads on certain key points, for more than superficial reasons. Those who have followed the story this far can appreciate—if only in broad outline—the impact left by the sources in forming such a chaotic picture of Quetzalcoatl and also weigh it against the thinking of some modern authors regarding the divergence of opinion. And some, looking ahead, may have anticipated the explanation that follows.

In any event, the full history of the biography called for by Nicholson in his doctoral dissertation has yet to be written. Whoever answers the call will find material to aid him or her considerably, and not only in the field of history but also outside it, in the literary sphere—with dramatic works, such as the play *Quetzalcóatl*, that did so little for Alfredo Chavero's reputation; or the theatrical piece, also titled *Quetzalcóatl*, written by the Mexican poet and playwright Berta Domínguez; short stories, like "Culculcan" by Miguel Ángel Asturias; and poetry, exemplified by Agustí Bartra's long poetic work "Quetzalcoatl." The material also encompasses cultural analysis, philosophical reflections, and psychological investigations. All three approaches were seemingly interwoven by Fernando Díaz Infante, when he sought to plumb the soul of the Nahua people by psychoanalyzing the figure of Quetzalcoatl,[1] or by Jorge Carrión, who did much the same, but on the larger canvas of the Mexican nation, in his essay "La ruta psicológica de Quetzalcóatl."² A pantheon of other authors, such as Octavio Paz, Ermilo Abreu Gómez, and Luis García Pimentel, have also sought to interpret the myth of Quetzalcoatl and its place in Mexican history and society. Also worthy of mention in this context are the irreverent epithets about Quetzalcoatl found in the writings of Carlos Fuentes and the nationalist-inspired project, dating to the times of Pascual Ortiz Rubio, under which Quetzalcoatl—to the dismay of a shocked public—would replace Melchior, Gaspar, and Balthasar as the dispenser of gifts to children on Three Kings Day.³ The prospective biographer of Quetzalcoatl can also contend with and compare such opposites as the demonic god described in all his ghastly horror by one sixteenth-century friar and an American Christ—though one who is "naturalized"—whose traces are so longingly searched for by a pious contemporary of the friar, the traces of a blond Christ moving among men who were such great sinners that their skin darkened. And finally, as fodder for a mass audience, the biographer will encounter the Quetzalcoatl well known to school children and others via comic books, a Quetzalcoatl presented as nothing less than a wise man from outer space, a cosmic traveler who provokes astonishment in the Indies with his flying saucers.⁴

**NOTES**

1. Fernando Díaz Infante, *Quetzalcóatl: Ensayo piscoanalítico del mito nahua* (Jalapa: Universidad Veracruzana, 1963).

2. Jorge Carrión, "La ruta psicológica de Quetzalcóatl," *Cuadernos Americanos* 8 (September-October 1949): 98–112.

3. Fuentes Mares, *La revolución mexicana*, 209.

4. This theme was used in the inaugural issues—February and March 1972—of the noxious popular magazine *Enigmas de la humanidad*.

# 6

## Men and Gods

While it is impossible to know how far back the tradition reached, the system of social, economic, and political organization found in sixteenth-century Mesoamerica revolved around units or groups whose membership was determined by ties of kinship. At the same time, however—and again, it is impossible to know how long the tradition had existed—the different cultures of Mesoamerica lived under regimes that were indisputably defined by instruments of state power. They had apparently been locked for a long time in an intermediate state, a prolonged transition that showed no signs of ending, so that what ought to have been a temporary condition turned into the norm.[1] The group's religion was one of the key elements that molded its cohesiveness, via a cultural patron, a type of divinity to whom the Spaniards gave the name protector god (*dios abogado*). Diego Durán states that every city, town, and settlement had a particular god "to whom, as the protector of the community, obeisance was paid through major sacrifices and ceremonies,"[2] and the Codex Magliabechiano underscored that each neighborhood or district had its own god, with a large temple erected for its worship, where *vecinos* (persons of a certain standing) held festivals in its honor.[3] In Nahua texts, these gods were frequently designated by the simple word *intéouh* (their god), following the name of the people of a given region or place; but the specific term is *calpultéotl*, or "god of the *calpulli*," this latter word signifying the kinship group and core social unit, considered by many as tantamount to a clan. The name of the *calpultéotl* leads one to think that, when it initially formed, a network of families consisted of those who, on the basis of blood relations, considered themselves to be descendants of a common being, the offspring of a particular divinity. Nicholson strongly emphasizes the wide spectrum, in terms of scale and size, of the social groups that the divinities protected. They ranged from extensive provinces or ethnolinguistic groups at one end to small sectors of the community at the other.[4] On this score, for example, the sources tell us about the god of the Otomíes;[5] or about the god who protects a given city;[6] or about the gods who belong to the different ethnic groups of which the city is comprised, each a separate population sector living in its own district;[7] or about the gods who—and here the interpretation reflects a clear Spanish orientation—belong to the districts themselves.[8] Among some present-day Mayan pueblos—and there should be no surprise that, from this point on, I draw constant comparisons with non-Nahua pueblos, since the Mesoamerican cultures can only be comprehended as constituent members of a cultural super area—the surnames are linked to the *calpulli*, which in turn are linked to a particular god.[9] At times, there is even the impression that a conglomeration of gods guides an ethnic group. And when the history refers to one in particular, it also distinguishes a god who looms over the ensemble: the Chichimeca were guided by the four hundred Mixcoas; but a community within the Chichimeca population—the Cuauhtitlanecas—were guided by Iztacmixcoatl, the younger brother of the gods who were called by the name Mixcoas.[10]

Two researchers have tried to define the specific characteristics of these protector gods. Nicholson notes as important factors the presence of the deities during times of migration; the existence of sacred images or bundles in which objects donated by the patron god are hidden; the fact that the privilege of carrying and transporting the image or bundle frequently belonged to the priest-rulers; the esteem garnered by these figures in their role as intermediaries between the protector god and the pueblo; the identification of the protector (god) with the ancestral tribe; the title given to the god as the "heart" of the community; the construction of a temple to the god as a formal act upon the founding of a settlement; the presence of the temple as a symbol of the community's independence and internal cohesion; and, conversely, the destruction that an image or bundle could suffer, or the theft it could experience, when a pueblo was defeated.[11] Luis Reyes classified these gods into three types: culture heroes or dema gods, the founders of pueblos, and priest-warrior-guides.[12]

The information contained in table 6.1 illustrates that reference to these gods in the sources is frequent and important. Column 1 provides the name of the protected unit—a people, ethnic group, or *calpulli*; column 2, the name of its protector god(s); and column 3, the respective source.

Presumably, during the period in which homogeneous ethnic groups inhabited fairly extensive geographic areas, they possessed common protector gods.

TABLE 6.1. Examples of protector gods of different peoples and cities

| Pueblo, Ethnic Group, or Calpulli | Protector God | Source |
|---|---|---|
| acxotecas | Acollacatl Nahualtecuhtli | Chimalpahin, Memorial, 37v |
| amantecas | Coyotl Ináhual | Sahagún, 3:61 |
| | Tizahua | |
| | Macuilocelotl | |
| | Macuiltochtli | |
| | Xiuhtlati | |
| | Xillo | |
| | Tepoztecatl | |
| Atenchicalcan | Iztacmixcoatl | Anales de Cuauhtitlán, 62 |
| Atitlalabaca [sic] | Amimictli (a rod of Mixcoatl) | Historia de los mexicanos por sus pinturas, 219 |
| coyohuacas | Tezcatlipoca | Chimalpahin, Relaciones, 154 |
| Cuauhtitlan | Fire God | Las Casas, 2:192 |
| cuauhtitlanecas | Mixcoatl | Anales de Chauhtitlán, 5 |
| Culhuacan | Cinteutl | Historia de los mexicanos por sus pinturas, 219 |
| | Cihuacoatl | Historia de los mexicanos por sus pinturas, 225 |
| | Ocotecuhtli, fire god | Historia de los mexicanos por sus pinturas, 219 |
| culhuas | The Sun | Serna, 173 |
| culhuacachichimecas | Tonan Quilaztli | Primeros memoriales de Sahagún, 60r |
| Chalco | Tezcatlipoca Nappatecuhtli | Historia de los mexicanos por sus pinturas, 219 |
| chichimecas | Mixcoatl | Sahagún, 2:81 |
| chichimecas neztlapictin teotenancas | Nauhyotecuhtli | Chimalpahin, Relaciones, 68 |
| Cholula | Quetzalcoatl | Motolinía, Memoriales, 70 |
| | Mixcoatl | Motolinía, Memoriales, 70 |
| Huexotczinco | Camaxtle | Motolinía, Memoriales, 70 |
| Huitzáhuac (district of Tetzcoco) | Tezcatlipoca | Pomar, 13 |

*continued on next page*

**TABLE 6.1**—*continued*

| Pueblo, Ethnic Group, or Calpulli | Protector God | Source |
|---|---|---|
| matlatzincas | Tlamatzincatl | Clavijero, 158 |
| mexicas | Tetzauhteotl Yaotequihua | Chimalpahin, Memorial, 23v |
| mexicachichimecas | Huitzilopochtli | Primeros memoriales de Sahagún, 60r |
| mexitin atenca | Huitzilopochtli | Chimalpahin, Memorial, 31r |
| Mízquic | Quetzalcoatl | Historia de los mexicanos por sus pinturas, 219 |
| otomíes | Huehuecoyotl | Códice Vaticano Latino, xxi |
|  | Otontecuhtli | Primeros memoriales de Sahagún, 60r |
|  | Mixcoatl | Sahagún, 1:204 |
| Teopancalcan | Iztacmixcoatl | Anales de Cuauhtitlán, 62 |
| tepanecas | Ocotecuhtli, fire god | Historia de los mexicanos por sus pinturas, 219 |
| Tepeaca | Camaxtle | Motolinía, Historia de los indios, 48 |
| Tetzcoco | Tezcatlipoca | Mendieta, 1:98 |
| Tícic | Iztacmixcoatl | Anales de Cuauhtitlán, 62 |
| tlacochcalcas | Tlatlauhqui Tezcatlipoca | Chimalpahin, Relaciones, 165 |
| tlacochcalcas nonohualcas teotlixcas | Tezcatlipoca | Chimalpahin, Relaciones, 201 |
| Tlacopan | Ocotecuhtli, fire god | Historia de los mexicanos por sus pinturas, 219 |
| tlailotlaques | Tezcatlipoca | Alva Ixtlilxóchitl, 1:289 |
| Tlaxcala | Camaxtle | Motolinía, Memoriales, 70 |
| toltecas chichimecas | Ipalnemohuani | Historia tolteca-chichimeca, 70 |
|  | Tezcatlipoca | Historia tolteca-chichimeca, 70 |
| totonacas | Great goddess of the heavens | Mendieta, 1:96 |
|  | Centeotl | Clavijero, 158 |
| Tzapotlan, in Xalixco | Xipe Totec | Sahagún, 1:65 |
| xaltocamecas | Acpaxapo | Anales de Cuauhtitlán, 25 |
| Xaltocan | The Moon | Sahagún, 1:262 |

*continued on next page*

TABLE 6.1—*continued*

| Pueblo, Ethnic Group, or Calpulli | Protector God | Source |
|---|---|---|
| xochimilcas | Cihuacoatl | Durán, 2:171 |
| Xochimilco | Quilaztli | Historia de los mexicanos por sus pinturas, 219 |
| Zacatlan | Camaxtle | Motolinía, Historia de los indios, 48 |
| zapotecas | Xipe Totec | Códice Vaticano Latino, xli |

Later, political rivalries and pressures caused their fragmentation and dispersion, either promoting the rise of the *calpulli* or, as is more likely, driving apart homogeneous *calpulli* that had initially lived contiguously. Separated and composed of families that came from different places, obliged to integrate settlements and live together due to economic exigencies, each *calpulli*—with its patron god over it— constituted an integral unit. Evidence of this pattern emerges from the *Relaciones geográficas*, in which there is no shortage of pueblos having Huitzilopochtli as a protector—the god whom belief had held was so closely connected to the founders of Mexico-Tenochtitlan. It was from these *calpulli*, as units protected by particular gods, and from the supremacy achieved by some of them in the formation of settlements and communities, that the patron god of the city arose. From the predominance of certain cities there then emerged, perhaps, a god who appeared to preside over the destiny of an entire ethnic group, although it is possible in some cases that ethnic groups were able to preserve a certain measure of collective political cohesion, and with it the unity of the patron god. Xipe Totec, according to the Codex Vaticano Latino, is *one of the gods* of the Zapotec,[13] and the persistence of the practice or custom whereby some *calpulli* have one particular god who gets elevated to become the god of the city is evident in Mexico-Tenochtitlan, where the priests of the protector god, Huitzilopochtli, came only from certain districts.[14] Examples also exist of a *calpulli* or community, cut off by the rebellion of the city in which it has lived under the domination of a different group, that returns to its erstwhile god and abandons that of the tyrant power. Such was the case for the Mexicas who, after abandoning the mysterious Aztlan (hence the name Aztecs, by which they came to be known) but before founding Mexico-Tenochtitlan under the mandate of their god Huitzilopochtli-Mexi, reaffirmed loyalty to their old cult and abandoned the humiliating name of those who had dominated them.[15]

Did the *calpulli*, however—through their travels and migrations and the contributions of their protector gods—gradually stitch together out of a patchwork of cults a religion that spread across Mesoamerica? Many have wanted to see it that way, with some parties having referred to the existence of gods belonging to the Pacific or Gulf Coasts or of a patron numen that was incorporated into or fused with an already existing one.[16] Yet the reality was apparently otherwise: a common base, a religion that covered an extensive area and possessed subtle regional differences, created a broadly accepted cosmovision—with one or another variant—across the cultures of Mesoamerica. Each social nucleus descended from a god, who often was named by a family appellative that no other men in the unit used. In the general scheme of things, this god was specific unto itself and could not be added to; it was here, by its own rights, in the divine place to which it had always corresponded. Or it could have been a patron god instead, precisely because it occupied in advance a fixed place in the world of secularly ordered numens. The *Historia de los mexicanos por sus pinturas* tell us that "these gods had these and many other names because according to how things were comprehended or attributed to them, so they were named, and [also] because each pueblo, by virtue of its own language, gave them different names, their names were many and various."[17] The sources, for example, state that Xomuco, the creator deity of men, is Itzpapalotl;[18] and that Tepoztecatl, worshipped in Tepoztlan, is Ometochtli.[19] Mexitli is Huitzilopochtli.[20] Although in this case there are elements which lead one to suppose that a sun and a terrestrial divinity were, in addition, fused.[21] Indeed, Pedro Carrasco—despite thinking that the phenomenon plays out on the level of tribal gods—takes the position that the Otomí Otontecuhtli, the Mexica Huitzilopochtli, and the Tarascan Curicaueri, Ocotecuhtli, Xocotl, and Cuecuex could all be the same numen.[22]

So proprietary is the god to a pueblo, and so proprietary the pueblo to a god that, depending on how it is looked at, one or the other imposes its name through its presence. Mexi is the god of the Mexitin or Mexicas. Tepoztecatl is the god of the Tepoztecas. Totonac is the god of the Totonacas.[23] Totec Tlatlauhqui Tezcatlipoca, the Red Tezcatlipoca, is the god of the Tlapanecos, "the native inhabitants of the Red Country."[24] Totollini is the god of the Chichimecas Totolimpanecas.[25] Taras is the god of the Tarascans.[26] And the list goes on.

Why is this proprietary relationship so fundamental? In the first place, because human groups have been created by the gods. And here research comes up against the problem of the creation of mankind, where mythmaking proliferates: "and since it is the case that some recount untrue fables, to wit: that they were born from some fountains and springs of water; others that they were born in and emerged from some caves; others that they sprang from the gods, etc: [all of] which are clearly and plainly seen to be fables, and they themselves are ignorant of their origin and beginnings, since they are forever attesting that they came from foreign lands."[27]

Out of the apparent chaos of the greatly varying myths it is incumbent to extract some concepts that, while they may not be present in all versions, nonetheless permit us to ratify the existence of some common benchmarks and principles. In the first instance, the creation is spoken of with reference not to the human species as a whole but to separate ethnic groups, in whom the time, the creator, the circumstances, and the place of their birth vary notably. Nor is the process of creation simultaneous. Instead, its appearance on the earth varies by year, century, and even, as Alva Ixtlilxóchitl tells it, by different suns and cosmic ages.[28] The year in which the creation occurs is especially important, and it is frequently called out in the sources. In some cases, the repeating or telling of cosmogonic myths seems to lurk, among the steps leading to the creation of men, leaving a sense of doubt about the relationships that obtain among figures in the storyline, whether they constitute astral gods or primordial human beings. A process apparently existed in the birth of different peoples that repeated the process under which their protectors had come into being—this correspondence serving as a model or guideline for men who, created in the same way as their patrons, had to ratify their dependent condition. The similarity between gods and men could be such that, in place of a god creating a first man, the four hundred Mixcoa gods led to the first four hundred Chichimecas. I recently committed to print an idea that not only has preoccupied me for some time but has also seemed to acquire, one element after another, greater validity with each passing day: the existence of a fundamental concept in Mesoamerica of the division of the world, based on a horizontally ordered break in which the upper part would be constituted by light, warmth, life, the masculine element, and the heavens (with the symbol of the eagle), while the lower part would contain the earth, water, darkness, death, coldness, and the feminine element (with the symbols of the ocelot and the serpent), to give but a partial listing of these oppositions.[29] Men, who dwell at the conjunction of the two, are created by the combination of the two worlds—the world of above (the heavens) and the world below (the earth). The process can be separated into four logical stages: the descent of the semen, conception, pregnancy, and parturition and separation of the children, as a way of schematizing the creation of pueblos.

Looking first at the process of fertilization, certain references lead to the supposition that the birth of humankind was due to the desire on the part of the gods to be worshipped. The sources, in fact, portray the need to obtain the nourishment that has to move the Sun with the blood won in battle. The supreme creator is the lord of heaven and earth, Teotloquenahuaque, Ipalnemohuani, who after having brought into existence all things visible and invisible, "created the first fathers of men, from whom all the rest came."[30] The problem arises when the texts call this creator by the name of one of the gods, the lord of the wind, Quetzalcoatl: "And they said thusly: he engendered people, he engendered us, he had the will to create us, he who is our inventor, Topiltzin Quetzalcoatl, and he invented heaven, the Sun, Tlaltecuhtli."[31] Why is a particular god cast in the role, assigned the place, of Tloque Nahuaque, the supreme god? There are three possible answers: (a) Quetzalcoatl is the creator god of a human group that, having gained power, exalted its patron as the originator not of simply a particular pueblo but of all humankind; (b) In addition to one or several gods being the specific creators of each pueblo, a greater body of numens had previously taken part in the creation, and among them Quetzalcoatl fulfilled an exceptional role, pointedly as a divinity of fertilization and as the very semen of heavenly divinity itself; and (c) Quetzalcoatl is one of the names of the supreme god, independently of being the name of a numen with a defined span of action—or this particular numen is one of the manifestations of the supreme god, as León-Portilla asserts in several studies.[32]

The last answers seem to get closer to the truth: the supreme god is repeatedly invoked under different names, some of which also correspond to the names of lesser gods. Among these names are those of Tezcatlipoca and Quetzalcoatl. On the other hand, in contradistinction to the first answer, it should be underscored that the presence of figures equivalent to that of Ce Acatl, and to his attributes as creator-ancestor-civilizing hero, exists both within and outside of Mesoamerica—in South America, as Metraux has noted,[33] and in both the Americas, as we earlier observed in the work of Brinton. Within the orbit of Mesoamerica, but outside the Nahuatl world, we encounter reference to the most beautiful indigenous literary work known to date:

> There was only immobility and silence in darkness, in night. Only the Creator, the molder, Tepeu, Gucumatz, the progenitors were in the water, encircled by light. They were concealed under green and blue feathers, and for that reason were called Gucumatz. Their nature is that of great sages, great thinkers. In this way the heavens existed and also the Heart of Heaven, which is the name of God. Thus was it told.[34]
>
> And they said, the progenitors, the Creators and Molders, who are called Tepeu and Gucumatz: "The time of dawn has arrived, may the work be finished and that those appear who are to sustain us and give us nourishment, the enlightened sons, the civilized vassals; let man, humankind appear over the surface of the land." Thus was it said by them.
>
> They arrived, gathered together and held their council in the darkness and the night; later they searched and confabulated, and here they steeped themselves in reflection and thought. In this way their decisions came forth with clarity and they encountered and discovered what should go into the flesh of man.[35]

At the risk of stating the obvious, Gucumatz is the Quiché equivalent of Quetzalcoatl.[36] Not only is he there, among the creator and the progenitors, but it is also difficult to know, from the phrasing and wording of the text, if (and what) differences and categories might come into play. All of the principals were called Gucumatz and all were in the heavens determining the birth of men. And soon thereafter, as will be seen, Quetzalcoatl, together with other gods, creates man, and he participates in this event in a very special way.

The descent of the fertilizing semen appears to take three principal forms: first, as an arrow, or dart, that plunges into the earth; second, as the fall of some gods, sons of the celestial couple; or third, an intermediate course, the blow of a big knife, to which Citlalicue—the consort of Citlalatonac—gives birth and which, upon falling to earth, turns into six hundred thousand gods.[37]

The arrow, the gods, or the big knife arrive at the feminine place, which is a rock, a cave, a place called Texcalco—"the rocky outcropping"—and get buried in the ground; or either a mother of pueblos, Chimalma, appears, "engendered by the rain and the earth's dust,"[38] or Iztacchalchiuhtlicue, who gives birth multiparously and who, "when [the Mixcoas] entered the cave, gave birth to them once again."[39] As the Codex Vaticano Latino makes abundantly clear, the pregnancy happens inside some caves,[40] in a place that bears such well-known names as Chicomóztoc and Tamoanchan.[41]

The act of conception may signify the moment of peak importance, when man is formed out of cold and hot matter. From their place on earth, the gods ask their heavenly parents to give them men so they can be worshipped by them, and they are ordered to take the bones from the world of the dead and form humankind out of them, spraying them with their own blood. This is the moment when Quetzalcoatl—or Xolotl—acts in a very special way, coming before Mictlantecuhtli and, by means of pleading, trickery, and chance, gives the bones to all of the gods so they can spray them with their blood, and, as a creative gesture, perforates his penis.

In the Codex Matritense de la Real Academia,[42] there is a protector god of a pueblo who is called *econitlacapixoani*—that is, "arrived," "creator of men"—and it further relates that they brought him (as an image) and that he spoke to the ancient ones who came first, the Mexitin. After the creation (in the myths) the birth takes place. The "arrived ones" (*econime*) are those who will themselves bring it about, who will cause the mountain to open so that the pueblo should commence its history. Or so we are led to deduce from the question put by the Chichimecas who, entombed in Culhuacan-Chicomóztoc, ask to be released, voicing the hope that those issuing the order shall be the creators.[43] In contemporary times, and outside the Nahuatl world, the Tzotziles continue to attribute to the creators both the function of granting the *ch'ulel*, one of the animistic entities—which was perhaps conveyed at the moment when the blood watered the bones—and of opening the caves in the hills that permitted their exit into the world.[44]

In the Nahuatl sources, it is Chicomóztoc—the "place of the seven caves"—from which they can make their way out. In the Mayan sources, the exit place has several names—Tulán, Pa Tulán, Pa Civán, Vucub Pec, and Vucub Ziván.[45] They emerge from here to see the Sun for the first time. As a general rule, groups of pueblos, varying in name but not in number, emerged successively. Seven groups, each from its own cave, come out of Chicomóztoc, although the order in which this passage occurs differs from source to source. For this reason, they are believed to be related to each other, even though the enumerations often refer to people who belong to different linguistic groupings. It is not unusual to encounter an allusion to a place of origin that lies beyond the sea, a place from where men must proceed by crossing the waters, a process that possibly conforms to the projection of a foundational myth.[46] In some cases, this narrative is not so explicit, relating only that upon their birth, men submerge themselves in the water and later are suckled by some divinity.[47] Some versions mention that, upon leaving the caves, the men are bid farewell by a goddess, possibly identifiable with the earth itself, who instructs them to go in search of the promised site.

Each tradition endows its first cohort of men with different features and attributes. They speak, variously, of human beings with half a body, who can only reproduce by means of sexual contact realized through their mouths, since they lack a lower part to their bodies;[48] of various primordial couples, who set out on the journey together, procreating groups linked by ties of friendship; of already-formed human groups that are presided over by the protector god, who may appear either as himself or in the guise of an animal; of children born to a single miraculous couple, each one of whom bears the name that belongs to the pueblo they will found;[49] of primal couples, in the manner of Adam and Eve—the *achtopa tlacaxinachtin*[50]—in whose names (Oxomoco and Cipactonal for example)[51] it is possible to identify gods; and of beings who, as the result of being the children of gods or having been formed out of parts of their bodies, partake of the divine nature.[52] Some gods are looked upon as being simply the direct predecessors—*inculhuan intahhuan*, "their grandparents," "their fathers," of the pueblo.[53] In general, whether deities or beings who seem to occupy an intermediate space, they are able to lead the group's migration. One day, the leaders die or go off, leaving the pueblo by itself upon the land. According to the Nahuas who live today in the municipality of Benito Juárez, in the state of Veracruz, all of their progenitors now find themselves in heaven.[54]

In his initial interactions with his now-constituted pueblo, the patron god serves as the guide, the "first captain," who must lead the pueblo in its migration. The Codex Telleriano-Remensis tells of this figure, imparting the idea that his leadership of the migration has led his followers to take a man as a god.⁵⁵ In some codices, the guide appears depicted in human form at the front of his group.⁵⁶ According to Muñoz Camargo, he is also presented *"en fantasmas"* (as a ghostly figure).⁵⁷ And in the case of the god of the Mexicas, it is noted that he precedes his people in the form of a white eagle that alights here and there to indicate the places where the group should bivouac.⁵⁸ The most recurrent form of his presence, however, once he had separated himself from the original company of men, was as the image that—carried on the ark of reeds or born on the shoulders of the priests, the *teomamaque*, in charge of it, or guarded in the same fashion inside a bundle—served to provide counsel to his community. These images, several of which are seen to be carried at the same time when the migration is composed of a complex of groups,⁵⁹ communicated privately to the leader-priests, dictating to them all of the important segments and stages of their journey. We can easily surmise the political force that a man held to be a divine intermediary would possess at all times in the eyes of his people. So venerated were the images themselves that some could not be looked upon directly, though the faithful would nonetheless come before them, offering sacrifices.⁶⁰

Once a settlement had been established, the patron god could continue, through its image—bundled or otherwise—to dictate needed actions.⁶¹ In some cases, it maintained its place throughout the entire history of a pueblo as an oracle in the temple, whereas at other times, in other pueblos, it mysteriously ceased to speak.⁶² This form of guidance has not been altogether lost. For example, the instances of the *cajas parlantes*, or so-called talking boxes, that have surfaced within Mayan political-religious movements are well known.

The bundles—*tlaquimilolli*—contained relics that the god had bestowed upon his pueblo, and they served as well as a medium to link the two. Some pueblos had obtained them as an offering, or gift, as far back as in their place of origin.⁶³ Others had found them during their wanderings, as is related in the history of the two bundles—the *chalchihuite* and the *maderos* (jade stone and fire sticks, respectively)—that the Mexica discovered, which, according to the sources, were the cause of the dissension that culminated years later in the community splitting up into two cities, Mexico-Tenochtitlan and Mexico-Tlatelolco. Both groups wanted the chalchihuite; the maderos, as shown by Huitziton, were more useful, since with them people learned how to light fire.⁶⁴ Still others had come directly from heaven, like the chalchihuite that fell onto the pyramid of Cholollan.⁶⁵ These precious possessions were always preserved in places accorded the most importance. They ranged from natural or simple handmade objects, such as the darts, or arrows, of Huitzilopochtli or the feathers, tinder, obsidian, and bow and arrows of Camaxtle,⁶⁶ to parts of the god himself—for example, the thigh bone of Tezcatlipoca and the beards of the Sun.⁶⁷ Some of these objects functioned as true instruments of communication, such as Tezcatlipoca's mirror, in and through which he appeared and spoke to his priests.[68] The Mixtec pueblos had a special predilection for the relics that were made out of jade, among which the piece discovered and destroyed in Achiutla by Fray Benito Hernández, one that its devotees called the "heart of the pueblo," particularly stands out.[69]

Through what the gods had passed down, the virtue of attracting the protection of the patron was present to such a degree that it could be obtained even when an enemy pueblo made use of it. Indeed, the practice followed by Mesoamerica's indigenous inhabitants of setting fire to the main temple of an enemy city, an action that signified the city's immediate downfall, is widely known. The reason behind this action is very clear: the protector is the supreme force of the pueblo. He may physically appear, armed, in combat, and beseech the heavenly god that he come to the aid, militarily, of his creatures;[70] although the assistance that he provides is more routinely transmitted via his image or relic. "He lives among them," as Alvarado Tezozómoc recounted,[71] and for that reason they place him, in the form of a statue or of his sacred bundle or both, as a guardian and means of defense, in the center of the city.[72] In Diego Durán's words, "He wages war for them."[73] Thus, some carry the sacred bundle, and the relics it contains, directly into battle.[74] If the pueblo's force resides in its god and his images and relics, then the enemy's penetration of the top of the temple, their capture and destruction of his image and burning the dwelling place, not only brings all of his protection to an end but also causes the pueblo—without any further resistance—to give itself up to the invader; to fight any more would be useless. The instances of such destruction, and even more frequently of robbery, carried out by the victors, are amply described in the sources.[75] The robbing of images and relics happened frequently for the simple reason that their power could be tapped and used if they were kept in a favorable relationship to the god, propitiating him with offerings.[76] To this end, the Mexica had constructed a temple in which they housed, as captives—and presumably treated well—the gods of defeated and subject pueblos.[77] The sources refer to an image celebrated for the force that it furnished its devotees and which for that very reason had to be treated with special care, even though that meant burying it in mud,[78] because of the danger that others who commanded power would succeed in taking it over. The most effective way to demonstrate submission to the victorious party was by relinquishing—though it might only be transitory—independence, through the act of handing over relics.[79] In more serious cases, when a pueblo had to concede defeat and submit to its enemy definitively, it would straight away, without qualification, renounce its founder numen and accept the imposed foreign cult. In this context, Durán describes the uncertain, doubtful attitude displayed by the Mexica in the face of the Tepaneca forces. It was proposed that the Mexica give themselves up completely to Azcapotzalco (*altépetl*, or city-state, of the Tepaneca), in which case the unity of the Mexica would be broken, since they would be intermingling with the Tepaneca community to the point of losing their own identity. Against this option, there was a counter opinion expressed, advocating that the group should enter and blend into Azcapotzalco, but with its gods concealed, as a way of preserving, with them, its integrity as a pueblo.[80] On other occasions, the requirement was such that the group that had fallen out of fortune had to accept the tutelage of a foreign god and receive as their new father and mother the gods of the owners of the lands that they were given as a favor.[81] The analog to this form of submission was the presentation by a dominant pueblo of a minor relic to a weaker pueblo, so that the latter would preserve and worship it.

The aid that was rendered was not exclusively military. As the sources note,[82] the protector god was the "heart of the pueblo"—*altépetl iyollo*. This name instantly recalls to memory concepts from ancient Mesoamerica that have lasted, in a notable way, into our times: Heart of Heaven (*Corazón del Cielo*), Heart of the Mountain (*Corazón de la Montaña*), Heart of the Hill (*Corazón del Cerro*), Heart of the Sea (*Corazón del Mar*), and Heart of the Lake (*Corazón del Lago*). "Spirit" or "soul" are closer to the idea conveyed in the word *qux*, so Brinton states when referring to the Quiché term, since the idea is associated with movement, and the Indians believe that life, intellect, and passion are found in the viscera.[83] Regarding the Nahuatl term, León-Portilla has written:

> *Yóllotl*: heart. As a derivative of *ollin*: "movement," literally meaning in its abstract form *y-óll-otl* "its mobility, or the reason for its movement" (understood of the living). The Nahuas therefore conceived of the heart as the dynamic, vital aspect of a human being. On that basis the person was "face, heart." Possibly, the Aztecs made an offering of the heart, the dynamic organ par excellence, that produces and preserves life and movement, to the Sun, because this same understanding was present in their own mystical-militaristic world view.[84]

The concept of the protector god as the "heart of the pueblo" clearly and indisputably has two principal elements. First, that of a conscious, volitional being who constitutes the reason that the pueblo exists as a social unit, a person who combines in himself the very essence and nature of the entire population, the *nahualli* of the pueblo, as Benson Saler heard it put in Guatemala.[85] Second, that of the first or motivating cause, the life of everything that lives in the pueblo. Sahagún records that the creator of the *petateros* (mat makers), Nappatecuhtli, gave the virtue of being born and of growing to the reeds, sedges, and stalks that his sons used to make mats.[86] William Holland relates the story of a contemporary Tzotzil Indian who, upon emigrating and against the indications of the divinity that had appeared to him in dreams, took some corn seeds that belonged to his community. The outcome was obvious; he had taken the seeds but not their spirit, and instead of germinating they turned to dust.[87] And the life of the individual human being? I earlier referred to how cosmogonic myths were adapted to overlay those associated with the creation of pueblos. The same relationship exists, extended in time, in the birth of a child. In the prayers that are said to accompany its birth, the midwife alludes to the divine collaboration between the heavenly gods and Quetzalcoatl that was needed to make the child, and she immediately sprinkles it with holy water. For their part, the protector gods watch out for each person, granting him the animistic entity that, belief held, originated through the element of heat-masculinity-heaven in the formation of men. Some present-day Nahua hold that the pueblo's protector goes out armed with a sword to fight against the evil being that takes possession of a sick person's soul (*tonalli*), defeats it, recovering that part of the patient that had been taken from him, at which point he is restored to good health.[88] In this same vein, many contemporary Mayans believe that the protectors of the pueblo, the "fathers-mothers," confer the soul (*ch'ulel*) upon each child while it is still in its mother's womb.[89]

The protectors or patrons possess a primordial attribute—their watery nature—that seems to have gone unnoticed. Their descent into the mountain's interior and their contact with the bones of the dead at the moment of man's creation perhaps explain why they partake of the qualities that belong to the entities of the underworld—among them their intimate connection to rain and water. The ancient Maya of Yucatán appealed to these gods—and this seems to confirm what was said above—for their aid in war, in attaining a long life, and in dealing with the elements.[90] Sources from the Nahuatl world relate not only that Huitzilopochtli,[91] Tezcatlipoca,[92] Nappatecuhtli,[93] or Tlatlauhqui Tezcatlipoca[94] were worshipped and propitiated as rain gods, but also that the twenty-day period of *tepeíhuitl*—the feast of the mountains—in which the rain gods were celebrated, is represented in the Códice Telleriano-Remensis as a hill, above water, with the symbols for rain and water, these being paper banners coated with rubber and the head of Tlaloc; and furthermore, that it was the feast of the "protectors" and of "all saints."[95] And should any doubts need to be dispelled, one need only examine the Códice Azcatitlan and its depictions of the gods Huitzilopochtli and Tezcatlipoca (represented as a hummingbird and a smoking mirror, respectively) that are carried, as images, on the migration by the priests who guide the group. (See figures 6.1 and 6.2.) These gods, like the pueblos they precede, have recently been in contact, in the mountain's interior, with darkness, cold, water, death, femininity . . . and serpents. A little carelessness on the part of the priest, or a little care on the part of the painter, and the secret is revealed: out of each of the bundles being carried there emerges a tail crowned by rattles!

**FIGURE 6.1.** Códice Azcatitlan, plate vi    **FIGURE 6.2.** Códice Azcatitlan, plate vii

The life of every migrant pueblo in the pre-Hispanic world, agriculturally oriented as it was, was inextricably linked to the availability of water resources. Rain was the gift of Tlaloc and his consort Chalchiuhtlicue, divinities surrounded by a true court of minor lords. The dwelling places of these beings were marvelous paradises of eternal springtime that produced every kind of thing that nourished and brought happiness to human beings. Moreover, they were located not in heaven but under the earth, very close to those who sought their favors. There is some interesting text in the Florentine Codex that explains the origin of the generic name of human settlements:

> The people of New Spain, the people of old, said: These [rivers] come—they flow—there from Tlalocan, they are the property of, they issue from the goddess named Chalchiuhtli Icue. And they said that the mountains were only magical places, with earth, with rock on the surface, that they were only like *ollas* or like houses, that they were filled with the water which was there. If sometime it were necessary, the mountains would dissolve; the whole world would flood. And hence the people called their settlements *altépetl* [*atóyatl*]. They said, this mountain of water, this river, springs from there, the womb of the mountain. For from there Chalchiuhtli Icue sends it—offers it.[96]

A settlement thus means "water-mountain," and its name derives from the hollow mountain that protects human abodes. As beautifully depicted in the frescoes of Teotihuacan's temple of Tepantitla, the damp court of the happy green family lives within these shells. Tlaloc, the lord, is the king of all the *tlaloque*, and among them are found, first and foremost, his four figures placed at the corners of the world. The lesser beings bathe in the springs or, amid claps of thunder, break pots of mud that lie in the heavens, letting their contents fall onto cornfields; or they blow at the clouds to make them move or carry the cold sicknesses that will invade and take possession of people's blood and joints; or they play, sing, and laugh inside the hollow mountains. It is the paradise of some, dead from watery causes, who become aids to the rain and the wind, and also of beings who cause problems with hailstorms or with painful, hurtful wounds. Each mountain is a god, and all of these gods transformed into mountains are gathered around Tlaloc and his wife:

> They also believed that all the prominent mountains and high mountain ranges shared in this condition and divine element, [and] they therefore imagined that in each of these places there was a god lesser than Tlaloc, subject to him, [and] through whose command that god brought about the clouds, and caused them to dissolve into water, which they awaited in the mountains and ranges throughout those provinces. For this reason, all of the inhabitants of those parts who shared in this water and rain were in the habit of coming to this place, where they saw that the clouds formed and built up, to worship that god who they believed presided over it, by the command of Tlaloc; and there are many of these places in New Spain.[97]

The lord of the gods of water was on Tlaloc's mountain, and on its promontory, to represent him, there was a temple in which the image of the divine ruler was encircled by other, smaller images—those of his underlings, the surrounding mountains.[98] Mountains that, among the Quiché, could cause either good or evil to those who came near them.[99] Male or female mountains that, according to contemporary Nahua belief, can also be favorable or damaging to the fortunes of people.[100] Mountains that, in the view of the ancients, are a couple—husband and wife.[101] Mountains out of which the god himself emerged to speak to people.[102] The mountains are the dead; they are the rain and must be continually worshipped by men.[103] But what is vital, the heart of the matter, is that the mountains are the protector gods: Matlalcueye,[104] Tezcatlipoca,[105] and Camaxtle[106] among the ancient Nahua; the protector gods, in Mesoamerica, of such distant peoples as the Zapotec—Coquebezelao, or the imaginary fantastic voice that bursts forth from the mountain.[107] For the Caxcane, their mother peak.[108] For the Quiche of Utatlán, their "*Mancebo* (young man) who helps [them]."[109]; They fulfill the same function as protector gods for the contemporary Tzotzil of Zinacantan,[110] within a religion that, tied to the land they cultivate, has operated for century upon century. Because they are one and the same, interchangeable, many of the gods and the rulers of pueblos bear the name of mountains: Gagavitz and Zactecauh, which according to the version of the Cakchiquel language offered by Adrián Recinos, mean "mountain of fire" and "mountain of snow."[111] By the same token, Huitzilopochitli is called Coatépec, "the serpent mountain."[112] The creators, protectors, oracles, guides, all of whom are interlinked and dwell together with their pueblos, are transformed into mountains, subordinated to Tlaloc and revered in caves, in high mountain sanctuaries, and on small rock mounds—those mounds that, in the judgment of the great persecutor of idolatries, Hernando Ruiz de Alarcón, who failed to grasp their importance, are unworthy of the splendid pathways that lead to the mountain summits.[113]

Water gods for pueblos that till and farm the land. And here it should be interjected that one must distinguish between the nature of the heavenly progenitor as such and its independent nature, established by the position it occupies in the pantheon of gods. Oftentimes, the coincidence is perfectly clear between the role of a water numen (Huixtocihuatl, for example) on the one hand and that of a god who provides rain on the other, specifically as the protector of a group of farmers who establish themselves alongside a mountain, where the protector—a pilgrim, like his pueblo—will dwell or into which he will be transformed. And what if, instead, the god is a god of the stars? The situation is analogous. Here on earth, beside his people, such a god will also have the role of a mountain filled with water, water whose course it will administer under the commandments of Tlaloc.

It is not difficult to suppose that, in the popular mind, for the campesino, *his* god—understood as the complex of god-image-relic of his pueblo—was independent of the god who dwelled in another part of the world, over the heavens, under the earth, in the water. A god who was different, even, from the god who—bearing the same name—presided over another human group. The god of one's own pueblo might even be reputed to be stronger and to work greater miracles than the same god in a neighboring pueblo.

At this point, we need to consider the cases of those who did not dedicate themselves exclusively to agriculture. The *calpulli* was a self-sufficient social collectivity in which the products needed to maintain daily life were produced by its own members.[114] Two factors contributed to this equilibrium: the simplicity of life within the peasant Nahua community and the presence of manual skills that so surprised and impressed the Spaniards. At the same time, however, the early chronicles make frequent mention of the existence of groups engaged in specialized tasks and labors. Furthermore, the sources indicated that crafts were inherited, passed down from fathers to sons.[115] Only with the permission of the *tlatoani*[116] could a man not born to merchants engage in commerce on a permanent basis.[117] The continuity of families, extending back to remote times,[118] within a profession was reported by many indigenous informants. With the exception of two obscure references,[119] I believe that all the sources are in agreement that the tradition of labor, as carried down in families, was the established norm. Moreover, work of a specialized nature occurred not only at a simple family level but at a wider group level as well; or, as the Spanish observed, the lines that separated identity grounded in kinship versus that based on territorial division, or the "district," were not clearly drawn. With reference only to the system of organization found in Mexico-Tenochtitlan, Arturo Monzón wrote, "I believe it can be shown, on the other hand, that these 'districts'—which most likely were *calpullis*, since in general their names do not coincide with those of the tlaxilacallis—were clans, and therefore that the division of work, like that affecting ownership of the land, the territorial distribution of the population, and social stratification, were the outgrowth of a clan-based organization of Tenocha society. Hence it is not anachronistic to speak either of clans of lords or of clans of pulqueros."[120]

The social system, then, was strictly ordered and regulated, and since the father served as his own children's teacher, he had no need to pay for their apprenticeship to a trade, contrary to the assertion made by López de Gómara, whose outlook on the matter was strongly shaped by the ideas underlying the tradition of guilds in Europe.[121]

Monzón's spot-on observation rested on his study of Tenocha social groups, a study that he synthesized and expressed in a table that groups *calpulli* or districts with their corresponding occupations and protector deities. It is reproduced in table 6.2.

In the breakdown of this same scheme, however, one will note a serious problem or discrepancy—namely, neither the trades, which are too numerous, nor the gods, who seem to be greater in number than their count within each *calpulli*, are clearly delimited. Of course, some groups undeniably fulfilled more than one artisanal trade—for example, the Amantecas, who dedicated themselves both to medicine[122] and to the elaboration of feather mosaics.[123] In addition, certain complexes of gods belong to just one group, as is the case with Coyotl Inahual, Tizahua, Macuilocelotl, Macuiltochtli, Xiuhtlati, Xilo, and Tepoztecatl.[124] It is also possible, as happened around 1930 among the Maya of Chan Kom, that small groups of individuals could have a common patron god.[125]

These cases were perhaps due to outside people—with their own gods and occupations—entering and embedding themselves into a *calpulli* at certain junctures, when it was open to such movement. It is also likely, however, that the interpretation of the sources has been subject to confusion, especially as concerns the term *calpulli*, which has sometimes been defined too liberally or imprecisely.[126]

TABLE 6.2. Correlations between districts-*calpullis*; temples-*calpullis*; occupations or offices; and deities in Tenochtitlan (source: Monzón, *El Calpulli*, 50–51)

| Calpulli or District | Occupation | Deities |
|---|---|---|
| 1. Yopico | silversmiths, goldsmiths, fabricators of offerings made of flowers, water, merchants, lords and kings, school for nobles | Totec, Xipe, Coatlicue, Coatlatona, Chalchiuhtlicue, Tlaloc, Tequiztlimayahuel |
| 2. Huitznáhuac | lords, fishermen, school for nobles | Huitzilopochtli, Opochtli, Huitznahuac, Centzonhuitznahuac, Tezcatlipoca |
| 3. Itepéyoc | rulers, functionaries | Huitzilopochtli |
| 4. Amantla | artists and artisans, embroiderers, artisans who painted designs on clothing, feather workers, painters | Tizahua, Macuilocelotl, Macuiltochitli, Xihui, Tlati, Xilo, Tepoztecatl, Coyotl, Inahual, Chicomexuchitl, Xochiquetzal |
| 5. Pochtlan | merchants | all the gods belonging to Amantla, plus Yacatecuhtli |
| 6. Auachtlan | merchants | |
| 7. Atlauhco | merchants | |
| 8. Acxotlan | merchants | Nahui Ehecatl, Chiconquiahuitl, Xomocuil, Cochimetl, Yacapitzahuac, Nacxitl, Chalmecacihuatl |
| 9. Tlamatzinco | pulque makers, tavern keepers, school for nobles | Tlamatzincatl, Izquitecatl, Coatlicue |
| 10. Atempan | healers and seers | Toci, Mother of the Gods |
| 11. Tzonmolco | makers of the main attire of the lord, school for nobles | Xiuhtecuhtli, Huehueteotl, Ixcozauhqui |
| 12. Tzapotlatenan | vendors of *úxitl* salve | Tzapotlatena |
| 13. | mat makers | Nappatecuhtli |
| 14. | lapidaries | Chicnahui, Itzcuintli, Nahualpilli, Cinteotl, Cihuacoatl |

Of course, the correlations drawn by Monzón were not limited to Mexico-Tenochtitlan. Another scholar who addressed this broad theme, formulating a list that dealt with the remote origin of certain occupations, was Úrsula Sachse.[127] On the other hand, the geographic extension of organized merchants, who occupied entire districts within the main cities, is well known. The sources go so far as to associate certain activities with particular ethnic groups. Some examples are: warriors with the Chichimeca Chicomoztoques;[128] artisans, painters especially, with the

Tlailotlaques Toltecas;[129] merchants[130] or potters,[131] with the Cholultecas; architects and carpenters, with the Xochimilcas;[132] hunters with the Chichimecas;[133] canoe fisherman, with the Mexica;[134] officials for the prime crafts with the Olmec, the Huixtotin, and the Mixteca;[135] singers, with the Tenochca and the Tetzcocanos;[136] architects, carpenters, silversmiths, metal workers, stone cutters, necromancers, sorcerers, wizards, astrologers, poets, philosophers, orators,[137] those with knowledge of the wheel of fate and fortunes and interpreters of dreams,[138] with the multifaceted Toltecs; and, far off in the Mayan area, another warrior group, the Cakchiquel, who in the name of their profession—the military, *ac chay*—bore that of the divinity Chay, the "Obsidian Stone."[139]

The link between the pueblo and its specialized line of work was such that the names of some occupations were forgotten in favor of a designation that in reality was nothing more than the name of a people from a particular region. Thus, Amanteca came to mean "he who fabricates objects made of feathers"; Pochteca, "organized merchant"; and Toltec, "artist," "artisan." Nor did the custom apply solely to those pueblos in which profession and social group were identified and aligned: the accomplished orator was called *tentoltécatl*, or the "artisan of the lips." Tollan, synonymous as the capital that brought together great artisans and builders in its districts, bestowed fame upon its men that lasted long after its disappearance.

Based on the writings of Torquemada, Monzón argued that in the beginning everyone labored in agriculture, although everyone did not perform the same tasks.[140] At the same time, routines were not unvaryingly agricultural because, among other things, the life of the *calpulli* could become destabilized. The historical sources reveal, in fact, that during the final centuries before the Spanish conquest, many pueblos in Mesoamerica alternated between periods of stability and periods of migration.[141] Insufficiently developed farming techniques, sociopolitical problems and unrest, and ecological disasters ultimately had grave results, such that the population, or, rather, its localized groupings, could not remain united. With the rigor of those who see ahead of them a possible rendezvous with tragic events, the distended *calpulli* drew back, went against the will of the sociopolitical entity to which it had been tied—an entity now impotent to prevent this breakup—and struck out in search of new lands where resources would be adequate to its needs and the presence of newcomers tolerated. It was a harsh social mechanism that partially supplanted the long-term inefficiencies of an agriculture that lacked draft animals and reflected a system of unjust and excessive domination. Put another way, it was preferable to exchange one's roof for the sky and twisting pathways among the trees for the alleyways one knew than to confront, at the cost of blood, a despotic ruling power organized for war. Under such conditions, a small lizard or a handful of *capulines* (a type of wild cherry produced by the *capulí* tree) was preferable to the sacred grain of corn that, in any case, was more a hope than a reality. During the pueblo's years of migration, while it stayed in provisional settlements, its life was that of sporadic hunter, sporadic gatherer, sporadic farmer, and sporadic fisherman. It journeyed with an unknown number of people, their endurance tested and constrained by what could be obtained for sustenance within a limited band of territory. The pueblo's wanderings went on for years, for decades, tracking over the signs of earlier generations, whose desiccated bones marked the way. Yet nonetheless, when the pueblo came to reconstitute itself, whether on its own or by reattaching itself, as a distinct unit, to a preexisting city, and a period of years had gone by, there flowered, like a mushroom and without any visible antecedent, a specialized knowledge and skill that could only have resulted from a tradition that survived and carried over from a previous time. What explained this occurrence? Beyond all else, those who migrated were not merely a collection of people; they were a *calpulli* that, together with its sacred bundles, had with it and as part of it its priests, its military chiefs, its teachers, and its enforcers of the proper ways. Linked by endogamous blood ties, in which marriages to outsiders were the exception, the group maintained a sense of common identity that never flagged. The schooling of the young went on as before and the pueblo kept, latent but alive, a special skill or trade that it would bring to the fore once the economic conditions of its new settled state allowed it.

Cities and urban centers formed in this way, were built up out of heterogeneous units, striving, perhaps, to find an equilibrium of internal production because, lacking both draft animals and carts, they could not easily or rapidly export products to distant markets. All goods were lugged on the backs or from the foreheads of people from an oppressed laboring class that was difficult to maintain but whose slow, methodical work was necessarily accorded high importance. Commerce, like the society based on agriculture, had to rely on perfecting a system of organization and maintaining a state of equilibrium to compensate for what the region lacked: beasts of burden, wheels that turned on an axle, and an adequate supply of animal dung.

Accounts of the organization and regulation of cities refer to ethnic groups corresponding to particular districts and districts corresponding to particular crafts.[142] Motecuhzoma Xocoyotzin, with the evident intention of undermining this tradition along with the unified strength of the groups that upheld it, may have begun its dissolution in Tenochtitlan by creating groups of artisans that were not only distinct from their respective *calpulli* but were also maintained directly by the state from within the palace complex.

The nobility also fulfilled a series of specialized tasks, which served to legitimate their position of supremacy. It is difficult to know how they arose, though one can surmise that at some juncture a surplus of production permitted it, but organized groups realized that they needed to engage, in a more dramatic way, the specialized talents of a singer, dancer, principal leader, or person responsible for saying prayers—all of whom were tied to the economic needs of the population, which in turn responded heavily to magical-religious suppositions. And they required that each virtuoso perform his tasks as a way of paying the tribute that everyone owed to cover the expenses of the community. When the surplus in production, the belief that specialized services were indispensable, and the protest offered by any who felt that his interests had been damaged by an excessive requirement all coincided, then communities collected as his tribute part of the specialist's work and made up the difference with some of the goods destined for the expenses of the community as a whole. To perpetuate their place in this order, the privileged specialists lacked only the vision to pass onto their children the knowledge and skills of their own well-paid trade. They would be the seed of the nobility in the later emergence of a social division that featured two groups that were complementary but had opposed interests.

On the eve of the conquest, the Nahua nobles—the *pipiltin*—did not pay any tribute. It was not necessary that they do so, since their services covered their participation in the tribute system. The specialized work that they performed was well rewarded—with their payments obtained from the overall body of tribute—and was the justification for their elevated status. They did not yet enjoy membership in the dominant group as an exclusively hereditary right. The deep seriousness with which these arrangements were taken is seen in the fact that the nobles not only publicly demonstrated the proof of their worthiness but also that the pueblo was convinced that a normal life was impossible without these officials who wielded certain powers. It was they who knew how to lead and direct communal work; how to judge, legislate, carry out highly complicated rituals that required intervention by the divinities of agriculture; how to lead and command the *calpulli's* military forces that were composed of the *macehualtin*, or commoners; how to engineer large-scale building projects, support militarily the actions of merchants who operated within networks that crossed the boundaries of different states; how to forge alliances with powerful pueblos, subjugate weak pueblos, or submit to another authority under the most favorable conditions; how to oversee and administer the *calendario de destinos* (calendar of fortunes, both good and bad), something that applied universally—in short, how to allocate to people their specific, designated place in the world. The mass of people who lacked the knowledge and skills that underlay these powers had to submit, by force, to the direction of those who possessed them if they wished to lead a civilized life—or so, at least, they had firmly been made to believe. The Mexica themselves, weary of the tyrannical government of the mysterious Aztecs, who exploited them as fishermen, left in the direction of another zone with lakes; but, as Motolinía indicated, they lacked a true government, as they were led only by captains[143] and thus, in the end, had to appeal, once again, to powerful dynasties to fill the vacuum and rule over them. When much later, after the conquest, the Spanish granted certain favors to the pueblo, the descendant of Motecuhzoma Xocoyotzin made sure to invoke and claim these past considerations, arguing that the Mexica had never been a people capable of governing themselves, and furthermore, that the true lords were the *pipiltin*, the descendants of the nobles of Culhuacan:

> I [beg to] inform Your Majesty that [in this land] there are [noble] people who come from high lineages, and who they are, and the mexicanos [commoners] have always sought to exceed the nobles, whom they call piles [pipiltin], but have never prevailed in this. And now that they see the disfavor with which the nobles are treated, how they were defeated, and [also] the fear we have of them because they become like one and rise up, the [Spanish colonial] authorities who rule the land on behalf of Your Majesty have curtailed them [the nobles] by not granting them any favors or any royal offices, [so now] the mexicanos are more honored and have more status than before, and they have much hatred and ill will toward the piles, who are [after all] their nobles.[144]

It was the Culhua people who held sway over those who possessed and exercised one or another special power, and so, when the Spanish inquired who ruled the lands to which they had come, they were told: the *Culhua tecuhtli*—Motecuhzoma Xocoyotzin. And because of how the name sounded to them, this reply gave rise to half of the Spanish name San Juan de Ulúa.

The nobles, too, had their school, in which they acquired knowledge of the law, religious rituals, the oratory of tears that was a frightful arm of dominion, military leadership, the use of the divinatory calendar, engineering, history, and the preparation and reading of texts. And the *macehualtin*, what could they do by themselves, without those who knew and could tell them what the future held in store for their sons and how to counteract evil influences affecting them, and of the possibility of their marrying particular women of whose signs—compatible and incompatible—they were unaware, or the days on which war ought to be fought, and the days on which the gods who had been offended should be propitiated? The nobility's school had doubtless been installed to protect "the tail and the wing"—the *macehualtin*—of the eagle that represented the social group. The pueblo had necessarily to be led by the hand, as conveyed in the expression *pachoa*, which simultaneously meant "to rule," "to bear down on or exert pressure," and "to sit on or over."

And since the possibility existed that the *macehualtin*, in less propitious times, might abandon their complementary or substitute trade of agriculture for something more profitable, what did the nobles do in such unsettled circumstances? The Toltecs, oppressors of the Nonoalcas, were farmers in Cholula but later earned fame as artisans. The *pipiltin* of Mexico-Tenochtitlan urged their sons to learn a worthy craft,[145] and some artisan schools were called *calmécac*, which was the same name given to the schools of the nobles. It is quite possible that education was structured and imparted so that different possibilities might be offered in the face of shifting conditions and contingent circumstance.

Yet the god that is the guardian and distributor of water for farmers is also the god who creates the craft of the specialist and places the needed instruments before him. This much is clear in the case of the Mexica, who receive the arrow, bow, and netted pouch of the hunter[146] from the same god who, as we have seen, had the aquatic tail of a serpent. According to Mendieta, each craft had its protector,[147] and each child, upon his birth—in repetition of the pueblo's receipt of the instruments of craft—likewise had them passed into his hands. The person who did nothing worthy in life, who harmed his fortunes by comporting himself badly, was condemned by the gods to lose his instruments, and they visited misfortune upon him. He was sentenced according to the terms of *in huictli, in mecapalli* ("the instrument for working the land, the sash for hauling loads")—that is, his status was lowered to that of the peasant or the bearer of goods, those who carried out the most burdensome tasks. In the account of Quetzalcoatl, the priest says that when he fled, he was obliged to leave behind all of the instruments pertaining to crafts and offices.[148] The god Quetzalcoatl was the protector of the Toltecs, the masters of all offices and crafts.

A brief list of gods and corresponding occupations, as given in table 6.3, illustrates this type of relationship.

These correspondences belonged to the Nahua world, but they were not exclusive to it. Among the Quiché, Tohil, as a rule, is the civilizing patron, a role that Quetzalcoatl plays in central Mexico and in addition is the inventor of fire.[149] Among the notable Mixtec gods are Toyua Yoco, Qhuav, and Cahuy (the lords of merchants, hunters, and peasants, respectively).[150]

It is unlikely that the location of the gods within the pantheon is invariably related to the work that they bestow upon men. In some cases it can be inferred, as in that of Amimitl—the protector of hunting on lakes—to whom it is sung, "fain follow the trail: it is your duckling, your duckling. ¡Ah!, what pleasure the obsidian gives me,"[151] perhaps in this way referring to a myth that coincides with the attribute. In other instances the relationship is more directly apparent, as in the case of Mixcoatl with hunter; Chalchiuhtlicue with water merchant; Mayahuel as the female lord of mead; and Pahtecatl, initiator of the process of fermenting pulque, because these are the principal characteristics of each god. In other cases, however, it is difficult to perceive some motive or reason, proximate or otherwise. In any event, does the image of the god modify the specialization residing in a craft? Or does specialization take up, select, a particular god from an extensive pantheon in whom some

TABLE 6.3. Correlation between crafts and the protection granted by specific patron gods

| God | Craft | Protection | Source |
|---|---|---|---|
| Camaxtle | hunting | patron | Mendieta, 1:89–90 and Códice Ramírez, 165 |
| Cipactonal and Oxomoco | threading, weaving, tilling the soil, healing and prophesying with corn, sorcery | inventors or first officials | Historia de los mexicanos por sus pinturas, 210; Sahagún, 1:139 |
| Cinteotl | precious stone work | inventor | Sahagún, 3:58–59 |
| Coatlicue or Coatlatonan | fabricating flower objects | inventor (female) | Sahagún, 1:122 |
| Coyotl Inahual | fabricating feather mosaics | inventor | Sahagún, 3:61 |
| Chalchiuhtlicue | water merchants | patron (female) | Sahagún, 1:51 |
| Chicnahui Itzcuintli | precious stone work | inventor | Sahagún, 3:58–59 |
| Huitzilopochtli | war | lawgiver | Fernández de Oviedo, 10:104 |
| Huixtocihuatl | mining and selling salt | inventor of salt (female) | Sahagún, 1:171 |
| Izquitecatl | making pulque | inventor of the process | Códice Boturini, 214 |
| Macuilcalli | precious stone work | inventor | Sahagún, 3:58–59 |
| Macuilxochitl | rulership | inventor of fire | Sahagún, 1:58 |
| Mayahuel | making pulque | inventor of honey (female) | Sahagún, 3:210 |
| Nahualpilli | stone work | inventor | Sahagún, 3:58–59 |
| Nappatecuhtli | mat making | inventor | Sahagún, 1:79 |
| Opochtli | hunting and lake fishing | inventor of oars, traps, nets, and the three-pointed spear | Sahagún, 1:64 |
| Otontecuhtli | gold smelting, stone work | patron | Carrasco, Los otomíes, 143 |
| Pahtecatl | making pulque | inventor of the process of fermentation | Sahagún, 3:210 |
| Papaztactzocaca | making pulque | inventor | Sahagún, 3:210 |
| Quatlapanqui | making pulque | inventor | Sahagún, 3:210 |

*continued on next page*

TABLE 6.3—*continued*

| God | Craft | Protection | Source |
|---|---|---|---|
| Quetzalcoatl | scientific activities | creator | Carrasco, Los otomíes, 147, based on the Diccionario castellano-otomí, manuscrito de 1640, Biblioteca Nacional |
| Quetzalcoatl | divination via the calendar | creator | multiple sources |
| Quetzalcoatl | commerce | inventor | multiple sources |
| Tepuztecatl | making pulque | inventor | Sahagún, 3:210 |
| Teteo Innan | medicine and healing through *temazcalli* | patron (female) | Sahagún, 1:47–48 |
| Tlaliyollo | medicine | patron | Francisco Hernández, Antigüedades, 136 |
| Tliloa | making pulque | inventor | Sahagún, 3:210 |
| Tzapotlatenan | the sale of medicine (*úxitl*) | inventor (female) | Sahagún, 1:49 |
| Xipe Totec | metallurgy | patron | Sahagún, 3:56 |
| Xochiquetzal | painting, fabric making, weaving, silverwork, tailoring | patron (female) | Durán, 2:193 |
| Yiacatecuhtli | commerce | inventor | Sahagún, 1:66 |

relationship is found with the craft and later elevate it to the category of patron, in the process identifying it with the patron god that was worshipped earlier? Or, as a third possibility, does the pueblo take up the specialized craft to which it deems it corresponds through the god from whom it believes it is descended? The lattermost answer is absurd on its face. The first is difficult to believe since, as a general rule, the gods occupy a firm place in a pantheon that seemingly extends back into the ancient past. The second answer appears to be correct, as long as one considers it possible that the attribution of patron in consonance with a craft could be grounded in some protector capable of being suitably modified at a given time.

The texts contain some references to a certain type of kinship relations among the protector gods of one or another group that carries on into the tradition of courtship, jealousies, and rivalries that obtains today, according to present-day Nahuas among Iztaccihuatl, Popocatepetl, and Teuhtli.[152] An explanation of kinship could offer us a better understanding of the history of pueblos or of the myths they hold. Yet this notion would seem to raise a host of other issues, to the extent that it is risky to offer judgments founded on its arguments. Let us use, as examples, Oxomoco and Cipactonal, whose marriage[153] appears to flow from their character as the creating couple and the brothers Yiacatecuhtli and Coyotl Inahual,[154] whose kinship may have possibly been acquired through the physical proximity of their protected pueblos, composed of artisans and merchants, but above all through the close economic relationship that joined the interests of both occupations. Respecting Iztacmixcoatl and his wives and children,[155] I would go so far as to infer a prior mythical relationship that serves to explain the ethnic origin of various groups. The family-like relationship of Yiacatecuhtli, Chiconquiahuitl, Xomocuil, Nacatl, Cochimetl, Yacapitzahuac, and Chalmecacihuatl[156] corresponds, in all likelihood, to a complex of gods that were adopted thus, in group form, as patrons. One can hypothesize that Malinalxochitl and Huitzilopochtli were brothers from the simple circumstance of the joining of one pilgrimage group with another; on the other hand, the identification of Opochtli with Huitzilopochtli, both left-handed and both the protectors of the same occupation,[157] could correspond to two pueblos originally linked by blood ties. In short, the kinship relationships among patron gods, at least for now, are neither the keys nor the road to unlocking and interpreting social and religious relationships.

One thing further must be emphasized. The worship of the protector gods was frequently performed in a way that was all but independent of the greater, more encompassing worship that was common to all pueblos. Perhaps at bottom, the widely popular opinion does prevail—that despite the special rites provided for Chalchiuhtlicue in the eighteen-month calendar, there should be another, distinct ritual directed to her within the limits of the *calpulli*, in her own temple, on the day dedicated to her according to the tradition of the *calpulli*, since she is conceived of as a different divinity. For there, at one remove, as part of the regular run of festivals, she is the goddess of the flowing of water whom everyone celebrates; but here, close in, she is our progenitor, the one who can be identified with the image that we possess and that lives in our time and our territory. It seems, all in all—and this should not be taken in an absolute sense—that there is a greater association between local, *calpulli*-specific festivals and the 260-day calendar on the one hand, and a stronger relationship between the more general festivals and the 365-day calendar on the other. For the time being, however, these problems go beyond the initial intention of lining up, if only in very broad outline, the coordinates that would enable us to situate our personage, the priest Ce Acatl Topiltzin.

The weight of the conquest and its religious arm, Christianity, notwithstanding, it was not possible for the indigenous population to renounce the protection of the creators of men. Yet together with the defeat and downfall of the Mesoamerican states, the edifice and framework of their grand official religion collapsed as well, with a mighty aftershock. The costly festivals and celebrations, the priesthood with its hierarchy and specialized roles, the numerous human sacrifices made possible by the continuous prosecution of war, and the panoply of ostentatious ceremony all came to an end. The art of foretelling destinies, of reading the future, lived on, now concealed from view and as nothing but a weak shadow of what it once had been. The social foundations of the grand native religion disappeared in a single stroke. In its wake, there remained a community of peasants tied to their water, to their mountain. Life, vegetation, shelter, health, work, group identity, and the hope of freedom continued flowing from a protector. Against the wishes of the conquerors, of those who now dominated them, the indigenous communities had to hold firm and not give themselves up to the new, unknown numens. The pressure exerted by the missionary friars soon presented an answer, a way out of the conundrum. The indigenous inhabitants could resort to the simple substitution of a name, of an image. They had found a satisfactory solution, or so it seemed, in a form of cultural parallelism: the patron saints of the pueblos.

All went smoothly until certain deceptions were discovered: in the mountainous area of Tlaxcala, Toci was found hidden under Saint Ann; Telpochtli Tezcatlipoca was located under Saint John the Baptist in Tianquizmanalco; and as the most serious outrage of all, Tonantzin was found under the Virgin of Guadalupe in Tepeyácac, to the great indignation of Fray Bernardino de Sahagún, who denounced the offending act.[158] Similar cases cropped up elsewhere. Pinopiaa, the Zapotec goddess, was found under the image of Saint Catherine of Siena.[159] Fray Diego Durán intervened to prevent a pueblo from installing Saint Luke as its patron when he discovered that its inhabitants had chosen him in place of Saint Paul or Saint Augustine, because the first saint corresponded to a key date in the indigenous calendar.[160] In the great majority of cases, however, the substitution held. For example, Tentzonteotl, the god of Coatepec de los Costales (a community in the present-day state of Guerrero), was successfully substituted, and this bearded pre-Hispanic divinity came to be called Saint Jesus.[161] Oztoteotl, "the god of the cave," became known as Saint Christopher of Chalma.[162] And so it went, across the length and breadth of Mesoamerica. The process by which figures in the Christian religion were adopted as a cover for those in the indigenous religion took so many turns that some missionaries preferred to support it.

This phenomenon forces us to consider the possibility of undertaking a study of the ancient protector gods, using as an aid the abundance of contemporary ethnographic material: saints who are related to each other; saints who have love affairs; saints who have a girlfriend or boyfriend; saints who are subject to the Thunderbolt, a pre-Hispanic god; saints who travel through the air, where they have their flyways;[163] saints bearing the same name who are believed to be the three brothers;[164]

and saints who were created by God so that they might found communities—as believed by the Tzotziles of Larráinzar, in Chiapas.[165] These and more can guide us to an understanding of an ancient religion, more of whose elements survive than is perhaps apparent at first view.

**NOTES**

1. It is interesting to compare this situation with what Karl Marx attributes to the Asiatic mode of production. See his *Formas de propiedad precapitalista*, 12–13; and *El capital*, 1:292.
2. Durán, *Historia de las Indias*, 2:118.
3. *Codex Magliabechiano*, folio 73v.
4. Nicholson, "Pre-Hispanic Central Mexico," 11.
5. *Códice Vaticano Latino*, plate xxi.
6. *Historia de los mexicanos por sus pinturas*, 219.
7. Alva Ixtlilxóchitl, *Obras históricas*, 2:74.
8. Acosta, *Historia natural*, 330–31.
9. Guiteras Holmes, *Los peligros*, 148; and Tozzer, *Landa's Relación*, 9–10.
10. *Anales de Cuauhtitlán*, 3.
11. Nicholson, "Pre-Hispanic Central Mexico," 11–12.
12. Reyes, "Los dioses tribales," 37.
13. *Códice Vaticano Latino*, plate xli; and Acosta, *Historia natural*, 239. See also van Zantwijk, "Los barrios sirvientes."
14. Acosta, *Historia natural*, 239. See also van Zantwijk, "Los barrios sirvientes."
15. Chimalpahin, *Relaciones*, 67.
16. Nicholson is one who supports this thesis. See his "Los principales dioses," 178.
17. Ibid., 210.
18. *Códice Telleriano-Remensis*, 2nd part, plate xxii.
19. "Relaciones geográficas de Diócesis de México," 6:238.
20. Herrera, *Historia general*, 3:226.
21. See the *Leyenda de los Soles*, 122–23.
22. Carrasco Pizanna, *Los otomíes*, 141, 146.
23. "Relaciones geográficas de la Diócesis de Tlaxcala," 5:128.
24. Sahagún, *Historia general*, 3:205.
25. Chimalpahin, *Relaciones*, 129.
26. Sahagún, *Historia general*, 3:207.
27. Durán, *Historia de las Indias*, 1:2.
28. Ibid., 1:11–15. The remaining sources present an opposed view, and based on them, Moreno de los Arcos posits the total destruction of men at the end of the fourth sun, in "Los cinco soles," 206.

29. López Austin, *Textos de medicina*, 21–41.
30. Alva Ixtlilxóchitl, *Obras históricas*, 1:19; 2:21.
31. Ana María Rincón Montoya, "Una justificación," 38.
32. See for example León-Portilla, *La filosofía náhuatl*, 336.
33. Metraux, "El dios supremo," 10.
34. Popul Vuh, 23.
35. Ibid., 103.
36. On this score, the value of comparing concepts, patterns, and institutions within the field of Nahuatl studies to their counterparts in other Mesoamerican cultures needs to be emphasized. In my view, the categorical division of Mesoamerica into separate and discrete cultures that we are accustomed to making in our research clearly undermines any effort at comprehension. Some methodological justification—for example, the knowledge of a particular indigenous language that a researcher has—perhaps exists for studying only sections of the super-area. Specialization, however, should be treated as a resource or lever that enables greater insight and understanding, not manipulated as an end in itself.
37. Mendieta, *Historia eclesiástica*, 1:83–84, 87–88; and *Historia de México*, 91.
38. Motolinía, *Historia*, 7.
39. *Leyenda de los Soles*, 122.
40. *Códice Vaticano Latino*, plate lxxxviii.
41. *Historia de México*, 106.
42. *Códice Matritense de la Real Academia*, Book IX, vol. 8, folio 46v, . . . *quinhualhuicaque, quinhualnotztia in huehueteque, in achto huallaque*.
43. Berlin and Rendón, *Historia tolteca-chichimeca*, 90.
44. Guiteras Holmes, *Los peligros*, 237.
45. Popol Vuh, 104–9; *Título de los señores*, 215; and *Memorial de Sololá*, 51.
46. I hope very soon to offer the results of this research, which, together with the background to this study, will form part of a larger investigation dealing with the concept of fate, or destiny, held by the Nahuas. In this connection, see my essay "La carga del destino en la tradición mesoamericana" (paper, Segundo Encuentro UBO-UNAM, Mexico City, May 6, 2013, publication forthcoming). For examples of the journeys pueblos make over the waters when they depart from their place of origin, see *Título de los señores*, 215; Fuentes y Guzmán, *Recordación*, 2:386–87; and the document reproduced by Mendizábal, *El lienzo de Jucutácato*. With respect to the connections and associations between and among various myths, see, for example, the ideas expounded by Eliade, *Mito y realidad*, 50.
47. *Leyenda de los Soles*, 122.
48. Mendieta, *Historia eclesiástica*, 1:87–88; and *Historia de México*, 91–92.
49. Motolinía, *Memoriales*, 10.
50. Molina, *Vocabulario*, v. Ombre y muger primeros.
51. Serna, *Manual de ministros*, 1:122.

52. *Historia de los mexicanos por sus pinturas*, 211–12, 215.
53. Dibble and Anderson, *Florentine Codex*, 9:79.
54. Reyes, *Textos nawas*.
55. *Códice Telleriano-Remensis*, part 1, plate ix.
56. *Códice Azcatitlan*, plate ii.
57. Muñoz Camargo, *Historia de Tlaxcala*, 143.
58. Cristóbal del Castillo, *Fragmentos*, 87.
59. *Códice Azcatitlan*, plate iii, in which each group is seen carrying the image of a different god.
60. Motolinía, *Memoriales*, 78.
61. Las Casas, *Apologética historia*, 1:643–44.
62. Pomar, "Relación de Texcoco," 13–14.
63. Among the Mayan pueblos, the Quiché speak of this tradition. See *Título de los señores*, 216.
64. Torquemada, *Los veinte*, 1:79–80.
65. *Códice Vaticano Latino*, plate xiv.
66. *Códice Ramírez*, 124; and Durán, *Historia de las Indias*, 2:126–27.
67. Las Casas, *Apologética historia*, 1:644; and *Historia de México*, 95.
68. Pomar, "Relación de Texcoco," 14.
69. Burgoa, *Geográfica descripción*, 1:332–33.
70. Tello, *Crónica miscelánea*, book II, vol. 1: 35.
71. Alvarado Tezozómoc, *Crónica mexicáyotl*, 12.
72. Torquemada, *Los veinte*, 2:139.
73. Durán, *Historia de las Indias*, 2:298.
74. Chimalpahin, *Relaciones*, 201.
75. Alvarado Tezozómoc, *Crónica mexicana*, 27; *Anales de Cuauhtitlan*, 51; and Durán, *Historia de las Indias*, 1:278 and 2:127, to list but several examples.
76. Torquemada, *Los veinte*, 2:151.
77. Sahagún, *Historia general*, 1:234; and Torquemada, *Los veinte*, 2:149.
78. *Origen de los mexicanos*, 266; and *Relación de genealogía*, 249.
79. *Historia de los mexicanos por sus pinturas*, 225.
80. Durán, *Historia de las Indias*, 1:70
81. Chimalpahin, *Relaciones*, 176–78.
82. *Proceso de indios idólatras*, 193.
83. Brinton, "Sacred Names in Quiché," 116–17.
84. León-Portilla, *La filosofía nahuatl*, 396.
85. Saler, *Nagual, brujo*, 18.
86. Sahagún, *Historia general*, 1:70.
87. Holland, *Medicina maya*, 80.

88. Briones and de Jesús, *Atla*, 163.
89. Vogt, "H?iloletik," 361; Vogt et al., *Los zinacantecos*, 114–15; Guiteras Holmes, *Los peligros*, 237; and Holland, *Medicina maya*, 80.
90. Landa, *Relación de la cosas de Yucatán*, 1:51–52.
91. Alvarado Tezozómoc, *Crónica mexicana*, 384.
92. Chimalpahin, *Relaciones*, 154.
93. Sahagún, *Historia general*, 1:70.
94. Chimalpahin, *Relaciones*, 165.
95. *Codex Telleriano-Remensis*, part 1, plate vii.
96. Translator's note: I have taken the text in this quote from the translation of the Florentine Codex done by Charles E. Dibble and Arthur J. O. Anderson. See Bernardino de Sahagún, *Florentine Codex: General History of the Things of New Spain*, book 11, chapter 12 (Santa Fe: School of American Research, 19–19), 247.
97. Torquemada, *Los veinte*, 2:46.
98. Durán, *Historia de las Indias*, 2:136–37.
99. *Título de los señores*, 218.
100. Briones and de Jesús, *Atla*, 160.
101. Muñoz Camargo, *Historia de Tlaxcala*, 131.
102. In the pueblo of San Martín Tutzamapa, whose members are Mexicano and Totonaca. See "Relaciones geográficas de la Diócesis de Tlaxcala," 133.
103. Sahagún, *Historia general*, 1:199; and 3:354.
104. Las Casas, *Apologética historia*, 1:643.
105. *Códice Azcatitlan*, plate vii.
106. Motolinía, *Memoriales*, 76.
107. Villegas, "Relación de los pueblos de Tecuicuilco," 125; and Burgoa, *Geográfica descripción*, 2:119.
108. "Relación de Nuchistlán," 66.
109. Fuentes y Guzmán, *Recordación florida*, 2:418.
110. Vogt, "Human Souls," 1152.
111. *Memorial de Solalá*, 47, note 2.
112. Alvarado Tezozómoc, *Crónica mexicana*, 270.
113. Ruiz de Alarcón, "Tratado," 37.
114. Katz, *Situación social*, 47–48.
115. See, for example, *Códice Mendocino*, plate lxxi.
116. The title given to the chief ruler of each pueblo.
117. Zurita, "Breve y sumaria," 12.
118. See, for example, Sahagún, *Historia general*, 1:341–42; and 2:17–18.
119. Durán, *Historia de las Indias*, 1:498; and 2:116.
120. Monzón, *El calpulli*, 49.

121. López de Gómara, *Historia general*, 2:393.
122. Salas, "Descripción de Tetiquipa," 116.
123. Sahagún, *Historia general*, 3:63.
124. Ibid., 61.
125. Redfield and Villa Rojas, *Chan Kom*, 107.
126. Pedro Carrasco has examined this problem.
127. Sachse, "Acerca del problema," 107–14.
128. Berlin and Rendón, *Historia tolteca-chichimeca*, 91–92.
129. Alva Ixtlilxóchitl, *Obras históricas*, 1:289.
130. Acosta, *Historia natural*, 232.
131. Rojas, "Descripción de Cholula," 159.
132. Alva Ixtlilxóchitl, *Obras históricas*, 1:455–56.
133. Sahagún, *Historia general*, 3:214.
134. Ibid.
135. Ibid., 205–6.
136. Motolinía, *Historia*, 150.
137. Alva Ixtlilxóchitl, *Obras históricas*, 1:40.
138. Sahagún, *Historia general*, 3:187–88.
139. *Memorial de Sololá*, 60.
140. Monzón, *El Calpulli*, 47; as supported by Torquemada, *Los veinte*, 2:430.
141. On this point, see López Austin, *Los señoríos de Azcapotzalco*, 17.
142. See the case of Tetzcoco, in Alva Ixtlilxóchitl, *Obras históricas*, 2:187.
143. Motolinía, *Historia*, 3.
144. *Origen de los mexicanos*, 278. The argument was made by order of Juan Cano, husband of Isabel de Motecuhzoma.
145. Sahagún, *Historia general*, 2:123–24.
146. *Historia de la Nación Mexicana*, 22–23. I think one should interpret in this sense that part of plate iv of the Codex Boturini, where an eagle appears to be giving a bow, arrow, and hunter's snood to an appreciative man.
147. Mendieta, *Historia eclesiástica*, 1:111.
148. Torquemada, *Los veinte*, 2:50.
149. Popol Vuh, 112.
150. Aznar de Cozar, "Relación del pueblo de Puctla," 157.
151. "Canto de Amímitl," in Garibay K., *Veinte himnos sacros*, 114.
152. Madsen, *Virgin's Children*, 128–29.
153. Mendieta, *Historia eclesiástica*, 1:106.
154. Sahagún, *Historia general*, 3:63.
155. Motolinía, *Memoriales*, 10–13.
156. Sahagún, *Historia general*, 1:68–69.

157. *Historia de los mexicanos por sus pinturas*, 223.
158. Sahagún, *Historia general*, 3:351–54.
159. Burgoa, *Geográfica descripción*, 2:331.
160. Durán, *Historia de las Indias*, 2:267.
161. Carrasco, "Quetzalcoatl," 89–91.
162. Carrasco, *Los otomíes*, 149–50.
163. Kelly, "World View."
164. Parsons, *Mitla*, 204.
165. Holland, *Medicina maya*, 79.

# 7

## Space and Time

According to the explanation frequently offered in the *Relaciones de Yucatán*, the names of indigenous settlements come from the names of an "idol who is taken to be a protector," the "protector of bread"—the one who causes corn to flower and sprout—three simple examples of whom, as given in the *Relaciones*, would be Canpocolche, Caquy, and Chochola.[1] This close association between the name of the creator god and that of the settlement was not limited to the Mayan world, though it may have been more conspicuous there than in other parts of Mesoamerica. According to Fray Alonso de la Rea, Ttzinzuni, name of the Michoaqueño equivalent of Huitzilopochtli, is the basis of the toponym for Tzintzuntzan.[2] Tolutzin, "the sloped," or Tolutépetl, "the sloping mountain," give rise to the name Tolocan,[3] "place of the slope," which is the name of the main seat of those who worshipped Coltzin, "the venerable stooped one." Similarly, the name Aculman originated from Aculmaitl.[4] The name Mexico itself simply means the "place of Mexi" or "place of Mexitli," that mysterious appellative of the divinity who is identified with Huitzilopochtli and occasionally with Tezcatlipoca.[5] Despite an abundance of work on the part of philologists, historians, and connoisseurs in general, the name Mexi still seems to resist interpretation.

Another phenomenon that warrants attention is the repeated use of the same name for pueblos, of which Culhuacan, among present-day place names, would be a signal example. In looking specifically for pockets of merchants and persons engaged in business, Miguel Acosta Saignes found that San Mateo Pochtlan turned upas the district or neighborhood name in the municipalities of Xochilmilco, Huitzilopochtli-Pochtlan, Hueipochtla, Tecuanipan-Amaquemecan-Chalco-Pochtlan, Pochtlantzinco in the province of Tochtépec, and Santiago Poxtla in the state of Tlaxcala.[6] Adrián Recinos refers to Vucub Ziván, "seven ravines," or Chicomóztoc, as translated into Mayan tongues in the chronicles of Yucatán and in Quiché and Cakchiquel documents, and to Tulán as the Mayan version of Tollan.[7] To the list of Tollans, Brinton adds the settlements of Tula near Ocosingo (in the present-day state of Chiapas), San Pedro Tula in the state of Mexico, and San Antonio Tula in San Luis Potosí.[8] According to Francisco Cervantes de Salazar, Mexico City had its predecessor in Mexico la Vieja (Old Mexico), the original homeland of the Mexica,[9] and also, based on the oral tradition heard and recorded by Roberto Weitlaner, Pablo Velásquez, and Pedro Carrasco, in a very small pueblo located some fifteen kilometers to the north of the city of Zumpango del Río in the present-day state of Guerrero.[10]

Thus, in the first instance, we find a reference to the city as a dwelling place of the protector god and, following that, the constant repetition of a name. We can then perceive one of the reasons for this relationship and combination: the alternation of periods of stability with periods of migration; and from these, in turn, we can hypothesize a point of departure, or starting place—the first or original home. Where is this first homeland to which all the others owe their origin? The world appears to have been torn away from an impossible Chicomóztoc or Tulán Zuivá or Aztlan; they are the birthplaces, wombs of inconceivable immensity, impossible starting points for all the Mesoamerican peoples, where men of diverse races and diverse languages coexisted. In this telling, Chicomóztoc is the region of which Aztlan and Teuculhuacan form a part,[11] or to which an undifferentiated Aztlan-Chicomóztoc belong,[12] or in which Aztlan-Nauhtlan-Colhuacatépec are located.[13] Moreover, the names get multiplied. What one source refers to as a place, or site, appears in another as two stages of the journey. In one source the Mexicanos are removed from Aztlan by Huitzilopochtli; in others the god is found within the curved mountain that gives its name to Culhuacan;[14] and in accord with still others the migrating pueblo is said to have gone forth from Aztlan in the year *ce técpatl* and to find itself in Chicomóztoc nine years later,[15] or to have had the protector with it until passing through Hueiculhuacan.[16] Such examples clearly indicate that within all these old documents and the tales they tell of the origin of pueblos, something more is at work than just a lack of verisimilitude.

The European and mestizo historians who wrote their accounts during the first years of Spanish dominion wanted to penetrate and grasp the mystery of this origin, but their intent was continually frustrated, despite the negligible distance—in time—that separated them from the historical traditions of pre-conquest Mesoamerica. They found themselves confronting a vast unknown. On the one hand was the myth about the beginning of humankind, fixed in history, that they clutched onto but could not place geographically. On the other, new myths needed to be slotted in and connected, as we can see, for example, in the tale of the Mayan peoples in the fortress city of Xelahuh:

> They went out from Ralebalheih, as from the place of Israel, and this according to another writer, we should understand as [being] Babylonia, and after a lengthy and protracted pilgrimage, burdened to the full with a frightening heap of cares, they reached the first unknown land of this all-powerful west, in the territory and country that is called Vucucinán, interpreted as [being] the seven cities in ravines ... soon and in a very orderly way they raised up a *tzaccoxtum*, a white castle, that was exceedingly imposing and well finished ... there went out from Pepolonia, which signifies Babylonia, thirteen heavily manned armies captained and led by notables; thirteen families of whom five were exceptional in the high quality and distinction of their lineage, and these were of the Capichoch, Cochoh-lam, Maliquinaló, Ahcanail, and Belehebcam.[17]

This new cadre of historians was unable to comprehend the meaning of a history that had served, instrumentally, to advance other ends, different from those with which they were familiar. In this history, Chicomóztoc had been the birthplace of Iztacmixcoatl and his children, those who spoke a different tongue, and who went off to settle in far-off lands to spread their seed. According to the Quiché, the different languages were created in Tulán.[18] Aztlan Chicomóztoc was the place "to which their fathers [and] mothers first came, [where] their generations began and were made."[19] The European conception of history, a foreign implant that allowed for no more myths than its own, required adherence to a rigidly realistic outlook, and it thus shredded the indigenous Eden into pieces. The attempt at reordering the pieces into a coherent narrative followed in due course.

Historians, however, did not resolve the problems and the confusions, and they continued to preoccupy a long line of scholars. From the end of the nineteenth century to the present, there have been three main currents of thinking, capped by utopianism and mystery, in the literature that treats the nature of the Mesoamerican settlements and populations.

The first of these denies the existence of Tollan in that it considers, following Brinton's line,[20] that the Toltec empire was nothing more than the historical expression of a myth; or, if one lines up with Seler,[21] it ascribes the meaning of Cuextecatl Ichocayan, Cohuatl Icamatl, Aztlan, Tollan, and Tomoanchan as being names that stand for the extreme positions of the world's horizontal plane and central axis—vitally important elements for indigenous religious belief.

Is there, expressly confirmed in the sources, a sufficient basis to state that some of the names of pueblos correspond to mythical cities? Absolutely. The homeland of the Mexica is called Mixtitlan, Ayauhtitlan,[22] "place of clouds, place of mist," or "place of mystery," when stripped of its metaphorical overlay. From the Quiché Pa Civán, Pa Tulán, the ancients saw the entire surface of the world so they could choose the place where it suited them to settle.[23] Xibalbá, the Mayan homeland of those who manufactured pottery and *metates* (flat stones used for grinding corn), is undoubtedly the world of the dead,[24] with whose numen, the sources relate, the men in those parts gained the capacity to speak.[25] Muñoz Camargo, among others, informs us that Tamoanchan is a celestial place,[26] and the *Manuscrito de la Biblioteca Nacional de México* likewise affirms that Tamoanchan is the place where man was created.[27] One Tollan, at least, is not of this world: literally translated, *Tollan Chalco on teotl ichan* means "Tollan Chalco, that dwelling place of God."[28] Once again, Mayan pueblos—so valuable as sources of information for anyone attempting to understand the culture of a wider circle of Mesoamerican peoples—tell us that there was not just one, but four Tollans, all of them places where man originated: "The people of Tulán arrived from four [places]. One Tulán is in the east; another in Xibalbay; another in the west; we [the Cakchiqueles] came from there, from the west; and another where God is. Thus there were four Tulanes, ¡oh children of ours!" So it was said. "We reached Tulán from the west, from the other side of the sea; and it was to Tulán that we came to be conceived and born by our mothers and our fathers." So was it told.[29]

There are four cities of Tollan, and if the text can be so interpreted, each lies at one of the extreme points of the sun's movement through the skies: in the east, at the zenith, in the west, and at the lowest point on the horizon. Like the Mexica, the Cakchiquel state that they come from the west. The place of origin of the Toltec lies in the east and the people of Xibalbá come from a place at the sun's low point, its nadir. Do people hail from all the different mythical places? How many birthplaces are there of mankind? Moreover, it is also a question of determining the level, since the remote heavens from which the seed of divine heat fell must be distinguished from the rock—the cave where, with the mixing of the maternal cold and the divine heat, the pregnancy took place and the cave opened at the birth. Tulán, the Mayan west, and Chicomóztoc appear to correspond to this maternal category.

The second current of interpretation is represented by Wigberto Jiménez Moreno. Jiménez Moreno argues that even in the case of the mythical Tamoanchan, elements exist in its description that enable it to be placed, as a physical site, on the northern coast of the Gulf of Mexico, between Boca del Río and the Huasteca region.[30] In his judgment, the celestial world, the world of the gods could in turn be imagined on the basis of this geographical description.

Moreover, the claim that there are cities that have the name of mythical places is quite easily substantiated. It would suffice merely to cite the many Tulas that lie within the territory of central Mexico. With respect, however, to the similarity between the description of a mythical place and a real place, we cannot let go of the fact that the first has been imagined on the basis of the place that is physically known. And while this assertion may at first glance seem risky or unguarded, the third line of interpretation, by concentrating on the replication of an archetype, will demonstrate its accuracy.

Several scholars have taken up the last of the three currents of opinion. Seler, who had denied the existence of certain cities, connects Coatépec to Mexico-Tenochtitlan: "This city [Coatépec] clearly has exactly the disposition of the true city, founded later."[31] Similarly, in his book *El pueblo del Sol*, Alfonso Caso declared that even in its mythical aspect, the city of Tenochtitlan was patterned on an anterior model city.[32] Subsequently, in 1970, Gutierre Tibón struck a much more explicit note by taking the phenomenon of a particular, restricted case as simply an instance of a generalized concept in history: "Aztlán, land of whiteness, and the moon lake of Meztliapan, are mythical archetypes, the same as Chicomóztoc, the place of seven caves, and Culhuacan, the crooked mountain. There existed, then, different Aztlanes, Metztliapanes, Chicomoztoques, and Culhuacanes that were turned into sacred centers. It is only of the Culhuacanes, [however], that we know of a sizeable number, from the hooked hill of the Sinaloan capital to the one in the Valley of Mexico."[33]

Finally, Paul Kirchhoff not only asserted, in principle, the existence of Aztlan but also the possibility that it could be sited geographically,[34] and he went on to postulate that it was the mythical-religious world (as exemplified in a general way by Aztlan), wherein the ordering of men, communities, and institutions was grounded. From Kirchhoff's interesting and compelling argument, I have extracted only the part in which he critiques the partial vision of Seler, as taken from one of the last pieces Kirchhoff wrote:

> Our demonstration that the mythical interpretation of a narrative that in reality is clearly historical falls into error should not lead to the opinion that the religious-mythical aspect was not present in the real occurrences and situations represented in the codices and historical texts. On the contrary, I would say that it played a much greater, far deeper role than Seler and his disciples ever perceived. For what was erroneously thought found within ordinary historical occurrences, namely, a cosmological grouping of four places conforming to the four or five celestial directions that were known in Mexico, which took on great importance for Seler's camp and for those who followed its mythological interpretations, was not recognized by them for what it is. It deals with the social order, that is, with not just a simple *interpretation* of the imaginary world but with a *practical intervention* in the real world that up to a certain point is controllable by man. That which Seler and his

disciples see in this society founded on a cosmological ideology is only a small segment, though it is indeed the central one; that is, planning in accordance with the four directions... they stay confined, as we see, completely within their unilateral ideological orientation, since this is precisely the part of the social order that is directly and obviously religious.[35]

All of the Mesoamerican pueblos fell within this scheme, even those of the Mexica, in whose supposedly barbarous history people wrongly believed. It is imperative that we begin to cast aside the old notion that the foundational pueblo of Tenochtitlan came about all of a sudden, as an entity absolutely unknown before that, within and to the land and peoples of Mesoamerica. The supposedly abrupt rise out of barbarity to civilization within the span of a few years has amazed us and caused us to commit any number of errors. We saw it as an exceptional, perhaps unique, case in world history. That such a case would defy explanation goes without saying. The studies carried out by Carlos Martínez Marín, however, have allowed the problem to be examined from a completely different angle. His is the only perspective that permits us to dismantle the false image that inspired the belief in the Mexica miracle: that at the moment they began to prowl about the lake zone, the Mexica were already Mesoamericans.[36] These people searched through the land for a place that would be similar to their lost paradise: a lake, an island, from which in the myth they had gone forth in a barbarous state—like children, as with any newly born—and needed to discover, as the means of initiating their history once more.

Not only was the mythical place interwoven in this way with history, but it also was not entirely closed to men. A magical song, a supernatural transformation—as practiced by the *nahuales* (persons with the shamanistic power to turn themselves into animal form)—could open the doors to this world that was uninhabited by the general run of men. By such means, for example, were the Toltec able to access the cave that housed within it the first men of the seven Chichimeca-Chicomoztoque groups,[37] and it was by the same practice, and under the same belief, that Motecuhzoma Xocoyotzin thought of going to Cincalco—the underworld of corn that guarded within it the life of ordinary men—when he learned of the arrival of those whom he believed to be the descendants of Quetzalcoatl.[38] In one of the most beautiful tales in which myth and history intermingle, Motecuhzoma Ilhuicamina dispatches his wizards to visit Chicomóztoc-Aztlan, site of the hill of Culhuacan, so they can deliver a message to the mother of his protector Huitzilopochtli, Coatlicue, who suffered in awaiting her son.[39] Tlaloc's mountain was considered so sacred, so near to the dominion of the supreme lord of rain, that nobody could eat there.[40] The Yucatecan Maya had managed to normalize their relationship, and their treatment of affairs, with the supernatural world: young maidens were thrown into the *cenote* (a sinkhole, or deep natural pit) with the hope that she who returned to the surface would bring a message from the gods of water that informed human beings of what the lords of the underworld had ordered them to do for the pueblo's next cycle of life.[41] The beginning of the last trek is almost always recorded as being the departure from these parturitional caves. Men must undertake a journey, must obey the command of that divinity—the earth mother perhaps—who, on expelling them into the world, had enjoined them to search for and to occupy *their* site, to find the place that the progenitors had seen from high Tulán. It fell to each pueblo to reach the replicated place where its progenitor god would dwell. Some went in search of an easterly heaven; others would transport their Xibalbá, their world of the dead, to earth.

When the start of the journey was linked to a historical event, the leave-taking is suffused with a very painful air; but the will of god, as expressed by priests who had indisputably to overlay their greater political vision with their function as intermediaries, moved the community in its entirety.[42] The voice emerged, encouragingly, directly from the creator numen: *Ca za achitonca tonnenemica mexiatl*, "a little more and we shall have gotten there, in the water of Mexi," said Huitzilopochtli to the Mexica,[43] and the pueblo continued on its onerous journey to take up its history once again. The priests anxiously sought out the exact moment and place for the new founding. Xelhuan, the Toltec, searched for the putrid, stagnant waters, the song of the Zacuan and of the quetzal;[44] Axolohua, the Mexica, lowered himself down into the water to ask Tlaloc if this should be the dwelling place;[45] Cuauhitzatzin performed a three-day penance before finding the site of Chiconcóac.[46] They were the ones who, through the miracle, communicated alone with the gods, appealing to them that they grant the wished-for site. Naturally, the place had to be equal, physically and geographically, to the archetype: a lagoon, such as that of Chilapa or of Huitziltépec, to which Huitzilopochtli descended in search of a seat;[47] the forest of the Quiché,[48] for a people who are known as "forest";[49] Tamoanchan, place of the peaks, where a mountain was so sacred that one had to defecate in another place, on Cuitlatépec or Cuitlatetelco;[50] the hillsides and mountain slopes of the Otomí;[51] perhaps the great ceiba tree where the pochteca, "the native inhabitants of the place of the ceiba,"[52] conducted their business affairs; the crooked-tipped mountain of the Culhua; the lake islet of the Mexica. Did the Mexica make, by hand, a lake in Coatépec? The historical account records that they did.

At times, it appears that a prior ritual needed to be performed, through which the priest prepared the miracle. Copil, the son of Malinalxochitl, served as a victim for the founding of Mexico-Tenochtitlan. Long before, his mother had been excluded from the pilgrimage group, and her son resorted to avenging her. An encounter with one of the Mexica priests ended with the death of the avenger, and his heart fell on Tlalcocomolco, the exact site on which the *nopal* (prickly pear cactus), where the eagle perched, would arise. In the Códice Azcatitlan, the city of Mexico-Tenochtitlan is represented as the place where, over the great temple, a nopal arises from the body of a prone Huitzilopochtli.[53] (See figure 7.1.)

Another version of the miracle relates that Chichilcuahuitl, a Culhua soldier, was sacrificed so that his body could be used to make the "heart of the altar" of the Mexica.[54] The Chichimeca ritual is described as the preparation of bundles of *malinalli* (grass) that are set on fire and the shooting of arrows toward the four directions of the horizontal plane.[55]

The god himself chose his place: "[Tetzauhteotl] brings us there, to where he will point with his finger, to where he will indicate,"[56] intone the Mexica on their pilgrimage, and the pueblo marches forward fired by the hope of the miracle. If these wondrous appearances are reduced to pure serpents, then a series of them can be noted: the strange grandness of the serpent of Coatlichan;[57] the enormity, the flying, and the great wings of the serpent from Coatépec;[58] the whiteness and great size of another serpent from Coatépec;[59] a gigantic serpent that encircles the hill, painted as a mat, in anthropophagous style, killed by the founder of the pueblo of Petlatzinco, in the land of the Mixtec,[60] and the seven-colored serpent of Chiconcóhuac.[61] It is not too extreme to say that the toponyms of these places that appear, that loom up, signify, respectively, "the home of the Serpent"; "the place of the serpent's hill"; in two instances, "the place of the venerable mat"; and "the place of Seven Serpents," this lattermost the name of the corn goddess.

The founding of Mexico-Tenochtitlan, the capital about which there is greater information because it was the scene of the tremendous clash with the Spanish, is described in multiple sources. The two fragments below are Diego Durán's:

> Thus they continued to roam from one place to another, seeking one that would be suitable as a permanent home. And wandering in this way, among the reeds and rushes, they came upon a beautiful spring and saw wondrous things in the waters. These things had been predicted to the people by their priests, through the command of Huitzilopochtli, their god. The first thing they beheld was a white bald cypress, all white and very beautiful, and the spring came forth from the foot of the tree. The second thing they saw was a group of white willows around the spring, all white, without a single green leaf. There were white reeds, and white rushes surrounding the water. White frogs came out of the water, white fish came out, white water snakes, all shiny and white. The spring flowed out from between two large rocks, the water so clear and limpid that it was pleasing to behold. The priests and elders, remembering what their god had told them, wept with joy and became exhuberant [*sic*], crying out: "We have now found the promised land. We have now seen the relief, the happiness of

**FIGURE 7.1.** Códice Azcatitlan, plate xii

the weary Aztec people; all we desired has come true . . .

Thus they again found the spring they had seen the day before. But the water on that day had been clear and transparent, and it now flowed out in two streams, one red like blood, the other so blue and thick that it filled the people with awe. Having seen these mysterious things . . . they continued to seek the omen of the eagle whose presence had been foretold. Wandering from one place to another, they soon discovered the prickly pear cactus. On it stood the eagle with his wings stretched out toward the rays of the sun, basking in their warmth and the freshness of the morning. In his talons he held a bird with very fine feathers, precious and shining. When the people saw the eagle they humbled themselves, making reverences as if the bird were a divine thing. The eagle, seeing them, also humbled himself, bowing his head low in their direction.[62]

The pueblo thus arrives at the place it *deserves*—the verb that is used is *macehua*, no different than the root of the word *macehualli*, "man of the pueblo," or simply "man,"[63] where its life will begin anew, and in so doing verify—for many—the miracle of sunrise; everyone waits, as had the gods in Teotihuacan, for the daytime star to rise from an unknown point on the horizon. Their wish is to see the Sun again, as they did upon exiting the maternal caves, but also to experience it as though it were the star's inception. In describing it, the Quiché sources are at once stark and beautiful: men have set off, in quest of their dawn, and when those guiding them discover the appointed place—on their feet, weeping, fasting, trembling with fear—they let time pass. The sun emerges, as the first miracle, and all rejoice in this initial dawn of day. The muddy land dries under the sun's rays as in the primordial breaking of light.[64] The Nahua sources make scant reference to the hope: *oncan tonaz, oncan tlathuiz* ("there the Sun will appear, there will it be dawn"), Camaxtle promises his people.[65]

Present time, then, vanishes and man returns, to fortify and strengthen himself, to his time of origin. Although in a very different context, Mircea Eliade sees the repetition of the primordial act as taking the same form:

> Through the paradox of rite, every consecrated space coincides with the center of the world, just as the time of any ritual coincides with the mythical time of the "beginning." Through repetition of the cosmogonic act, concrete time, in which the construction takes place, is projected into mythical time, *in illo tempore* in which the foundation of the world occurred. Thus the reality and the enduringness of a construction are assured, not only by the transformation of profane space into a transcendent space (the center) but also by the transformation of concrete time into mythical time. Any ritual whatever ... unfolds not only in a consecrated space, that is, one different in essence from profane space, but, also, in a "sacred time," "once upon a time" (*in illo tempore, ab origine*), that is, when the ritual was carried out for the first time by a god, an ancestor, or a hero.[66]

One is in the other world, in the archetypal world, giving to the city that is born names that are already consecrated: among cattails, among reeds, where the yellow and the greenish blue waters flow into each other, in the eating place of the eagle, where the snake hisses, or in rank, stagnant water where the zacuan and the quetzal sing. They are names and words that interconnect with and are joined to the dwelling place of the gods.[67]

Later, the city, Mexico-Tenochtitlan, will be given the name that often carries a deep, transcendent meaning. "The place of the serpent's hill" and its temple, Coatépec, was accorded the same name;[68] the Cakchiquel, worshippers of the Obsidian Stone, gave the name "the stone of God"—*Qabouil Abah*—to the city that was Xibalbay on earth;[69] "Lord of [bark] paper dress" the god asked to be called, and the place will be Amaquemecan.[70] The foundation is thus laid in accordance with the design that had been foreseen, everything constructed in the right order.

Is the ownership of land a miracle that god grants? For the people who take possession of it, the world in this moment is reborn; for those already living on it, there is simply the arrival of a people who may be a source of disturbance or who appropriate for themselves what is not theirs. Everything will be determined according to how strong, how powerful the new holder of the land feels. If he believes himself capable, he will neither have to bend to anyone else's will nor acknowledge any submission on his own part, since his god has given him this place.[71] If not, he will be fully aware that he is on land belonging to others.[72]

It seems all but given that similar traditions exist in settlements with like names. In discussing the tradition found in Coatépec de los Costales (Guerrero)—that of the enormous, great-winged, flying serpent mentioned earlier—Pedro Carrasco compares the current stories of the god who has left his handprints on a stone and that of the great serpent with those told in the pueblo of Coatepec-Chalco, in which the tradition of a great snake also held sway and where the god Quetzalcoatl had similarly left traces of his presence on stone. "It would be interesting," Carrasco wrote, "to ascertain whether the rest of the Coatepecs in Mexico also had Quetzalcoatl as a patron deity."[73] Be that as it may, we can unearth still more similarities. For example, in the account of Coatepec-Chalco we can see that the hill's reptile is a "serpent covered with green feathers," that it is the same being as the god that leaves its traces on the rock and that both call out, hissing and howling loudly, from the top of the hill.[74] And by the same token, there is the heralded Tzatzitépetl, "the mountain of clamors, or calling," the promontory of Tollan from which, on the command of Ce Acatl Topiltzin, great cries were heard to summon the people.

In addition, the spatial distribution of pueblos also seems to have followed the requirements of archetypes. On this matter, the opinions of Miguel Acosta Saignes, Paul Kirchhoff, and Carlos Navarrete are extremely interesting. Acosta Saignes underscored the possibility of tracking merchants' districts by searching for the names Pochtlan, Acxotlan, and others that are known.[75] For his part, Kirchhoff believed it possible, using the reports in documents, to reconstruct an empire that had situated its administrative seats geographically in accordance with a religious scheme, and he drew up a hypothetical map showing their location.[76] Finally, Navarrete indicated that he had observed the repetition of toponyms in geographic areas that were quite distant from each other and in a way that grouped them not randomly but always similarly, to the extent that one can search for the placement of a pueblo with a fixed name solely by finding those with companion names.[77] It is cosmography itself, transplanted onto earth. One is motivated to risk a comparison of the norms of these peasants of high culture with the nomadic bands that populated the region far to the north of the Mesoamerican frontier:

Groups of hunters may be considered a settlement that frequently moves from one place to another. As a rule, the encampment of any hunting group follows a precise, pre-arranged pattern, according to which certain families would always live close to one another, and others [would] always [live] at one edge of the encampment. Among the Comanches, when the group reached the place where the new camp was to be set up, the group's chieftain chose the spot for his tent, and the rest of the families automatically lay hold of their places in relation to his. If some family had fallen back on the trek, a place was reserved for it until it arrived. The layout of the land itself had some bearing on the arrangement, but the chieftain took this into consideration when selecting his own dwelling spot. The families that adjoined one another in one encampment invariably did so at every site.[78]

This description implies that different groups, related culturally, could have migrated separately but have always anticipated or allowed for the possibility of establishing a new arrangement within a scheme in which the balance of production and the exchange of goods had been created through the day-to-day experience of a common life. Underpinned by channels of distribution in a territory that was seen to be a copy of the supernatural world, this type of grouping could have gone on to incorporate more complex bodies, in which the political balance, too, had been designed on the basis of a previous scheme. The assertions made by Acosta Saignes, Kirchhoff, and Navarrete are a good starting point for a needed study of political relations in Mesoamerica.

All of the foregoing raises a serious problem in the interpretation of indigenous history. Is there, as Krickeberg says in referring to the issue of migrations, a first mythical part, in which the description of the route is simply the indication of a return that terminates in the center—Tollan—from where every pueblo declares it will abandon barbarism to accept a civilized life?[79] Can one affirm, as Kirchhoff does, that the apparent mythical places can be placed geographically? If one starts not only with Kirchhoff's assertion, but also with the possibility that the copy of the supernatural world on earth is not single but multiple, then there may be a third answer: the real existence of cities that correspond to mythical places—again, ordered according to this kind of template but repeated various times geographically and temporally, always arising out of a pilgrimage, from a history whose course follows a mythical prototype.

Tollan and Chicomóztoc, Aztlan and Tamoanchan—all, then, truly existed. As we already know from the multiple references made to it, Tollan has been situated in various locations. Chicomóztoc, despite being considered man's place of origin, also appears in history as a stage in the pilgrimages.[80] In the pilgrimages, which were not composed of just a single, unitary group but were formed by very different groups—though all represented the same current—the places that are cited are, generally speaking, the same. Were there pilgrimage routes that were all too well established, that served, in effect, as a "beaten path," as Acosta Saignes claimed?[81] Or perhaps the track itself was not as clear and unvarying as the one delineated in the myth.

Martínez Marín has indicated that one of the narrative devices employed in the Codex Boturini is that of flattening historical reality down to a schematic order, under which the majority of departures and arrivals by different populations occur in a year *ácatl* and *técpatl*, respectively.[82] The repeating of this pattern in the codex is definitely not mere coincidence. There are two possible explanations: either history, in the setting down of events, has been fabricated or people—in particular, the group to which the Codex Boturini refers—operated under the rigid imperatives of a belief system, religious or magical in character, that obligated them both to begin and end journeys and to act more broadly in strict fidelity to the calendar.

The sources need to be examined to see if they bear out Krickeberg's thesis. Earlier, I mentioned that communities had to cross a stretch of sea to commence civilized historical life. The Cakchiqueles arrive, coming from the west, after crossing the sea.[83] The Chichimec start out on their migration routes once they make landfall, after passing through an inlet of the sea.[84] On their journey, both the Mexica and the Tetzcocanos likewise cross the sea.[85] The Olmec and the Xicalanca people arrive from the east, with boats and ships,[86] and the Tlaxcalteca passed through the straits of a sea.[87] Did no one by chance come from the north, by land? Undoubtedly the notion of undertaking a passage over water is, as I noted earlier, the repeating over land of a schematic element of the cosmogonic myth in which the central figure crosses the sea. This part of the myth will stand out more clearly if other sources that refer to the way in which the passage occurred are also mentioned. The Cakchiquel, after reaching the seashore, drove into the sand the red staffs that they received in Tulán as emblems of their race;[88] the Mexica, upon leaving Chicomóztoc-Quinehuayan, passed between the waters, which opened to allow them through;[89] another source claims that the sea opened up after the Mexica leader produced a blow with a rod, that leader being Papa (Ce Acatl).[90] In another telling, Balam-Quitzé, at the head of the Quiché, touched the sea with his staff to part the waters;[91] other texts relate that as the waters parted, the Quiché went between them, crossing over stones that lay in a row on the sand.[92] On the simple face of it, if one analyzes just a single case, it would seem that the tale smacked of biblical history,[93] and Diego Durán himself—though initially overjoyed in believing that he had discovered that the Indians were Jews—later suspected that they were simply reciting the story of Exodus back to him. Upon examining the texts together, however, any such claim must be called into question. Above all, we need to recognize that a fundamental Mesoamerican myth is at play, such that in territories very distant from each other, but within the same context, a similar history is being recounted. Separating fact from fiction, we have clearly come up against a first mythical part of the history of the pilgrimages.

Consider another example: Coatépec is the mountain where Coatlicue gives birth to Huitzilopochtli, the rising Sun. The myth of Teotihuacan tells of an extended night before Nanahuatzin, turned into a star, appears on the horizon. Before reaching Coatépec, the Mexica suffer, like Nanahuatzin, a prolonged period—three days and four nights—during which the Sun did not move along its path.[94] (See figure 7.2.)

In the face of such examples, can one credibly assert the existence of a purely historical narrative?

Another episode in the Mexica migration involves an *ahuehuete*, or sabino tree, that broke apart. The god Huitzilopochtli had warned the people who found themselves at the foot of the tree that they should move away from it.[95] In this tale, a real incident—

**FIGURE 7.2.** Códice Azcatitlan, plate iv

the simple breaking apart of a tree that because of the girth of its trunk seemed miraculous—was mythologized, with the part about the message from the god added as an embellishment. Nonetheless, the rest of the narrative helps illuminate what, exactly, it deals with. The tree that fractures is that of Tamoanchan, and its breaking apart represents the moment of the heavenly descent to earth of a god, to take charge of a human group. After the incident, the god commands his people, who come to know who they are in the very moment of the miracle, to break off from the rest of the pilgrims, to acquire a separate identity as symbolized by changing the name Aztec for that of Mexitin, and to stick eagle down on their ears—all as a sign of recognition. In addition, he gives them the bow, arrow, and netted pouch, all instruments of work (See figure 7.3.)

**FIGURE 7.3.** Códice Boturini, plate iv

There is a further remarkable occurrence in this tale: the death, by sacrifice, of men who are slit open over great cactuses. Here we observe the reference to another myth—or to another part of the myth—of creation. One can compare this "history" with the narrative of man's creation in the *Anales de Cuauhtitlan*,[96] and the coincidence will be apparent.

Moreover, the incident of the broken tree is not unique, since at least two other similar cases can be directly noted in which the protector god uses this device, or happening, to spark a recognition of him by a community of people as their god. Chimalpahin describes one of these in the following way: the totolimapanecas shot an arrow toward heaven that, on its descent, fell onto a jaguar; after the jaguar is offered to the god—who is represented by a white eagle—he descends to devour it. At the same time, thunder claps rumbled through the heavens—a message that the god had recognized these people, who from earth had implored his intercession, as his children.[97] The second incident occurs to the Mexica as they celebrate before Cocoxtli, the ruler of Culhuacan, the new fire ceremony, the binding of years. Again, the boom of thunder is heard—the tree of Tamoanchan? The eagle descends and receives the offering of the sacrificed Xochimilcas.[98]

The number of cases is still larger. In Atlacuihuayan, once again during the Mexicas time of migration, the *átlatl* gets "invented," spear-throwers that are characteristic of people who hunt and fish on lakes.[99] The story that people whose primary mode of obtaining sustenance revolved around lakes should just then have invented, or come to know, an instrument that was among the oldest weapons in Mesoamerica is very strange. A much more likely interpretation is that it deals with a renewal of the pact between the god of communities that specialize in fishing on lakes and their people. Clearly, Atlacuihuayan means "the place where the *átlatl* is taken." Furthermore, another geographic name is expressive of a different etiologic myth: Pozonaltépetl, "the mountain of foam." It was on this site that another pueblo "invented" pulque, with its frothy head, and a drunken huasteco—the original huasteco—"invented" the nudity of his people, who it seems were ill-disposed at any time to cover their genital organs.[100]

Perhaps this reliving of the myth by Mexica historians, within their remembrance of the journey and its geographical markers, accounts for some apparent contradictions in the sources— for example, that the Mexica, taken out of Aztlan by Huitzilopochtli, do not encounter him until later, at the time they pass through Colhuacan.[101] At any rate, this puzzle reserves its place among the many that the Mexica migration still guards.

However, as Kirchhoff asserts, the existence of some of these cities can also be deduced very clearly from the sources. And if they are plural in number, is it not possible to think that they bear a name that refers to their function? According to Mayan sources, Tollan, where in Krickeberg's telling every people becomes civilized,[102] is the place where the power of kings is confirmed. Cholollan acquired its fame as the city to which kings journeyed from distant places in search of confirmation, and its name, as we have seen, was Tollan-Cholollan. As Sahagún relates it, Teotihuacan, which also was Tollan, received the former name because those who were going to rule over other pueblos were elected there.[103] Perhaps all of the Colhuacans were places of reception for the image of the protector god, just as all or almost all of the Panutlans, Panoayans, or Panocos were places in which the landing by boat from the other side of the sea, or the arrival by walking across the parted waters, was renewed or reenacted. Similarly, the Chicomóztocs were the sites in which a new birth was simulated and the Coatépecs the places where the gods of light were born.

In this way, the history of pueblos on migration would not be the simple account of a past event, overlaid with a religious covering, but a true process of reliving in which new places may have acquired the name that the magical passage of some pilgrims had imprinted on them. Consider that Mixiuhcan is still called the place where a woman delivered a baby, and its name signifies "the place for giving birth." The woman was a very important Mexica noblewoman, who later, in Temazcatitlan—"place of the steam bath"—took the postpartum bath that was indispensable for recuperation. Where is the record of all the women who gave birth during all of the pilgrimages? It is nowhere, of course. To have been recorded, the act of this woman giving birth, in the place that she did, must have represented something of much greater importance.

The felt need to revitalize time by returning to the origin had a transformative effect on history; elements of the real, as lived by people, and of the ritualistic, as relived by them, were thrown together and amalgamated. In this way, in agreement with Mircea Eliade's ideas vis-à-vis societies that he classifies as archaic, man would acquire on earth the anchorage that spontaneous existence had not been able to furnish him:

> This "transcendent" world of the Gods, the Heroes and the mythical Ancestors is accessible because archaic man does not accept the irreversibility of Time. As we have repeatedly seen: ritual abolishes profane, chronological Time and recovers the sacred Time of myth. Man becomes contemporary with the exploits that the Gods carry out *in illo tempore*. On the one hand, this revolt against the irreversibility of Time helps man to "construct reality," on the other, it frees him from the weight of dead Time, assures him that he is able to abolish the past, to begin his life anew, and to recreate his World.[104]

This fluid orientation toward time and the past implied, wherever it was manifest, that history possesses a cyclical nature. In the case of Mesoamerica, the region's two principal calendars were the instruments that gave meaning to the presence of human communities on earth. One of them, given the name *tonalpohualli* in Nahuatl, was divinatory, warning men of the day-to-day influences that held sway, within a circular frame of time that lasted 260 days. The other calendar, known as the *xiuhpohualli*, was organized around a count of fifty-two years of 365 days each. On an annual basis, this calendar allocated the great ritual ceremonies into eighteen periods of 20 days each, plus a minor period of 5 days; and in the sequence of years, it aided man by allowing him to foresee destiny and also offered rules to guide his actions within the public sphere. In broad outline, these were the distinct uses of the two calendars, although they also shared some in common, which stands to reason, given that the two were ultimately part of a single system of calculating time. In other words, the function of the calendars was dual: on the one hand, to regulate ritual conduct, thereby maintaining human beings in their designated place; and on the other, to defend against bad times or to instruct men on how to take advantage of the good. The first function caused the indigenous inhabitants to submerge themselves in a time outside the present, a time that was not real, such that their conduct became simply the covering of an archetypal action; the second, in contradistinction, caused them to confront a reality that was all but set—and the influence of this belief was strong—against one that called for them to struggle, drawing on the capacity for spontaneous, intelligent, nimble action. Here were two radically opposed positions, and mental attitudes, toward time—one that entailed only the passive acceptance of its continually repeating cycles versus another that required a harsh engagement with its passage. In the case of the former, the use of ritualized action predominated; with the latter, the historical record loomed large. For this reason, historical texts were imbued with a sense of total knowledge of time: they demonstrated the circle of time and history, describing that which had happened and would always happen, within the circle, on particular dates. With the purpose of obtaining a precise knowledge of man's futures through the record of cycles past, the layers of history could be superimposed on each other, perfecting an image, in each return, the vague outlines of which the far-seeing and well-ordered man was able to sketch out. Originally, then, history was neither of the past nor of the future. It was the discovery of a circle, a perfectible discovery, that could serve powerfully to explain what had transpired in the present as well as what had happened in the past and would happen in the future.

In this way, it had been possible to discover the danger posed by the years *ce tochtli*. In each return, every fifty-two years, there was the danger of hunger, which on one occasion so devastated the Mexica that many of the pueblo's members were forced to sell themselves into servitude. This strong indigenous belief clearly colored the reading that one early colonial period missionary made of the Codex Telleriano-Remensis, convincing him that the phenomenon needed to be studied under the norms of Old World astrology: "In this year [of] one rabbit, if this account is looked into closely, hunger and death will be seen to have reigned down in this year, and so in this year of 1558 there have been the heaviest frosts that the natives can remember, and shortages in some areas, and so has it befallen to them this year, the great omen of which is always brought by this year one rabbit. He who is a good astrologist looks at which stars and planets line up in these years, because they themselves [the native inhabitants] count the day from midday until the midday of the next day, and their year has 365 days like ours."[105]

There were other causes that gave rise to the record of unique actions and occurrences, among them, the need to have a document that attested to and spelled out the rights that a pueblo had acquired vis-à-vis the interests of other pueblos or the case that a group holding power made to justify its dominance of a pueblo, since the subordinate population might with some regularity ask by what title the group exercised its right to govern, what exploits its ancestors had performed, how it interceded with the gods, or what benefit its kin had brought to the community.

Here, perhaps, is where the difference lies between the history of the pilgrimage, or of its initial phase, and the history of the period of settlement. In the first, the peasant community holds itself up as worthy—*macehualli*—of a distinctive place on the land, of the right to assert its interests in a world in which neither the land nor the peasant, cut off and separated, can be fully considered as a good on the one hand or a worthy man on the other: their reason for being arose from the condition of their being joined in production. This link did not depend on a powerful person but on the gods, and on the fact that the entire world was ordered accordingly. For the Mexica, the primary justifying title lay in the knowledge of the cycle of divine origin and of their own role and permanent location within it. Once a pueblo was established, a new set of interests necessitated the creation of a new type of history, the record of unique, discreet events and actions: the fixing of boundary lines, at the founding of the pueblo; the distribution of the *calpulli* on different parcels of land within the pueblo's overall territory; the permanence of the group in power; the tie—and this also obtained during the pilgrimage, with its appropriate characteristics recorded—between a pueblo having the right to its own rulers and the powerful pueblo, next to the gods, grantor of governments; the right of exploitation, by means of tribute, over pueblos that had been conquered, or at least, for the defeated, the right to owe no more than a fixed periodic tribute.

In the great majority of cases, the history of a particular deed or action, to so designate it, did not extend much beyond the life of the city-states that needed it as a tool, or it began, in both the telling and the record, to get twisted this way and that, thereby enriching the myth. The centuries of the Classic period came and went without leaving us the inheritance of a single word.

The history of the years spent in migration is not the history of an unbridled chaos. On the contrary, the problem is one of perspective: we are incapable of fully comprehending the rationale for something that lies well beyond the boundaries of our own cultural canons. All the same, it is only logical to infer that the recorded history met urgent needs and met them to such an extent that the material from the Postclassic period survived in abundance down to the present. The effort to uncover either myths or history, however, will yield no more than a partial answer. What Kirchhoff attributes to space can also be applied to time in the Mesoamerican cosmology and worldview. There existed heavenly schemes that *indeed* had reality on earth, and it was by means of them that man rooted himself—before his fellow men, within his *calpulli*, and on the land that he worked and cultivated.

The present-day historian must confront a chronological question of considerable gravity: the diversity of days on which, according to the different calendars, the years began or of the years that marked the beginning of a century. Both Jiménez Moreno and Kirchhoff have paid substantial attention to this problem, and both participated in the 1955 symposium organized by the Mexican Society of Anthropology to study it. According to the sources, the calendrical differences result from the fact that the counting began either at the moment that each pueblo came into the world or, in Motolinía's telling, at the moment of creation of the Fifth Sun.[106] Torquemada wrote that three things—the departure from the place of origin, the first year, and the first century—all corresponded;[107] and Muñoz Camargo wrote that the Chichimeca arrived on the mainland in "the year that the natives reckon by their [own] count."[108] This lattermost version is indicative of which date should be taken as year one in the case of those who, like the Mexica, set out from two different places—Aztlan and Chicomóztoc—in different years. The year that merits attention is that of the last departure. There exists a place of origin; the great womb is reached, and from it men are born, and with their birth begins the calculation of their age. That is, the first year—at least in the case of the Mexica—begins at the conclusion of their birth year.

The Nahua celebrated a rite that was called *tóxiuh molpilía*, "*se atan nuestros años*" (our years are bound up), or *xiuhtzitziquilo*, "*son asidos los años*" (the binding of years), at the precise moment in which a fifty-two-year century had ended and, it was hoped, a joining to the next one was accomplished. This crucial instant was greatly feared because it was the date on which all humankind would come to an end. The sign that this express moment had not arrived and was yet postponed was the shooting up of the flame in the chest of a recently sacrificed captive, a fire that was immediately parceled out to replace the one that had been completely extinguished throughout the region. The rite was celebrated by each pueblo in a particular year: by the Chichimec in *chiconahui técpatl*;[109] by the Acolhuas in *ce técpatl*[110] by the Totomihuaques in *chicome ácatl*[111]; by the Tecpanecas Culhuaques in *ome ácatl*[112]; and by the Mexica in *ome ácatl* as well,[113] despite some confusion about the lattermost celebration, stemming from Alvarado Tezozómoc's attribution of it to *chiconahui ácatl*.[114] This particular beginning of the century led to the use of possessive pronouns in references to the rite: *to-* in *toxiuhmolpilía*, "*our* years are bound up," or *in-* in the case of a sentence in which another pueblo is mentioned—for example, *inxiouh molpilli in mexicah*,[115] "the binding of *their* years, of the Mexica."

The date was considered crucial because, as just noted, it was thought that the world would cease to exist in the moment that one century was bound to another. Apparently, the idea of the general vanishing of men stands in contradiction to the continuing force, and life, of the ceremony. Yet at this moment there was no need to place one's faith in a temporal correspondence. To have arrived at a fixed point in the count of years demanded a celebration in which the rite joined a time that ended—the extinguishing of all fire—with original time, so that in this moment, when the original time, not the present, was validated, the union of the two was sealed. As a result, the lack of concordance with a purely temporal reality had no importance whatsoever.

For the Mexica, as mentioned earlier, the calamitous year is that of *ce tochtli*. The Mexica sing of their personal travail when in a *ce tochtli*, one that commemorated their abandonment of Chicomóztoc and they fell under the power of the Culhuas, who vanquished them on the field of battle in Chapultepec. I have translated a poem that speaks of the fate that befell a group of people; once again, the poem relates, it is necessary to begin the count of years with the *xiuhmolpilli*:

| | |
|---|---|
| In tlalli tentlapa topa machiztic, yehuaya, | From the edge of the earth we came to be known of, ¡ay! |
| topa matzaya[n] in ilhuicatl, | the heavens cracked above us, |
| topan temoc Ipalnemohuani ic oncan Chapoltepetl icatya, ayyo. | that one for whom one lives descended over us there in his place in Chapultéptl ¡ay! |
| Icuepca icuac topan mochihua, yetihuaya | Then over us his return happened, ¡ay! |
| ce in tochtonalli xihuin tlatquitl. | of the charge of the destiny of the year |
| Yahuaya, choquiztli, yehuaya. | *ce tochtli*. |
| Ye huicallo in mexicah ye nican Cha-Poltepetl icatca, iyao oamoiye. | ¡Ay, I weep, ay! Now the Mexica are carried off from here, |
| Aocnello quitohua mexicatl, aya Caninelhuayo ilhuicatl[116] | from their place in Chapoltéptl, ¡ay, ay! Now it is said the Mexica have no foundation, ¡ay! Where is the foundation of heaven . . . ? |

Days, months, and even *suns*—eras—also possessed particular attributes along with those who venerated them. The *chicome ácatl* was especially celebrated in Cholula, because it was the day of Quetzalcoatl's birth, as was the *ce ácatl*, the homonymous day of the year of the priest's death.[117] Also considered special was the *chicunahui itzcuintli*, the day of the gods of those who cut and worked stone.[118] A twenty-day period, like that of *xócotl huetzi*, was the object of much celebration in Coyohuacan,[119] and every four years, or always under the same annual sign, the festivals of a particular group of pueblos were held. Despite the statement made in the majority of historical accounts that men were destroyed before the present Sun, the fifth, reigned; Alva Ixtlilxóchitl asserts that both the Olmec and the Xicalanca were men of the third age, and the Códice Vaticano Latino says that Tollan arose in the fourth.[120] The phases of the night star had an influence on their worshippers; the Metztitecos, for example, fought against their enemies on "the nights that produced a moon, and wondrously they went into battle by day."[121]

There were favorable and unfavorable times. For the Mexica, the *ce tochtli* was unfavorable,[122] for the Toltecs, the *ce técpatl*.[123] The *ce ácatl* counted as a highly unfavorable day for the Mexica commoners, since it provoked gossiping and disagreements, but it was notably favorable for the nobles because it was the sign of Quetzalcoatl.[124] A particular sign could hold sway over a territory, though its affect was felt by only one group of people, with its malign arrival leaving neighboring groups unaffected.[125]

In my case, an essay by Alfonso Caso, "El águila y el nopal," had a liberating effect because it gave me the sense that I possessed an interesting key to studying the concept of history held by the Mesoamericans. Caso stated that the founding of the city of Mexico-Tenochtitlan and, fifty-two years later, the naming of the first *tlatoani* (the supreme ruler, or head, of the city-state)—Acamapichtli—corresponded to the years *ce técpatl* because *ce técpatl* was the date consecrated to Huitzilopochtli. The Mexica had left Aztlan in the original year of *ce técpatl*, which made Caso's proposition all the more appealing. Caso did not leave it at that but rather extended his line of reasoning to the Toltec, who had left their city in the year *ce ácatl*, which, as we have noted, corresponded to the name Quetzalcoatl.

A short time later, Kirchhoff gave a sharper edge to the argument concerning the symbolic value underlying the category of years by applying it to numbers as well. In his words, "The influence of ritual numbers in not just the thinking but also in the ceremonies and the social institutions of the Indians of Mesoamerica is an indisputable fact. Without such recognition, it will never be possible for us to understand the complexities of their life and culture."[126]

Yet, for all the persuasive logic that informed Caso's proposition, a comparison of the sources resulted in a very different picture. Kirchhoff himself published an article in which he highlighted the many discrepancies regarding the year of the city's founding.[127] Part of the reason for the confused picture, of course, stemmed from the fact that there were different calendars used and different traditions followed inside the city itself, so that not only could a unique event or act have been calculated as having fallen under different dates, but also the time for ritualistically celebrating the founding of the city could have been several in number. Nonetheless, the date *ce técpatl* assigned by Caso does not even appear in Kirchhoff's tables. The problem could not be shrugged off. Evidently, Caso was mistaken; yet the pull of his argument was such that I could not drop it just like that. Instead, I decided to see if, despite the error that he made in settling on a particular year, Caso's larger point was valid—that is, whether there was in fact some chronological base that served to guide the life of the indigenous population. The majority of the sources and, more particularly, those that related most directly to the Mexica community, gave *ome calli* as the date of the city's founding. To begin with, that date drew me away from the starting points of the *trecena* (the 13-day period) that were so important: *ce* being "one" and *ome* being "two." It followed that the date *ome calli* was no longer bound to the years *ce técpatl* and *ce tochtli*—"one flint" and "one rabbit"—the exit dates, respectively, from Aztlan and from Chicomóztoc. Then I remembered what I had observed earlier: the Mexica abandoned Chicomóztoc in the year *ce tochtli*, but their century begins to be counted in the following year, *ome ácatl*—"two reed." The same thing, I thought, could occur with the date *ce técpatl*. I added one to it, and the result was *ome calli*—"two house." The thought experiment worked to my advantage, for among my notes I came across a number that, to that point, was not familiar to me as having any special significance in Nahua culture: the number twenty-eight. I had initially encountered it in a reference to the celebration of the first new fire ceremony, coming twenty-eight years after the group had left Aztlan. It was mentioned explicitly that a period of twenty-eight years had transpired, but to confirm that this was actually so, the year in which the departure took place must also be included in the total.[128] The second appearance of the number occurred with reference to the group's arrival at the lake, and the source mentions that twenty-eight years passed between the year in which the group reached the lake and the year that Mexico-Tenochtitlan was founded.[129] Taking the date *ome calli* as a base point, and folding it in, as in the earlier case, I counted in reverse and arrived at the year *ce tochtli*. I thus had two groups of pairs:

| DEPARTURE | ARRIVAL |
|---|---|
| ce técpatl-ome calli | ce tochtli-ome ácatl |
| ce tochtli-ome ácatl | ce técpatl-ome calli |

Since the first group of two pairs referred to the beginning of the migration and the second to its conclusion, I began—with the valuable aid of Víctor M. Castillo F.—to scrutinize the pictorial codices that might give some meaning to this key. The two that provided concrete information were the Codex Mexicanus and the Códice Azcatitlan. In one the departure takes place from Aztlan in *ce técpatl*, and in the other it occurs on the same date, but from Culhuacan. This distinction was not a stumbling block because in the Códice Boturini Aztlan and Culhuacan are located next to each other. In one codex, according to Ernest Mengin,[130] *ome calli* is associated with Tlatzallan, whereas in the other it is connected to Tepemaxalco. The meaning of the first place name is "intermediate place," or "a mountain gorge between two ranges," while the second means "separation between mountains." Both are illustrated with glyphs in which the migrants traverse a pass between two mountains. As the information contained in numerous sources has made it widely known, the year *ce tochtli* corresponds to the departure from Chicomóztoc, and that of *ome ácatl* to the departure from Coatépec. The group of years that cluster near the end of the pilgrimage are the *ce tochtli*, noted always as a year of hunger and misfortunes, in which the lot of the Mexica comes to an end, according to the verses cited earlier. The year of the *xiuhmolpilli* is the *ome ácatl*; the year *ce técpatl*, obviously, celebrates the departure from Aztlan, to which the sources were always making reference. Although I should note here that I do not find any particularly significant event during the epoch of the city's founding and the *ome calli* is the year of the founding of Mexico-Tenochtitlan. Both the second and the fourth are consequences of the presence of the first and the third, since for some reason there is a celebration held in the years "two," not in the years "one." I am omitting all of the intermediate details to focus solely on the first two and last two pairs of years of the first series and last series of the pilgrimage.

I believe, as expressed diagramatically in figure 7.4, there can be a projection of the first pairs of years *ce técpatl-ome calli* in the last pairs of years *ce tochtli-ome ácatl*, and another of the first *ce tochtli-ome ácatl* pairs of years in the last *ce técpatl-ome calli* pairs of years. The presence of the number twenty-eight that unquestionably forms the units of a process, occurring both at the beginning as well as at the end of the journey, underlie my contention. If, as a point of departure, one takes the interpretation of the myth that I offered in referring to man's creation, then a possible correspondence can be seen:

a) Aztlan, "place of whiteness," or "place of white eagle down," is the heavenly place from which creation comes: the semen descends.

b) Tepemaxalco and Tlatzallan are the way station for the beings that come from heaven: the penetration of the semen. For the time being, some intermediate sites, spanning a lapse of twenty-four years, are left uninterpreted.

c) Chicomóztoc is the place of birth, a mountain full of caves that open so the people can leave.

d) Coatépec is the serpent's mountain, the place in which, armed, the Sun is born, to fight against his brothers, the Moon and the stars. The dikes that hold back the waters are broken there. It is the place of birth that corresponds to the city's beginning.

For now, these relationships remain purely hypothetical and await a deeper study of the Mexica migration, one that I hope some scholar will soon undertake.[131] Jiménez Moreno has observed an interesting relationship with regard to the matter of place names. He points out the existence of certain places that bear the same name as cities, but to which a diminutive suffix has been added: Tetzcoco becomes Tetzcozinco; Mexico becomes Mexicatzinco. He further notes that, although the name of the first is what gives rise to the second, the settlements that bear the

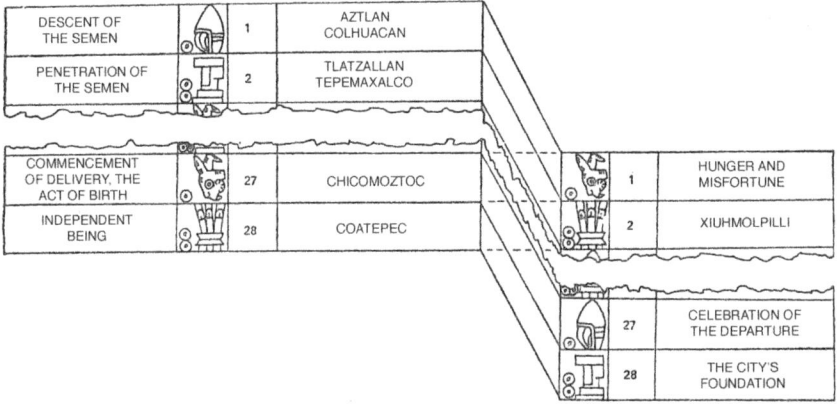

**FIGURE 7.4.** Hypothetical relationships between occurrences related to the beginning and the end of the Mexica migration

derivative names were actually founded earlier.[132] This sequence is expressly related in the *Relación de Mexicaltzinco*.[133]

The case of Tollantzinco and Tollan Xicocotitlan can help us untie this apparent knot. Tollantzinco predates Tollan Xicocotitlan.[134] Upon arriving in Tollantzinco, the Toltecs counted one age[135] (in the year *ce técpatl*). They began to build Tollan in the year *ce calli*, thirteen years after their arrival in Tollantzinco.[136] The particle *tzinco*, which is generally interpreted as a diminutive, can also have the meaning of "place of the foundation." It is evident that it pertains to pueblos that are founded "provisionally"—that is, *to await* the arrival of the date on which the life of the principal city has to be ritually begun. The suspicion could still exist, however, that these pueblos, in turn, had to be founded on a precise date. The thirteen years during which Tollantzinco preceded Tollan leads one to suppose that such a correspondence existed between other places. Mexico, which as already noted is founded in the year *ome calli*, must have had an antecedent in *ome técpatl*. I have not found any mention of the date on which the Mexica occupied Mexicatzinco, but both this occupation and that of Tetzinco take place in the immediate vicinity of what would be Tenochtitlan, on a date that is close to the birth of Contzallan, the son of Quetzalmoyohuatzin, an important Mexica woman.[137] His birth took place on *ce ácatl* or on *ome técpatl*, thirteen or fourteen years before the founding of Mexico-Tenochtitlan, and the event was apparently so important that, as noted earlier, it gave the name *Paridero* to Mixiuhcan. Preparations were made for founding the city on the same site as that on which Axolohua and Cuauhtlequetzqui had discovered the eagle perched on the nopal. Axolohua had gone down there into the water and remained submerged for an entire day, conversing with the god Tlaloc, who did not object that it was the site of Huitzilopochtli's house. The Mexica killed a captain from Colhuacan, and his heart served as an altar heart, thirteen years before the founding of Mexico-Tenochtitlan. In addition, the Tlatelolca branch (we have to assume) of the Mexica celebrated a highly important ceremony in Iztacaltzinco in the year *ce técpatl*, thirteen years before that of *ce calli*, the latter marking the date on which they split off from the Tenochaca to found their city of Mexico-Tlatelolco.[138]

After choosing the place and waiting for the proper time, all that was lacking was to designate the place in which the protector god would dwell. On one hand, this could be the temple; on the other, the same mountain from which he would send down water. Moreover, the temple was a mountain, for which reason the name given by Alvarado Tezozómoc to Coatépec—the great pyramid of Tenochtitlan, dedicated to Tlaloc and Huitzilopochtli—was "temple and mountain."[139] As for the temple of Quetzalcoatl in Chololan, its worshippers believed that it truly was a mountain, hollow and filled with water like all the rest:

> And they said that when a layer of the whitewashing was scraped off, in the time of their paganism, water flowed from there; and because they were not flooded by it, they sacrificed children of two or three years of age, and with their blood, mixed with lime, they made a kind of mastic and with it stopped up the springs and founts [of water] that so poured forth: and fulfilling this the cholutecas said that when some reversal happened to them in the war of the white gods and the Tlaxcaltecas, they would scrape off and chip away all of the whitewashing, whereby fountains of water would flow that would flood them.[140]

## NOTES

1. *Relaciones de Yucatán*, 1:283; 2:95, 127, 181.
2. de la Rea, *Crónica*, 25–26.
3. Sahagún, *Historia general*, 3:200.
4. Mendieta, *Historia eclesiástica*, 1:87.
5. Muñoz Camargo, *Historia de Tlaxcala*, 234; Motolinía, *Historia*, 205; and Motolinía, *Memoriales*, 204.
6. Acosta Saignes, "Los pochteca," 29–30.
7. In his introduction to *Memorial de Sololá*, 41.
8. Brinton, "Toltecs," 92.
9. Cervantes de Salazar, *Crónica*, 1:50.
10. Weitlaner, Veláaquez, and Carrasco, "Huitziltépec."
11. *Códice Ramírez*, 17–18.

12. Castillo, *Fragmentos*, 88; and Alvarado Tezozómoc, *Crónica mexicáyotl*, 14.
13. Chimalpahin, *Relaciones*, 63.
14. *Códice Boturini*, plate i; *Códice Azcatitlan*, plate iii.
15. *Codex Mexicanus*, plates xviii, xx.
16. Torquemada, *Los veinte*, 1:78.
17. Fuentes y Guzmán, *Recordación florida*, 3:157.
18. Popol Vuh, 124.
19. Castillo, *Fragmentos*, 88.
20. Brinton, "Toltecs."
21. Seler, "Aztlan."
22. Chimalpahin, *Memorial*, folio 22v.
23. *Título de los señores*, 215.
24. Popol Vuh, 100.
25. López de Cogolludo, *Historia de Yucatán*, 192.
26. Muñoz Camargo, *Historia de Tlaxcala*, 155.
27. Ángel María Garibay K., "La divina elección," in *Poesía náhuatl*, 2:139.
28. Ángel María Garibay K., *Cantares mexicanos*, in *Poesía náhuatl*, 2:77.
29. *Memorial de Sololá*, 48.
30. Jiménez Moreno, "El enigma," 131–32.
31. Seler, "Algo sobre los fundamentos," 299.
32. Caso, *El pueblo del Sol*, 50.
33. Tibón, "Mito y magia," 679.
34. Kirchhoff, "¿Se puede localizer."
35. Kirchhoff, "El imperio tolteca y su ocaso," 4–5, emphasis in original.
36. Martínez Marín, "La cultura de los mexicas," 180.
37. Berlin and Rendón, *Historia tolteca-chichimeca*, 88.
38. *Florentine Codex*, trans. Ángel María Garibay K., in Sahagún, *Historia general*, 4:97.
39. Durán, *Historia de las Indias*, 1:219–27.
40. Ibid., 2:139.
41. *Relaciones de Yucatán*, 2:25–26.
42. Berlin and Rendón, *Historia tolteca-chichimeca*, 76–77.
43. Alvarado Tezozómoc, *Crónica Mexicana*, 8.
44. Berlin and Rendón, *Historia tolteca-chichimeca*, 70–71
45. Chimalpahin, *Relaciones*, 94.
46. Ibid., 134–35.
47. Weitlaner, Velásquez, and Carrasco, "Huitziltepec," 68.
48. Popol Vuh, 119.
49. From a personal communication with Otto Schumann.
50. Chimalpahin, *Memorial*, folio 41r–42r.

51. Sahagún, *Historia general*, 3:212.

52. The *Códice de Calkiní* relates (folio 27–29) that all of the pueblo's dealings took place under the ceiba tree of the well of Halim.

53. *Códice Azcatitlan*, Plate xii.

54. *Historia de la Nación Mexicana*, 41.

55. Alva Ixtlilxóchitl, *Obras históricas*, 1:87.

56. Castillo, *Fragmentos*, 90.

57. Pomar, "Relación de Texcoco," 7.

58. *Relaciones geográficas de la Diócesis de México*, 118.

59. Ibid., 41–42.

60. *Relaciones geográficas de la Diócesis de Tlaxcala*, 70.

61. Chimalpahin, *Relaciones*, 135.

62. Translator's note: These passages are taken from Doris Heyden's critical translation of Durán, published as *The History of the Indies of New Spain* (Norman: University of Oklahoma Press, 1994): 40, 43–44.

63. See, for example, Alvarado Tezozómoc, *Crónica mexicáyotl*, 66.

64. Popol Vuh, 119–26.

65. Muñoz Camargo, *Historia de Tlaxcala*, 33–34.

66. Translator's note: I have taken this passage, from Mircea Eliade's *The Myth of the Eternal Return*, from the English-language translation done by Willard R. Trask; whereas López Austin uses the Spanish-language translation done by Ricardo Anaya. The differences between the two are purely stylistic. See Eliade, *The Myth of the Eternal*, 20–21; and Eliade, *El Mito del eterno*, 27.

67. As Caso affirms in his article, "El águila y el nopal," 100.

68. Krickeberg, "Mesoamérica," 47.

69. Adrián Recinos, *Memorial de Sololá*, 79n124.

70. Berlin and Rendón, *Historia tolteca-chichimeca*, 71. Amaquemecan signifies "where the one attired in [bark] paper is."

71. Durán, *Historia de las Indias*, 1:41.

72. Ibid., 46.

73. Carrasco, "Quetzalcóatl," 89–91.

74. *Relaciones geográficas de la Diócesis de México*, 45–46.

75. Acosta Saignes, "Los pochteca," 25–28.

76. Kirchhoff, "El imperio tolteca y su ocaso."

77. Personal communication with Carlos Navarrete, February 28, 1972.

78. Linton, *Estudio del hombre*, 214.

79. Krickeberg, *Las antiguas culturas*, 43.

80. *Historia de los mexicanos por sus pinturas*, 220; and Sahagún, *Historia general*, 3:212–13.

81. Acosta Saignes, "Migraciones," 40.

82. Personal communication with Martínez Marín.
83. *Memorial de Sololá,* 48.
84. Muñoz Camargo, *Historia de Tlaxcala,* 39–40.
85. Mendieta, *Historia eclesiástica,* 1:158–59.
86. Alva Ixtlilxóchitl, *Obras históricas,* 1:19.
87. Muñoz Camargo, *Historia de Tlaxcala,* 5.
88. *Memorial de Sololá,* 58–59.
89. Chimalpahin, *Memorial,* folio 30r.
90. Durán, *Historia de las Indias,* 1:5; 2:76.
91. *Título de los señores,* 216.
92. *Popol Vuh,* 118.
93. See Durán, *Historia de las Indias,* 1:5n1.
94. *Códice Azcatitlan,* plate vi. See Robert Barlow's comments in *El Códice Azcatitlan,* 108. A partially rubbed-out drawing that appears in the *Codex Mexicanus* (plate xxiii) appears to refer to the same phenomenon.
95. Alvarado Tezozómoc, *Crónica mexicáyotl,* 19–20; Chimalpahin, *Relaciones,* 67; and *Historia de la Nación Mexicana,* 20–23.
96. *Anales de Cuauhtitlan,* 3.
97. Chimalpahin, "Memorial," folio 45v–47r.
98. *La historia de Tlatelolco,* 40–41.
99. *Códice Ramírez,* 32; *Historia la Nación Mexicana,* 30; and Alvarado Tezozómoc, *Crónica mexicáyotl,* 48.
100. Sahagún, *Historia general,* 3:210–11.
101. Torquemada, *Los veinte,* 1:79. *Códice Azcatitlan,* plate iii; *Códice Boturini,* plate i; Chimalpahin, *Relaciones,* 63, etc.
102. Krickeberg, *Las antiguas culturas,* 43.
103. Sahagún, *Historia general,* 3:209.
104. Translator's note: I have taken this passage, from Mircea Eliade's *Myth and Reality,* from the English-language translation done by Willard R. Trask; whereas López Austin uses the Spanish-language translation rendered by Luis Gil. As in the case of note 66, the differences between the two are merely stylistic. See Eliade, *Myth and Reality,* 140; and Eliade, *Mito y realidad,* 158.
105. *Códice Telleriano-Remensis,* part 4, plate xxxviii.
106. Motolinía, *Memoriales,* 389.
107. Torquemada, *Los veinte,* 1:78.
108. Muñoz Camargo, *Historia de Tlaxcala,* 39.
109. Berlin and Rendón, *Historia tolteca-chichimeca,* 108.
110. Alva Ixtlilxóchitl, *Obras históricas,* 1:93.
111. Berlin and Rendón, *Historia tolteca-chichimeca,* 13.

112. *Codex Mexicanus*, plate xxii.

113. *Códice Boturini*, plates vi, x, xv, and xix, as examples of a large number of sources that confirm the practice.

114. Alvarado Tezozómoc, *Crónica mexicana*, 10.

115. Ibid., 14.

116. This fragment of the poem is from *La historia de Tlatelolco desde los tiempos más remotos*. I have taken the paleography from the facsimile edition of *Unos annales históricos de la nación Mexicana: Manuscrit mexicain No. 22 bis*... (Corpus codicum Americanorum medii aevi), 2:78, corresponding to page 31 of the original manuscript. The translation is mine. For the entire poem, in a different translation, see *La historia de Tlatelolco*, 94–95.

117. *Códice Telleriano-Remensis*, part 2, plate v.

118. Sahagún, *Historia general*, 3:58.

119. Durán, *Historia de las Indias*, 1:89.

120. *Códice Vaticano Latino*, plate viii.

121. Chaves, "Relación de la provincial de Metztitland," 532.

122. *La historia de Tlatelolco*, 49.

123. Alva Ixtlilxóchitl, *Obras históricas*, 1:29.

124. Hernández, *Antigüedades de la Nueva España*, 171.

125. Alva Ixtlilxóchitl, *Obras históricas*, 1:23–24.

126. Kirchhoff, "La historia tolteca-chichimeca," xxxviii.

127. Kirchhoff, "Mexican calendar."

128. Chimalpahin, *Memorial*, folio 24v.

129. *Historia de México*, 101.

130. Mengin, "Commentaire," 419.

131. Translator's note: The year 2011 saw the publication of *Los orígenes de los pueblos indígenas del valle de México: Los altépetl y sus historias* (Mexico City: Universidad Nacional Autónoma de México) by Federico Navarrete Linares, a student of Alfredo López Austin.

132. Jiménez Moreno, *Notas sobre historia antigua*, 26–27.

133. *Relaciones geográficas de la Diócesis de México*, 194.

134. Sahagún, *Historia general*, 3:212.

135. Torquemada, *Los veinte*, 1:37.

136. Alva Ixtlilxóchitl, *Obras históricas*, 1:65.

137. Alvarado Tezozómoc, *Crónica mexicáyotl*, 59–61.

138. *La historia de Tlatelolco*, 42–43.

139. Alvarado Tezozómoc, *Crónica mexicana*, 318.

140. Muñoz Camargo, *Historia de Tlaxcala*, 212.

# 8

## The Nature of the Man-God

In their struggle to stamp out paganism, the New World's Christian colonizers seized on an old argument, from the third century CE, concerning the origin of the gods, which held that all of the gods had been simply men, of flesh and blood, who, at a later date, were deified because of the great worthiness of their lives. After the Europeans reached the shores of America and discovered its intricate array of gods, the old argument gained fresh life and, moreover, could be put to two specific uses: it could allow Christians to make sense in their own minds of the multiplicity of numens and it could be deployed as well to convince the indigenous inhabitants that there was no bona fide reason that their gods—who were none but illustrious men—should be worshipped. What is more, if these men were branded and cast as sorcerers, the supposed miracles attributed to them would necessarily amount to—in the Christian world and its heaven—no more than satanic interventions, thereby undercutting any counterargument the native population might make based on its traditional belief in supernatural powers and events. For the Europeans—psychologically, culturally, spiritually—the explanation also had a calming effect: a world buffeted by the new and the unexpected was kept intact.

Camaxtle,[1] Quetzalcoatl,[2] Tezcatlipoca,[3] Huitzilopochtli,[4] Yiacatecuhtli,[5] Tzapotlatenan,[6] Chicomecoatl,[7] Nappatecuhtli,[8] Nahualpilli,[9] Huemac,[10] Opochtli,[11] Titlacahuan,[12] and Tetzahuitl[13] had all been men, independently of the fact that, according to other sources, all of the remaining gods partook equally of the same human origin.[14] This claim is also made in documents pertaining to the Mayan world; the case of Itzmat, king of Itzmal and possessor of the power to cure sicknesses and even to resuscitate the dead, is one example from that region of Mesoamerica.[15] That celebrated men should have been taken as gods was attributed by the early chroniclers to several causes: the invention of some craft or skill (this is the reason given most frequently); exploits performed in battle; serving as a priest or ruler;[16] the ability to employ trickery and wield magic; the imposition of the belief through force and fear, as was the case with Huemac,[17] and—since doctrine and explanation were as one—the close contact with demons that was attributed to Quetzalcoatl.[18]

The opinions of the first generation of European and mestizo historians, however, were not engineered from without. On the contrary, the indigenous sources themselves helped inspire and promote them. Centuries later, Eduard Seler,[19] Pedro Armillas,[20] Pedro Carrasco,[21] Wigberto Jiménez Moreno,[22] Ignacio Bernal,[23] Yólotl González,[24] and Luis Reyes[25] continued to uphold the actual existence of persons who were subsequently taken as gods. There is sufficient basis, above all in the case of Huitzilopochtli, to affirm that this or that god should be seen, no differently than the majority of historical personages in Mesoamerica, as a human being. This being so, how does one explain the process of transformation? Seler's explanation is that a dead warrior, one famous for his exploits, was turned—according to popular belief—into a hummingbird that dwelled in heaven, a belief that was applied to all soldiers who fell in battle; once the dead warrior had ascended to his new dwelling place, he was identified with the god of fire. Armillas theorizes that a group of men bore the same title; collectively, they passed over into the category of a unique civilizing hero, and this figure was later deified. In discussing Otontecuhtli, Carrasco points out that the divinization of the ancestor ruler is commonplace within indigenous cultures and that the defining step is the ruler's assumption of certain attributes, whereby he declares himself to be the god's representative; this action results in the formation of a new tutelary divinity that takes on a life of its own. Bernal proposes a human origin for Huitzilopochtli; he was a priest who rose up from a common background and, by performing acts of magic, convinced people that the god spoke through him—and not just any god but Tetzauhteotl, the god of the group in power. Upon dying, he is divinized, first given the name Tetzahuitl-Huitzilopochtli, then later called Huitzilopochtli alone; simultaneous to this change, another occurs that takes him from being a numen of the god of the Moon to being a numen of the Sun god.

These are quite logical explanations that are based entirely on the sources, which include, notably, the fragmentary parts that survive from the history written by Cristóbal del Castillo. Still, they are not the last word; another phenomenon seems to have been in play. The *Relaciones de Yucatán* relate that the blessings of water and of a long life were asked of these celebrated figures and worthy personages.[26] It was said of Malinalxochitl, who was abandoned during the Mexica pilgrimage, that she resorted to a "thousand wiles . . . to later make herself worshipped as a god[dess]."[27] These personages not only have miraculous acts attributed to them but also a great power of self-transformation.[28] The Spanish naturalist and humanist author Francisco Hernández, who led a scientific expedition to the viceroyalty of New Spain in the 1570s, maintained that "they were men, but [also] heroes and a seedbed of gods and of immortal strength."[29] The reader will thus have comprehended that a relationship undeniably existed between historical personages on the one hand and the protector gods of pueblos on the other, with the latter possessing the particular attributes noted earlier.

Those who functioned as guides on the pilgrimages figure prominently among these personages, but they also include the rulers of pueblos as well as people who were said to know and to be practitioners of sorcery. Something that crops up frequently, and can also serve as a clue or identifier, is the use of the name of some god. At the very least, we can reasonably posit that the person who uses the name maintains some kind of link with his pueblo's protector gods. A select but still substantial number of cases, illustrative of this linkage, are given in table 8.1. The first column contains names that belonged equally to historical figures and to gods; the second, the people or settlement to whom or to which these historical figures belonged; and the third, some of the sources in which these historical personages are mentioned.

Many additional examples of such correspondences could be added to this list, including those that feature names of relative obscurity that some pueblos gave to their protector gods. Indeed, one of the most interesting personages of the Mexica migration should perhaps be included in this category: Copil, the son of Malinalxochitl, who appears in the Codex Mexicanus wearing the headpiece of the god Xipe Totec.[31] It should be borne in mind that this figure, to whom the name Itztapaltetl[32]—"*Laja*" (slab)—is also given, carried the meaning, as Copil, of "*gorro*," or "*tocado*" (headpiece, headdress), which might well refer to that worn by Xipe.

The case of Ce Acatl Topiltzin Quetzalcoatl is noteworthy: Ce Acatl is the calendrical name of the god Quetzalcoatl. In the *Primeros memoriales* of Fray Bernardino de Sahagún,[33] however, the name Topiltzin—attributed by some authors to the priest alone—*is that of the god* Quetzalcoatl, creator of earth, heaven, and the Sun; and the Nicarao refer to one of their gods as Theotbilche[34] (i.e., Topiltzin in their Nahuatl dialect).

The references made to guides or important persons, who become the source of place names and of names that denote places of origin, are also of interest. Of course, to maintain that the importance of these men was such that even pueblos were given their name is going too far.

TABLE 8.1. Examples of gods and ruling leaders mentioned in the sources as guides

| | | |
|---|---|---|
| [Ce] Tecpatzin | mexicas | Serna, 168–69 |
| Coatlicue | mexicas | Historia de los mexicanos por sus pinturas, 220 |
| Chalchiuhtlicue | Coyohuacan | Chimalpahin, Relaciones, 154 |
| Chiconcoatl | mexicas | Leyenda de los Soles, 127 |
| Chimalma | mexicas | Códice Boturini, plate i |
| Ehecatl | Ehecatlan | Relaciones geográficas de la Diócesis de Tlaxcala, 139–41 |
| Huemac | Cholollan and Cuauhquecholan | Muñoz Camargo, 6 |
| Huitzilopochtli | mexicas | Chimalpahin, Memorial, 24r |
| Ilancueitl | colhuas | Relación de genealogía, 249 |
| Itzpapalotl | chichimecas cuauhtitlanecas | Anales de Cuauhtitlán, 5 |
| Ixtac Mixcoatl | mexicas | Alvarado Tezozómoc, Crónica mexicáyotl, 19 |
| Mexi | mexicas | Durán, Historia de las Indias, 1:43–44, 47 |
| Mixcohuatl | mexicas | Anales de Cuauhtitlán, 62 |
| Nauhyotzin | Culhuacan | Chimalpahin, Memorial, 20r |
| Opochtli | Culhuacan | Chimalpahin, Memorial, 17v |
| Quilaztli | Xochimilco | Alvarado Tezozómoc, Crónica mexicana, 528 |
| Tetzauh | mexicas | Anales de Cuauhtitlán, 62 |
| Xipehuehue | Huehuetlan | "La Relación de Chiepetlán," 252–53 |
| Xolotl (Tezozomoc) | Azcapotzalco | Anales de Cuauhtitlán, 40 |

Rather, as noted above, the names of three things—the protector gods, the people attached to them, and the settlements that these men found—do on many occasions coincide. True, it apparently was the case that men, in their role as founders, gave their own name to the places they had reached, as Boturini underlines with respect to the seven Tollans,[35] and as Diego Durán mentions, in referring to the practice as coming from Jewish tradition;[36] but at bottom there was something else at work. The bestower of the name does not seem to be an ordinary human being; and if he [or she] does seem to qualify as one, this identification results from a spurious or contrived linkage. The granting of the name is connected to some circumstance that, by being wrongly incorporated into history or through simple confusion, implies that strong reasons exist—reasons that are shrouded in obscurity but nonetheless exert a powerful influence. An example of such obscurity is the case of Cuauhnene, the wife of Huemac, who gives her name to the place where she delivers a child. Table 8.2 lists the names of personages (some of whom are gods, others historical figures, and still others a combination of the two), the name of the place or human group, and the source, in the left, middle, and right columns, respectively.

Another phenomenon that is repeated among these figures is their lack of singularity, a condition that led J. Eric Thompson to observe that the name Quetzalcoatl was found as often in the annals of indigenous history "as [that of] the Roosevelts or the Adams in the public life of the United States."[37] Their propensity to appear in multiple guises, or to appear, and reappear, in ways that are inconsistent with each other, seems to be confirmed in the sources. On the same page of the *Anales de Cuauhtitlán*, for example, our central protagonist is said to have died first in the year *ome ácatl* and then in the year *ce ácatl*.[38] Nor has history done full justice to Huemac, the Toltec whose multifaceted or plural life makes him no less worthy than Quetzalcoatl of inspiring a multitude of biographies.

Indeed, Huemac can be seen as an astrologer or political ruler, as a youth who asks his pueblo to secure for him a woman with enormous *nalgas* (buttocks) and who dies as a consequence of the political turmoil unleashed by his capricious antics and whimsical conduct, as a venerable guide who leads the Toltecs, as a devout priest, or as a cruel and ruthless warrior; his life—in the event it is reduced to just one—would span centuries. And Huitzilopochtli, in Yólotl González's judgment, was in all likelihood yet another leader who took the name of the god in the sacred site of Coatépec.[39]

Taken as a whole, these elements suggest either the chance existence of persons who bore the same name or, more pointedly, a relationship that obtained between political office and family line, passed down through inheritance, as illustrated in the case of Cuauhtlequetzqui, one of the most mysterious figures in the Mexica pilgrimage. The lives of Totepeuh, who lived some 100 years; of Xolotl, who ruled for 112 years; and of Acatonale, lord of the Xochimilcas, whose life spanned more than 600 years, would be explained on this basis.[40] At the same time, however, the sources also maintain that the persons who brought the Mexica out of Aztlan and Chicomóztoc are the same figures who appear centuries later, when the migration ends and the city is founded—a repetition that is painted on a codex that depicts the entire journey on a single sheet[41]—and that one can deduce from the question asked by an elder of the Mexica wizards who are sent by Motecuhzoma Ilhuicamina and Tlacaelel to the mythical world of Coatépec: What has become of those guides of the pueblos who left the serpent's mountain at the beginning of the migration? Their names are the same as the names of those who, gathered together, centuries later began the life of Mexico-Tenochtitlan.[42]

**TABLE 8.2.** Examples of the names of peoples or cities bearing the names of gods or human eponyms

| *Personages* | *Place or Human Group* | *Source* |
|---|---|---|
| Acolhuatl o Aculli | acolhuas | Motolinía, Historia de los indios, 7 |
| Apepetz | Apepetzpan | Chimalpahin, Relaciones, 77 |
| Aztlal | aztecas? | Alva Ixtlilxóchitl, Obras históricas, 2:62 |
| Copil | Acopilco | Alvarado Tezozómoc, Crónica mexicáyotl, 43 |
| Coacueye | Coacueyecan | Anales de Cuauhtitlán, 12 |
| Cuauhnene | Cuauhnénec | Anales de Cuauhtitlán, 14 |
| Cuextecatl | Cuextecas | Sahagún, Historia general, 3:211 |
| Chichimecatl | chichimecas | Alva Ixtlilxóchitl, Obras históricas, 1:16 |
| Ehecatl | Ehecatla | Relaciones geográficas de la Diócesis de Tlaxcala, 139–41 |
| Itztapaltetl | Itztapaltetitlan | Alvarado Tezozómoc, Crónica mexicáyotl, 41 |
| Ixputzal | Azcapotzalco | Alva Ixtlilxóchitl, Obras históricas, 89 |
| Malinalxochitl | Malinalco | Alvarado Tezozómoc, Crónica mexicáyotl, 41 |
| Mazatl Tecuhtli | mazahuas | Sahagún, Historia general, 3:201 |
| Mexi | mexicas | Burgoa, Geográfica descripción, 1:369–71 |
| Mixtecatl | mixtecas | Burgoa, Geográfica descripción, 1:369–71 |
| Moquihuix | cuauhtinchantlacas moquihuixcas | Kirchhoff, "La historia tolteca-chichimeca," xlv |
| Nicarao | nicaraos | León-Portilla, "Religión de los nicaraos," 19 |
| Olmecatl Huixtotli | olmecas huixtotin | Sahagún, Historia general, 3:210 |
| Otomitl | otomíes | Motolinía, Memoriales, 11 |
| Tenoch | Tenochtitlan | Durán, Historia de las Indias, 1:47 |
| Tezcatzin | Tezcatépec | Relaciones geográficas de la Diócesis de México, 31–32 |
| Tutul | Tutulla | Relaciones geográficas de la Diócesis de Tlaxcala, 169 |
| Tuzantzin | Tuzantlalpan | Relaciones geográficas de la Diócesis de México, 31–32 |
| Xicalancatl | xicalancas | Motolinía, Memoriales, 11 |
| Xipehuehue | Huehuetlan, Chiepetlan | "La Relación de Chiepetlán," 252–53 |
| Xolotl | Xóloc | Códice Xólotl, plate i, d–2 |

Even some figures whom we know all too well as living, historical persons fall, through this process, under suspicion: their names are encountered—projected back, perhaps, from actual time?—in the non-time of myth. Two men aid the gods in bringing about the creation: Coatemoc and Izcoaclt,[43] who indisputably are Cuauhtemoc and Itzcoatl, respectively. And in far-off Aztlan, where boats ply the waters and palaces rise, there was a king called Motecuhzoma.[44]

Evidently, there are men who possess very special qualities and characteristics; they are indelibly connected in some fashion to the protector god and to directing the activities and life of their group. Their central role takes shape and develops during the course of the pilgrimage yet is not limited in any way to that time and experience. The reason why it is so difficult to study these men is that the core of any such study must contend with and focus on the pilgrimages, a period in the history of the Mesoamerican pueblos that takes us furthest away from a demythologized account of events that can be isolated and placed concretely. The journey made by the Mexica gives us the greatest amount of information, so it behooves us to look into their narrative most closely. However, we run up against an immediate obstacle in that an event that is presented as being seamless and self-contained—the single route of a united pueblo—could not have been so. The Mexica migration was not carried out and accomplished as the great movement of a mass of people who swept away all that came before them. It was composed of groups—possibly *calpulli* isolated from one another most of the time—that little by little filtered individually into a region, settled down in particular places for varying periods of time, and by fits and starts came selectively to band together in an area removed from the direct interests and sway of powerful pueblos. Indeed, a defining characteristic of Mexicatzinco was the role it played as a meeting ground and place to take stock for the people of the different *calpulli* that made up the Mexica migration. The *calpulli* were not even of the same ethnic origin, as evidenced, at least, by the composition of the city of Mexico-Tenochtitlan, whose population was extremely heterogeneous. An outgrowth of these circumstances is that, even in the mythical aspect of the story of the journey and despite the later sifting of the official version of events, the tales were rife with dissimilar episodes.

Another factor that makes it difficult to penetrate and grasp the accounts of the pilgrimages is the apparent wish on the part of those who created and narrated them to leave a trail of confusion and misdirection. There is a *desire*, a *necessity* that the distinctive profiles and marks of certain figures get blurred, stretched out over time, and joined not simply to the first rulers but to the creator gods themselves. In this way, a permanent presence and continuity are forged that, reflective of divine support, serve to aid and sanction all of the actions and interventions of the traveling migrants.

Still another factor that obscures the picture is the multiplicity of functions of some figures whose talents and disposition make them suitable, in the eyes of the pueblo, to perform the role of guide, to have authority over families, to exercise leadership in warfare, to preside over rituals, and to communicate personally with the protector god. The complex range of functions entrusted to and associated with these persons made their position, vis-à-vis the group at particular moments in time, ambiguous, enigmatic.

Cuauhtlequetzqui is a classic example of the man with a confusing biography. He is the close comrade of Huitzilopochtli before the migrants;[45] a great priest and the one who carries the sacred bundle containing the image of the god;[46] he dies on a particular occasion before the founding of Mexico-Tenochtitlan;[47] succeeds Tlohtepetl in Tlatzallan; renounces the charge of guide-ruler-interpreter of the will of god in Chimáloc and from then on participates only in collective authority and leadership;[48] takes possession of Mexico-Tenochtitlan together with other leaders; and through all this we can clearly see that he is Cuauhcoatl himself.[49] What, exactly, occurs with him, comes over him? It is his condition of being more than a mere man, of being confused overly with the god. And here it bears emphasizing that the case of Cuauhtlequetzqui is but one example of a phenomenon that applies to all the pilgrimage leaders whose names turn up time and again in the texts concerning migrations that span the centuries.

The wish to set down the history of the one who guards the god, and of that figure alone, likewise leads to the confecting of narratives that makes any simple reconstruction by historians an all but impossible task. To begin with, the indigenous narrator aims at being no more than a faithful interpreter of the beliefs of his community. For him, whoever devotes himself to the protector god connects his life to those who have done the same in the past. The names of both—the god and the one who guards the god—may come and go, become separated or confused. Cristóbal del Castillo's account, for example, grants names to two distinct persons: on the one hand, the numen continues being called Tetzauhteotl, while the man is called Huitzilopochtli, a name that he takes from the moment in which, as ruler, warrior, and priest, he dedicates himself to the divinity.[50] Elsewhere, del Castillo relates that he was called this for having first been known as Huitzil and for being left-handed;[51] but one can clearly see that this is a very free, open-ended explanation of the origin of the name. The name Huitzilopochtli is that of the god, and so it appears in old religious hymns, in which he is called both Huitzilopochtli and Tetzahuitl.[52]

The names of this pair vary to an excessive degree. In one source, Huitzilopochtli is the god and Tlohtepetl Xiuhcoatl, the man.[53] In another, the name of the god is also Huitzilopochtli and that of the man is Chalchiuhtlatonac.[54] In another source, the god is named Tetzauhteotl Yaotequihua and the man, Huitzilopochtli.[55]

And elsewhere, the name of the man is Iztacmixcohuatzin and that of the god, Tetzahuitl Huitzilopochtli.[56]

This designation of different names frequently means that one cannot know with any degree of certainty who it is who is being talked about or if the words that are attributed to one or another figure spring from the lips of the god or reflect the interpretation made by the one who guards him, since the god, too, can roam the land, whether in a divine form, during moments of great danger,[57] whether transformed into an animal during the pilgrimage,[58] or whether as a person of flesh and blood.

Despite such confusion, the following concepts can be clearly identified:

a) The protector god (*altépetl iyollo*)—one for each pueblo, the creator of man.
b) The first fathers (*in achtopa tlacaxinachtin*)—the first guards and representatives of the god and from whom the entire pueblo descends. Their appearance is not always a given, and their human character is often blurred.
c) The god's representatives or impersonators (*teixiptlahuan, teotl ipatilohuan*), his guards (*iteopixcahuan*), and servants (*teotlayecoltianime*)—endowed with the ability to interpret the divine will (*tlaciuhque*) to hear the god's message and to transmit it to the pueblo.
d) The *cargadores* of the god (*teomamaque*)—that is, those who carry the sacred bundle containing the image of the god and are the only ones who can approach either the image or the bundle.
e) The pueblo's guides (*teyacanque*)—who execute the god's commands.

These, it should be stressed, are concepts and not distinct persons who invariably stand alone since, as I noted earlier, the functions coincide and overlap. The first fathers are "images." The representatives are also "images" but date to a later time. The cargadores frequently converse with the god and on some occasions their names coincide with those of the "images." The *calpulli*'s guides may or may not coincide with the "images" and the cargadores.[59]

Despite all the divergences, the particularities of distinct traditions, and the changes to these concepts wrought by the course of history, the abundant presence of these personages gives rise to certain commonalities out of which emerges the figure of he who can be called *hombre-dios*—the man-god, or collectively, men who partake of godlike qualities and characteristics.

The belief in hombres-dioses in the relationship between two distinct persons, one human and the other divine, with the former being the spokesman and representative of the latter, was detected by historians some time ago, easily deduced from the texts of chroniclers such as Cristóbal del Castillo or from Quiché or Cakchiquel documents—still vivid in this regard—or from tackling the problem posed by the life of Ce Acatl Topiltzin Quetzalcoatl. Every author who has become aware of the problem has expressed some opinion concerning the nature of this relationship, or bond. Antonio León y Gama (1735–1802), realizing that the phenomenon had a broad sweep, entertained the idea that there had been priests in charge of recording and transmitting the history of the origin of the gods and of the times in which the principal captains and rulers had lived—those captains and rulers who had, supposedly, turned themselves into gods.[60] Many years later, Daniel Brinton interpreted the problem as the belief in an avatar, whereby Hueman was none other than the god Quetzalcoatl who descended to earth.[61] Walter Krickeberg agreed with this opinion, stating that "the king-priest is also the incarnation of a divine being who originally resided in the starry heavens and was subsequently related to the morning star."[62] Miguel León-Portilla is not so categorical but, instead, offers two possible solutions to the problem, each intriguing in its own way: Quetzalcoatl's returns could be new reincarnations of the great priest, in the style of those found in Tibetan Buddhist doctrine; or the explanation may lie in a new, later identification of the great priest Quetzalcoatl with the ancient concept of Quetzalcoatl—god.[63] Finally, Román Piña Chan, in referring to Quetzalcoatl, unqualifiedly makes the claim that "the priests who preside over the god's cult will be called by the same name, will display his attributes, will magically acquire his power; that is, they can be rulers and priests, wizards or sorcerers, and able to turn themselves into his *nahual* (take animal form), thus sparking the confusion between the myth and what is real."[64] In Piña Chan's view, these multiple functions and roles explain the character of civilizers who, in serving as the nahuales of certain gods, exhibit diverse personages.

Before rendering my own opinion, it is necessary, I believe, to address some aspects of the problem, the first of which concerns the origin of power.

The departure from the place of origin presupposes the existence of a tutelary god and of a leader of the pueblo. From the myth we learn that the relationship was born and then developed with the pueblo itself. The god had already participated directly, bringing into being the men who would worship him. The advent of life was followed by difficult conditions, and the pueblos' leaders appealed for great efforts and sacrifices. The demands made by the tutelary god—that is, by the rulers who spoke for him—ran the risk of provoking a reaction on the part of the pueblo, a possibility that was damped down or silenced through a story about the genesis of a contractual obligation. This link, or tie, existed because at the time of the departure, the god and the man-god had agreed on the terms of their respective obligations. By this means, on the initiative of the ruler who wanted to free his pueblo[65] or on that of the divinity who descended to request the covenant,[66] the numen promised protection, leadership, counsel, land, and all else that could be enjoined to maintain the common interest in the expectation of what lay ahead, while the man-god, in the name of the pueblo, made a vow of faith and of worship to his particular creator. The covenants that came later were more dependent on the will of the group. For a brief period, however, after the European conquest derailed the political institutions of the indigenous population, leaving it awash in confusion and hopelessness, a ruler once again needed to emerge, spontaneously, to take on the charge of leading the group. One covenant was struck in the midst of a dream. Some years after the conquest, Andrés Mixcoatl, moved by the great needs of his pueblo, prayed and did penance; one fine day, asleep, he received the message of his election. Thus did he declare it later in a court of law.[67]

Under normal conditions, the hombres-dioses appeared in a less dramatic and spontaneous fashion; at the very least, a more institutionalized form of election was the norm, in which the god seemed to be directly interceding, perhaps by indicating, in some cases, who the person was who ought to be his representative. The pueblo chose him as soon as the sign was detected. At times, it manifested itself in a child.[68] On other occasions, it seemed necessary to search among a specialized group of men. When a pueblo was absent this figure, the counsel of other hombres-dioses, of those who mediated between heaven and earth, was sought. Upon the resignation of their hombre-dios—and such occurred because the person chosen could apparently step out of the role when the labors intrinsic to it complicated his life—the Mexica, after three years without an earthly protector, had to choose a successor, Apantecuhtli, after erecting a ritual "stone seat."[69] The search apparently had to be conducted among men who had already concluded their own "pact." And with whom? Possibly, with any god. Such previous experience could help smooth the way toward instituting a new covenant and representing another numen. The requirement of such a pact, however, was not absolute; a life steeped in the devotion to solitary religious worship could be sufficient to elevate someone into becoming a man-god. Quetzalcoatl—that is, a particular Quetzalcoatl—was discovered when he was found doing penance.[70] When the Quiché leader Iqi-Balam died, it was necessary to replace him. The two remaining hombres-dioses, who were his brothers, learned of the existence of a certain penitent, Qotuha; they found the elder and invited him to fill the position of their brother and take his name and that of the pueblo.[71] It is possible that a ritual of initiation was frequently expected of a new hombre-dios and, as the sources indicate, previous instruction was indeed required.[72]

My initial point of criticism is directed at those who, in their study and analysis of the indigenous belief system, have interpreted the man-god as being an incarnation, or the avatar, of the god. There is a clear distinction, at least in the history of Huitzilopochtli and in Quiché and Cakchiquel sources, between the two parts of the covenant, or contract. One person, who may be Tetzahuitl, commands another, who may be Iztac Mixcoatl;[73] one, turned into an eagle and from among the clouds, precedes the group, while on earth the leader Huitzilopochtli follows with his hooked staff.[74] One advises, the other questions, in a relationship in which the dialogue constitutes the necessary and strongest link between the two. The Mayan sources, employing the Nahuatl language, use the very term nahual,[75] which Piña Chan correctly employed in dealing with and contextualizing the concept.

And why are they nahuales? Let us turn to that question. Elsewhere, I referred to the term *nahualli*—which in a general sense means the person who possesses the power to transform himself or the person or animal into which he transforms himself—indicating that it can be translated as "what my clothing is," "what I have on my exterior, on my skin or surrounding me."[76] For the moment, let us hold the matter there and see if the same conclusion can be reached, and the same meaning ascertained, via a different route. In their frequent references to the man-god, Nahua texts state that he is the *ixiptla* of the protector god. For example, Cristóbal del Castillo declares, "*Huitzilopochtli ixiptla in Tlacatecolotl Tetzauhteotl*."[77] What is meant by *ixiptla*, a word that has been translated as "image," "delegate," "replacement," "substitute," "personage," or "representative"? A fine-grained study of the term would carry on for pages and is not something that I wish to undertake here. I attest to the importance of the problem, and those who wish to examine it at length may consult the studies carried out by Leonard Schultze-Jena,[78] Ángel Garibay K.,[79] Johanna Broda de Casas,[80] and Arild Hvidtfeldt,[81] all of whom have concerned themselves with analyzing the terms *xipe* and *ixiptla*. The problem is a complicated one, above all with respect to the composition of the word *ixiptla*, which Hvidtfeldt deals with extensively. So as not to exceed what is necessary at this stage, I am going to refer to the particle *xip*, which, as is readily apparent, is common to both *xipe* and *ixiptla*.

If we take the words that begin with the particle *xip* contained in the Nahuatl-Spanish dictionary compiled by Fray Alonso de Molina,[82] we will find that the letter *p* from *xipétztic* belongs to the verb *petzoa* and that the *p* in *xipochehua* corresponds to the verb *pochehua*, for which reason both words are eliminated. The words *xippachoa* and *xippalli* are another matter, since in them the first *p* is the *uh* of the syllable *xiuh*, which means "grass" and "turquoise"; coming before the *p*, the letters *uh* change into *p*. We are thus left, as foundational grammatical elements, with only the *xip* of *xipehua*, "to flay, to strip, or to peel," and the *xip* of *xipintli*, "foreskin." In the case of *xipehua*, *ehua* means "to raise," and from the context we can deduce that *xip* is "skin," "rind," "husk," or "covering." In addition, if we take the two eliminated words as valid, considering that although the *p* forms part of the two aforementioned verbs, there could have been another *p* to which it was fused. It is quite logical that *xipétztic*, which according to Molina is "a smooth thing," and *xipochehua*, which his dictionary translates as "to produce lumps or swellings," should literally be, respectively, "the one who has the skin burnished" and "to raise the darkened skin." If this is true, *xipe*—contrary to the general rendering—would not be "the flayed," or, as Schultze-Jena states, "the flayer," but simply *xip* and the possessive *e*: "the possessor of skin." Unquestionably, the particle *xip* is the most important component of *ixiptla*, the concept of which corresponds to the idea of "skin," "covering," "rind," or "husk"—very similar, in other words, to what I proposed for *nahualli*.

Walter Lehmann has translated another pertinent word formed by the verb *copina*. It is the saying of an hombre-dios who, in referring to his god, chants *ninecopinaliz e huehuentzi e yohualcohuatla*, which Lehmann translates as "I, the reproduction of the One of Old, of the serpent of the night."[83] It should be understood that the hombre-dios is the likeness, as well as the covering, of the god. There is yet another highly interesting verb—*itech quinehua*—that is related to everything set forth thus far. I have taken three short fragments from Chimalpahin and one from a sacred song, all of which contain this verb:

> Chicomoztoc quinehuaqui zan niahueponi, zan inzan teyomi.[84]
> ... ihuan itocayocan Quinehuayan inic motenehua Quinehuayan yuh mitohua inicuac oncan quizaco mexica intech quinehuac yuhquin yollococox catque...[85]
> ... inic motenehua Quinehuayan oncan intech quineuh in mexica in ihcuac oncan quizaco...[86]
> Chicomoztotl oncan intech quinehuaco mochintin in mexitin.[87]

Ángel Garibay K. translates the first fragment as follows:

> Only under a spell did I undertake the trek from Chicomóztoc.

If we give the same sense to the verb, the remaining three fragments can be translated in the following way:

> ... and its name is Quinehuayan; thus is Quinehuayan called because, it is said, when the mexica came to leave they were [cast] under a spell, they were sick at heart [crazed]...
> ... Quinehuayan it is said because the mexica were cast under a spell there when they came to leave from there ...
> Chicomóztotl, they came to cast all the mexica under a spell there.

The sense that is ascribed to the verb is correct; Charles Dibble and Arthur Anderson, however, focus more on another text and render it as "to be possessed"[88]— that is, to have within the body a being that unhinges one. They clearly adhere to the broad meaning given by Molina ("possessed by the devil," "to have a demon [in one])"[89] and by Rémi Siméon ("bewitched" and "possessed by the devil"),[90] but set aside the European idea of the devil himself—a belief grafted on by the Spanish, beginning with Molina and his contemporaries, which Siméon copied in the nineteenth century. These Nahuatl terms must be understood on their own terms and in their own context.

Among the synonyms given by Molina for "possessed by the devil" (*endemoniado*) is *ipammoquetza*. Garibay K. has published a text, from among those gathered by Fray Bernardino de Sahagún, pairing up both verbs, which indicates—in keeping with Nahuatl syntax—that they carry a similar meaning: *teutlipan moquetzaya, itech quehua*. Garibay K. translates the two as "he who appears or presents himself as a god, he who represented him."[91] The translation is correct, though if one can ignore how the rendering grates, the two would literally translate as "the god in him rose [up]," "concerning him, it rises." The true essence of the earlier-cited four fragments is that in Chicomóztoc, which is also Quinehuayan, men received "something" divine within their bodies, something that caused them to become disturbed in their minds, at least momentarily.

"Something" penetrates them and, in so doing, causes them to partake of the nature of the gods. This "something" that everyone receives at the moment of birth apparently registers more intensely in the hombres-dioses in their role as intermediaries and repositories. That is why, following a very biblical line, Topiltzin was seen as a representation of a god on earth when he was referred to as "child son of Bel."[92] He was compared to the Babylonian dragon worshipped as a living god, whom Daniel kills with pitch, fat, and hair.[93]

There are certain moments in which the "something" is so strong, the representation so faithful, that there seems to be a transitory confusion of personages, and men can be led into a mortal duel in an encounter among gods. When he enters into combat against Cuauhtlequetzqui, the representative of Huitzilopochtli, and falls before him in Tepetzinco, Copil is none other than a god.[94] In the symbolism of the gods, it is men themselves who occupy the site when the sign appears that sanctions the founding of Mexico-Tenochtitlan: Cuauhtlequetzqui, who also had the name Cuauhcoatl ("Serpent-eagle"),[95] said to Tenoch ("hard prickly pear"), in referring to the future portent signaling the place where the city would be, "And when this appears, Tenuché, because you are that, the Ténuch . . . and the eagle that you will see, Tenuché, that eagle will be me, I myself, Tenuché, [with] lips bloodied from what I devour, because I am that: Cuauhtlequetzqui."[96]

To have an idea of the force of this relationship between men and gods, it should be pointed out that it was not only the covenants reached with and sent by the gods that allowed the body to be its receptacle. For example, intoxication was punished, but the momentary unsettling of the mind was seen to be the product of the action of a "rabbit" god.[97] The multiplicity of these rabbit gods—they numbered four hundred—in turn explained how those in the inebriated state comported themselves so differently. Whoever insulted a drunken person received a punishment from on high, because at bottom he was insulting the numen whose influence, at that juncture, was playing out in the body of the drinker.[98]

In the majority of cases, the manifestation of the god or godlike properties in someone quite possibly came about as the result of an impersonal force. According to Hvidtfeldt, the idea of force had always existed, while the idea of god had not so much as made an appearance in Nahua religion.[99] This claim is exaggerated, and Krickeberg does well to counter it, arguing that the presence of personal gods in the Nahua pantheon is beyond question;[100] yet in some cases it is undeniably impersonal forces that lie outside human will that give rise to the actions of those who are possessed. Men retain their own personality. We need to see if the sources contain any indications regarding this phenomenon, whereby impersonal forces are introduced into human beings and possess them.

Texts from the Mayan world speak of a divine fire that the hombres-dioses conserved in their bodies,[101] of an intense brightness that emerged over them in the night, while they made the earth quake,[102] or of a grace, a dew, or a substance that came down from heaven.[103] There is a reference in the Nahua world to a subtle air of the protector god that aids the pueblo[104] and express mention of the fire when, in speaking of the laws dictated by the king, it is said that they are "like sparks shot off of the divine fire that the great Motecuhzoma had planted in his breast."[105] The force required an object that would receive it, in which it stayed put, out of which it later emanated. The images of the gods must be seen as sacred objects capable of serving as a tie that connected the divinities and men. They likewise served as a conduit that brought the offerings of the faithful to the numens and through them the gods, "with their divine influences, their virtue, and great power," could send down to earth "all that was needed."[106] The search for a force close at hand necessitated the construction of temples in the mountains and cities,[107] and the small images of the gods, those that were found in populated settlements, were taken into the hills, together with others, to be honored there.[108] It was probably thought, in a mechanical way, that by making these sacrifices, the images would be revitalized, obtaining amid the mountains the force that had been lost in the city.

To attract this force that was projected from the world of the gods to the images, mothers dressed their sick children in the attire of the god, hoping in this way that their children would be healed.[109] Although less in evidence with each passing day, this custom—aligned with its Old World counterpart—still evokes the sight of children dressed in the clothing that is particular to one or another Christian saint. Similarly, and possibly motivated by the hope that the deceased would find an easy path toward their final resting place, the dead were dressed in the clothes that suited them, in keeping with the manner of their death,[110] which, as is known, determined the place where one of man's animistic entities was conducted. What is more, since the sovereign rulers were also, in a particular way, representatives of the divinity, the nearness of important images could, on certain occasions, work seriously to their detriment. It was customary when the king fell ill to veil or put a mask over the figure of the god that, it was supposed, represented the sovereign, and it was not unveiled until he had either been restored to health or died.[111] If the image was covered, all of the force reached the sickened king and aided him in recovering his lost health. If luck deserted the sovereign and he died, the effort to impede the images from taking in the share of the force that corresponded to them was now useless. They were uncovered, and the force then flowed in its usual way inside the chapels of the temples. As it passed through the temple's lofts, the power of the force suffused the weapons that were stored in them.[112]

The relics of hombres-dioses functioned equally as receptacles of the divine force. First Lewis Spence, and later Karl Nowotny, drew a comparison between the sacred bundles of Mesoamerica and the bundles containing curative items found in some indigenous communities in the present-day United States. Nowotny remarked that, according to a belief held by the Oglala, the divine forces of important men were stored in them.[113] Among the fetishes contained in the bundles belonging to medicine men in the indigenous communities of North America are dried fingers,[114] and according to Nahua belief, the fingers of women who died while in their first delivery enabled warriors, who fastened the fingers to the inside of their shields, to blind or weaken their enemies.[115] Cristóbal del Castillo very clearly states that the force of Tetzahuitl would continue to reside in the bones and skull of Huitzilopochtli;[116] and it was also reported that an hombre-dios—Quetzalcoatl—had been turned into a stone image in Coatépec and that through it, the priests conversed with the "demon" that the colonial-era author identified with Quetzalcoatl.[117]

At this point one must interject the concept of the heart, which can perhaps be interpreted as the optimal receptacle and center of movement of the power of the gods. This power was the reason that, and explained why, everything possessed a heart. The city, the mountain, bodies of water, granaries, men, animals, the images of the gods—theirs was of stone and was placed in their chest. The bodies of the dead—theirs, too, was of stone—the earth, and the heavens themselves; each and all possessed a heart. And when the statue of Huitzilopochtli—made of a dough of amaranth seeds—was parceled out so that the faithful might ingest it, it was the *tlatoani* who received the heart.[118]

The artist, to be truly an artist, had to receive the god's force in his heart. The translation that León-Portilla made of part of a text furnished by indigenous informants to Sahagún reads as follows: "the accomplished painter: understood, God in his heart, who divinizes things with his heart, talks with his own heart ... as if he were a Toltec he paints the colors of all the flowers."[119]

The fire of heaven, sacred energy that it was, was dangerous in the extreme. When particular images, such as Camaxtle in Tlaxcallan and Coatlicue in Tenochtitlan, or certain hombres-dioses (for example, the representative of Ometochtli) were reputed to hold excessive amounts of the god's power, no one dared to train his eyes on them.[120] Perhaps for this reason, and with the intention of seeing that their children would not fall ill, fathers covered the images of the goddesses Cihuateteo with paper on the days when they exercised their malign influence.[121] (*Goddesses* plural because they are the women who had died while giving birth and were divinized.) The artisans and craftsmen in Yucatán frequently refused to fabricate the images, fearing that illness and even death would strike them,[122] and the fear existed among the Zapotec that, upon touching a sacred white stone, the fire would fall from heaven, burning the one who had committed sacrilege.[123]

The divine force endowed hombres-dioses with military power.[124] Hence, it is not surprising that their prestige, including that belonging to a particular hombre-dios among all who bore the name Quetzalcoatl, should be based on their capacity for overcoming challenges and conquering others. Even today a Nahua shaman, living quite close to the country's capital, claims that "people can have hopes of killing me, but nobody can actually do so, because I carry God in my heart."[125] This attribute compelled the hombres-dioses to seek out power, to gather into themselves the energy and power of the gods: *moteotía*—that is, to "deify" themselves, especially, as Hvidtfeldt proposes, if one associates the term *téotl* more closely with the concept of manna than with the concept of god. I think he is right in this case.

It is the divine power that affords the possibility of a long life—one spanning 160 years in the case of the primordial Huitzilopochtli;[126] the divine power that enables the foretelling of future events;[127] that permits the intercession on behalf of men, with the rain gods;[128] that allows the hombre-dios to transform himself into a dog, ocelot, or jaguar; or to journey to one of the worlds in which the gods dwell and return to his earthly abode.[129]

One of the ways in which divine power and energy were obtained was through contact with the garments and dress of a god; and not merely some article of clothing that bore a similarity but, rather, something that was preserved as a relic—the *máxtlatl* (loin cloth) of Huitzilopochtli, for example.[130] Those who commanded objects such as these were feared and respected. References to the bundle that Nacxit—the mysterious Mayan god-king of the East—gave to the hombres-dioses who submissively came before him, seeking the power they needed to become ruling authorities, illustrate this phenomenon.[131] It was this magical-religious process that enabled the rulers of the great urban centers—Chololan, Tollan, Teotihuacan—to employ the power it brought them as one of their key instruments of domination, since, to receive the sacred paraphernalia of rule, other lords would have to come before them from quite distant lands.

Just as meditating, observing penitence, and having contact with objects in which divine power resided promoted the acquisition of such power, other acts caused it to withdraw. The latter included the ejaculation of semen, though—to be more accurate in the interpretation—only when it occurred as a result of contact with a woman, and in some cases, perhaps, only when it resulted from the act of copulation.[132] Sadness and tearfulness also occasioned the loss of divine power, for which reason it was essential that particular living images of the gods, who were going to be sacrificed, not be overcome by sadness.[133]

Upon the death of the hombre-dios the divine force had to return to its place of origin, at least in its greater part. Since it had lodged in the recipient heart of the hombre-dios, and the heart was the center of conscious life—the entity that made its way to the world of the dead—the deceased carried this entity with him and placed it next to the numen that he had represented in life. The last words of the priest-guide Huitzilopochtli reveal the journey as one undertaken by the two in the company of each other; were this not so, the following utterance attributed to him, a dialogue between the dying man and a "something" which forms part of himself, would be inexplicable: "No more then, be gone, that I too [shall] come along."[134]

It appears that at times, the final journey is preceded by another miraculous journey to the divine world. On the eve of his death, the ruler Huitzilopochtli was able to travel to Hueicolhuacan and there, on its hooked mountain, found himself together with the gods.[135] Upon dying, he returned to this place, where he continued to be the companion of Tetzauhteotl, the two in heaven, together; although in his character as an image he continued to be seen as a very near likeness of the god.[136] The priest Quetzalcoatl also departed at the side of his impersonator:

> After garmenting himself, he set himself aflame and burned up; that is why [the place], here, where Quetzalcoatl came to set himself on fire is called the burning ground. It is said that when he burned up, when his ashes had piled high, all the precious birds that soar up to and visit heaven appeared to witness them: the *tlauh- quéchol*, the *xiuhtótotl*, the *tzinitzcan*, the *papagayos tozneneme*, the *alome*, the *cochome*, and so many other lovely birds. In the moment that his ashes finished [accumulating], they saw Quetzalcoatl's heart lift high up. From what is known, it was heaven and his heart entered heaven. The elders said that it turned into a star that comes out at first light; thus it appeared, they say, when Quetzalcoatl died, and for that reason they called him the Lord of dawn. When he died, they said, he did not appear for four

days, because he went to dwell among the dead . . . ; and in another four days he was equipped with arrows; whereby at eight days the great star (the morning star) they called Quetzalcoatl appeared. And then they added he was enthroned as a Lord.[137]

God is in heaven, flanked by those who on earth bore his fire. Accordingly, Quetzalcoatl directed his prayers upward, to all who were his ancestors, and prayed "to those who dwelled here, who had lived prudently and in sadness"[138]—that is, to those who had consecrated themselves to the way of penitence.

Once dead and raised into the worlds divine, the hombres-dioses retained their capacity—like the primordial capacity of the tutelary god—to press advice on the rulers and priests of their pueblos and, under different guises, could even return to earth.[139] The men who were sacrificed in representation of the gods also went with them, and people could charge them with fulfilling special tasks and missions.[140] In the worlds of the gods, life was eternal, a belief that allowed Andrés Mixcoatl to say, "We who are gods never die."[141]

What transpired, then, was neither the transference of the identity nor the incarnation of a god, nor a process of consubstantiation after death, nor the appearance of an avatar of a god. Rather, as Román Piña Chan stated, there was an acquisition of his power, or the conversion of the man into the nahual of the god, as related in Mayan texts: the nahual understood strictly—I do not want to offer generalities here—as a receptacle, a covering of the divine force; a covering such as the inebriated constitute when they harbor the crazed energy of the four hundred rabbits.

I remarked earlier that it was obvious in some cases that men were possessed by forces through no agency of their own. That the personality of the hombre-dios was preserved intact is proven in the dialogue that needed to be established between the protector god and his representative, a dialogue that became operative after the hombre-dios had received miraculous admonitions. Still, we cannot be completely sure of the innermost workings of this conversation. Was it realized by the hombre-dios through his entering into an ecstatic state? How, then, was this mental state triggered? Did the god's will transitorily pass into and dictate the man's, causing that "rising up in him" or that "disturbance of his heart"? Did the man undertake a journey to the region of the divine? The state of ecstasy was very likely brought on by the use of a drug, a proposition that is reinforced by present-day indigenous practice. At the very least, there are reports that in pre-Columbian times, among the Mixtec, the natural lords chewed mushrooms in order to converse with their protector god.[142] The same was done by Andrés Mixcoatl, the rebel hombre-dios, as a device to oppose Spanish dominion; and those mushrooms, it was said, were the body of his god.[143] The hombre-dios was a covering, a husk, the skin of a divine force granted for a people's protection. His actions were directed by the admonitions of the one true guide. Consequently, when Martín Ocelotl, Andrés Mixcoatl's predecessor as hombre-dios, had been exiled to Castile, Andrés, being simply a skin, could assert that Martín was his brother (that both were the same).[144] Upon setting forth, his brother had been unable to continue being the receptacle of the protector god's force but, instead, could delegate the fire to Andrés, which is what truly mattered during the critical time when the Christian interlopers imposed their ideas and theology on the native population in detriment to indigenous belief.

Women of this same nature also appear in the accounts and narratives. Among them is the wife of Huemac, Coacueye, who serves as ruler of her pueblo and who endows the divine power to first one and then another representative of Quetzalcoatl, as her successive husbands. She is called, mysteriously, *mocihuaquetzqui*,[145] a name that was given only to women who died during their first delivery and who, because of the manner of their death, accompanied the Sun, amid chanting, from its zenith into its twilight. My opinion is that she was given this name because she was placed in the same category as the *mocihuaquetzque*, and not because she was thought to be deceased. In the etymology of the name, the verb is found, used reflexively, away from the front of the word—*quetza*, as it appears, for example, in *teutlipan moquetzaya* and *ipammoquetza* ("the deity in her rose up" and "it rises up in her"). Again, we are dealing with the receptacles of divine forces, but in this case, with the qualification that the receptacles are female. The distinct element *cihua*, which indicates the gender, derives from this condition. In this way, *mocihuaquetzque* would carry the meaning of "those women in whom [the numen] arises." The women who expired during their first delivery received, in this final moment of their lives, the presence of Cihuacoatl Quilaztli, and because of this momentary infusion they went off into the western heavens, now dedicated to accompany the Sun in its diurnal movement.

The sources contain references to a number of women who play determinative roles in the life of their communities. For example, Malinalxochitl takes up an important part of the story of the Mexica migration. In another instance (as the record tells), Huactli delegated the governing of his pueblo to his wife, Xiuhtlacuilolxochitzin, because she conversed with the goddess Itzpapalotl;[146] and among the Chichimeca Cuauhtitlaneca, she seems to have commanded an assemblage of lords, some bearing the names of gods, and of women, some having the names of goddesses.[147] In other instances, there are accounts of children, engendered by hombres-dioses, who possess very special characteristics, such as those twins, called "*animalejos*" (animal-like), who were reputed to be images of one of the "devils."[148] The women who conceived them seem to have been the images of goddesses.

It should be noted that the particles *moyóhual* or *moyáhual*, appear in the names of some of these women. Xicomoyahual was the daughter of Copil. When Copil perished by the hand of Cuauhtliquetzqui, Xicomoyahual remained with her father's slayer, and the two produced Cohuatzontli from their union.[149] The story is also told that in Tlatzallan two notable deaths occurred on the same date, those of the hombre-dios Tlohtepetl and of his "older sister," Huitzilmoyahual,[150] on whom this kinship relationship, or supposed kinship relationship—a very relative or imprecise one in the Nahua world—is conferred. The woman who gives birth to Contzallan, or Coatlicue—the latter name is definitely that of a goddess—and through her delivery gives the name *"Paridero"* ("birthing place") to Mixiuhcan, is called Quetzalmoyahuatzin.[151] For my part, I do not find any special motive behind the possible meanings of the root *-moyóhual,* or *-moyáhual*. It may perhaps be related to a peculiar verb, *yahualpoloa,* that is conjugated reflexively and appears with specific reference to Maxtlatzin of Azcapotzalco, a lord whose relationship to the god Cuecuex is reasonably well known. The words in this case are *moyahualpollo* and *canchollo,* which Adrián León interprets as meaning "he [Maxtlatzin] was lost in the night" and "he fled."[152] The Códice Carolino also includes a word pertaining to the same family of words: *moyohualittoani.* The name is given to a type of shaman, and the códice says—when rendered literally—that "they are harmful, they let it be understood that they were nearly immortal or immovable. May God see that they do not now deceive women. Nor men, either, but in another way."[153] It could be conjectured, if only remotely, that the verb employed here, *yohua,* or *yahua,* bore some relationship to *nahualismo,* and in particular to some magical action whereby one transformed oneself, or made oneself vanish. Should this be the case, the names Xicomoyahuatl, Huitzilmoyahual, and Quetzalmoyahuatzin would mean, respectively, "she who changes herself into a bee," "she who changes herself into a hummingbird," and "the venerable one who changes herself into a precious feather."

It is not off the mark to think that some men should represent goddesses. Indeed, on particular occasions the priests functioned as such, even dressing themselves in the garments of the female numens.[154] In this connection, the Spanish conquest recorded an episode that provides considerable food for thought. While engaged in battle against the native inhabitants of Cuitzeo, Nuño de Guzmán was taken aback upon observing a woman who fought with great energy and resolve, only to discover—after capturing her—that she was actually a man. The warrior confided to Guzmán that he had dressed as a woman from the time he was a small child. Under the pretext that in his guise as a woman the Indian had devoted himself to prostitution, the conquistador ordered that he be burned at the stake.[155] One must be careful, however, with the judgments or pretexts to which a man like Nuño de Guzmán would resort to justify putting an adversary to death.

With respect to the succession of hombres-dioses, considerable importance seems to have been attached in some cases to maintaining a direct line of descent while still factoring in, of course, the requirement that a new hombre-dios received adequate previous instruction. On this point, it was mentioned that when one of the Cuauhtlequetzque died, his place was left vacant because "he did not leave anyone with sufficient instruction in how to deal with the devil Huitzilopochtli."[156] As just noted, Copil was the son of the woman-goddess Malinalxochitl and the father of Chuahtlequetzqui's wife. Following the Spanish conquest, the indigenous noblemen thought that if they delivered their daughters to Andrés Mixcoatl they would establish a caste of gods.[157] The Mayan sources contain a fetching tale in which Balam Quitze, Balam-Agab, and Mahucutah find themselves, along with their sons, on the mountain of the gods. After the three guides disappear from the site, their sons assume their names.[158] The line of descent should be considered valid on both the paternal and the maternal sides. There is a group of hombres-dioses that collectively could be known as those who come from the branch of the god Cuecuex. Among them is Tzutzumatzin, and together with him, the *Crónica mexicana* identifies Tezozomoc, Chimalpopoca, and Maxtlaton as the "lords of the mountains and sierras."[159] Three of them are Tepaneca lords, and the fourth, Chimalpopoca, is Mexica-Tenochca, the grandson, through the maternal line, of Tezozomoc; it is solely through this family line that his link to the god Cuecuex can be established.

At times it appears that the power that the hombres-dioses bequeath to their children loses its religious character and retains solely its political aspect.[160] This reformulation is the response to new social conditions. Radically different, however, is the situation in which some descendants of hombres-dioses are apparently perceived more as ritual objects than as men. Some hombres-dioses were asked to give up their children—and they did—so that the youngsters could be ritually sacrificed.[161] Might this also have been one of the functions intrinsic to their position? Unquestionably, some relationship existed between hombres-dioses who fulfilled a political role and those who, dressed as gods and bearing the names of gods, perished on the sacrificial stone during great religious festivals.

The lives of the hombres-dioses abound in miracles. One such personage, a celebrated king of Coyohuacan, was reputed to be a wizard of all things connected to water—recall the intimate relationship that the tutelary gods had with water—as well as a prophet and soothsayer.[162] He had fallen foul of Ahuizotl, the lord of Mexico-Tenochtitlan, over an interchange related to water. Apparently, this hombre-dios had warned Ahuitzotl not to channel water from Acuecuexo to the Mexica capital because its course was variable, and there was a danger that the city might be flooded. Ahuitzotl took offense and ordered that the king of Coyohuacan be executed. To defend himself, the king resorted to magic and in front of his persecutors changed himself into an eagle, a jaguar, and a serpent until he saw that escape was impossible, and then he died at the hands of his adversaries.[163] Immediately thereafter, the course of the Cuecuéxatl grew in size;[164] its waters rose, overran their banks, and flooded Tenochtitlan. Bent on fleeing the city, Ahuizotl received a blow to the head, from which he died sometime later. The body of Tzutzuma was flung onto the rocks, from where a natural spring has flowed ever since.[165]

As noted above, Tzutzumatzin is one of the representatives of Cuecuex. The channel of water that caused the flooding was called Cuecuexatl, or "water of Cuecuex," and the spring out of which it flowed bore the name Acuecuexco, "place of the water of Cuecuex." Copil was killed in Acopilco ("place of the water of Copil")—the nopal of the future Tenochtitlan rose out of his heart as did the thermal springs of El Peñón from his body.[166]

Another life bound up with miracles was that of Gucumatz, the Quiché king who seven days went to heaven; seven days took the road down to Xibalbá; was seven days a snake, an eagle, and a jaguar; and seven days became a pool of blood—all portentous events and transformations that he occasioned with the purpose of provoking fear and submission.[167] Likewise, in Quiché territory, the hombres-dioses, using their expert skill and knowledge, fashioned and summoned lightning bolts, thunderclaps, and hail to defeat their enemies.[168]

Timal, the Nonohualca conquistador, had the rain and the wind as his allies in battle;[169] and after falling into water, the Tetzcocano king Nezahualcoyotl was conducted by the gods to Poyauhtécatl so that he could fulfill the penance needed to secure military power.[170] Malinalxochitl was a great practitioner of the wizard's arts, capable of harming men through various means, and both she and her son possessed and commanded the divine power that allowed beings to be changed from one form into another.[171]

Despite his power and his nature as a man-god, Tzutzumatzin was put to death, an act that led the king of Tetzcoco to protest to Ahuitzotl that he had offended the gods whom Tzutzumatzin represented.[172] The same thing transpired with Huemac, as related in the *Historia tolteca-chichimeca*, who was persecuted and killed by the Nonohualcas who rose up in revolt; the latter, fearful of having a curse brought down on them, abandoned the city in which they had lived in service to the Toltecs[173] and fled to lands far from their reach.

Still another case of the assassination of an hombre-dios was that of Tepetecuhtli, the lord of Cuetlaxtlan. Motecuhzoma Ilhuicamina and Tlacaelel, who had bested him in battle, wanted to end the life of the Cuexteca lord but hesitated to do so because of the danger that was posed in paying so little heed to his divine nature. In the end, they crafted a solution that was truly horrific: they would have his neck cut off, but from behind.[174]

The fact that a Huemac had been chosen as an hombre-dios, or been discovered to be such a personage, from the time he was a child and that Coacueye should have the enormous buttocks that history credits her with,[175] suggests that in some cases the love of the gods needed to be expressed in a material form or made manifest through some obvious mark. The dedication to the gods of individuals who are expressly called out, either physically or psychically, is not unusual. The belief existed among the Zapotec that dwarfs had been created by the command of the Sun and that he requested sacrifice of them.[176] Wanting to save his people from the hunger and death brought on by a drought, Motecuhzoma Ilhuicamina sacrificed the albinos, dwarfs, hunchbacks, and those suffering from macrocephaly by having them thrown into the recess that served as a natural outflow for Lake Texcoco.[177] According to the *Memoriales con escolios*, albino men were offered as a sacrifice whenever an eclipse of the sun occurred.[178] Albinos were also sacrificed when they reached the age of five, a Toltec custom that, in the telling of Alva Ixtlilxóchitl, became engraved in law following the appearance of a portentous white-skinned child, born with a withered head, who caused the downfall of the capital.[179] Those afflicted with leprosy and other maladies and contagious diseases were sacrificed to the god Iztaccinteutl.[180] In another case, an Indian from the wild whose arms and legs were extremely hairy was worshipped and sacrificed in Tzutzumpa, a site whose name means "in the thick hair."[181] In ministering to the indigenous Mames of San Juan Atitlán, the Mercedarian friar Marcos Ruiz discovered that its inhabitants worshipped an Indian in their community who was deaf and mute—as well as decidedly filthy, according to Ruiz—whom they had draped with the ornaments of the Catholic faith.[182] One must keep in mind that some characteristics, among those that can be seen as divine signs, stemmed from the nature of heavenly influence. For example, those born on the day that was dedicated to Huitzilopochtli, the "left-handed hummingbird," quickly became left-handed themselves, and once they had matured, acted with great bravery but also paid the price of dying an early death in battle.[183]

All of this logically poses a question: Did the Quequetzalcoah have some physical attribute by which they were deemed to be people whom the gods had chosen. According to the tale related in the *Anales de Cuauhtitlán*, the sorcerers, motivated by the desire to defeat Quetzalcoatl, brought out a mirror in which "they would give him his body," show him the face of which the priest was ignorant due to the life he led of ceaseless penitence and confinement. In front of the mirror, Quetzalcoatl came face-to-face with his hideous ugliness—eyelids covered with warts, eye sockets sunken in, a face swollen and deformed.[184] Did the tradition of the white-skinned Quetzalcoatl, as the lord of the light of dawn, necessitate the leukocytic condition of priests? The *Relaciones de Yucatán* tell of a man called Zacmutul, the leader of a people who came from the east, who reached the place called Mutul. He was white but of indigenous blood.[185] In addition, it is known that Don Gonzalo Tecpanecatl

Tecuhtli, lord of the head town of Tepetícpac, foreswore his religion, handing over to the Spanish a sacred bundle in which they found, among the ashes, some strands of blond hair that, according to tradition, had belonged to a man with white skin.[186] Quetzalcoatl, the penitent, was white—like the first light of day—so tradition has it. Furthermore, he was a man who fled from the light of the Sun.

Another criterion that demonstrated that a person was beloved by the gods was the day or year of his birth. The god Quetzalcoatl had *ce ácatl* as a calendar date, and, according to many sources, the priest Quetzalcoatl was born in the year *ce ácatl*. Meconetzin, the personage of whom Ixtlilxóchitl speaks in order to give his audience a different version of the life of Quetzalcoatl, is born in the year *ce ácatl*.[187] According to other sources, Quetzalcoatl arrives in a year *ce ácatl*.[188] Quetzalcoatl's flight from Tollan and the city's destruction take place fifty-two years after his birth, in a year *ce ácatl*. Can there, then, be any doubt about the existence of a fixed temporal scheme? As further evidence, the god Huitzilopochtli has as a symbol the year *ce técpatl*. Huitzilopochtli the man leaves Aztlan with his people in the year *ce técpatl*, and he dies, upon arriving in Culhuacan, in the year *ce técpatl*, "when the hour of his death arrives," as he realizes from the journey he makes to the mountain of the gods, where the gods tell him that the time for his departure has come.[189] Under the sign *ce técpatl*, which expressly applies to Huitzilopochtli, a certain Cuauhtlequetzqui, some of whose representatives also bore his name, began his period of rule.[190] And in the year *ce técpatl* this priest of Huitzilopochtli died, the victim of sacrifice at the hands of his enemies: "Year 1-flint, 1275 . . . It was in this year 1-flint when they killed their *huei teopixqui tlamacazqui*, "great priest" of Huitzilopochtli. It had also been in a year 1-flint when the great priest and sacred guardian took up his office."[191]

Some are born, already hombres-dioses, fifty-two years before their death. Others die fifty-two years after receiving their command. Still others, according to Alva Ixtlilxóchitl, will rule for a period of fifty-two years. The lattermost, it seems, are no more than simple rulers: "They issued an order that their kings not reign for more than fifty-two years, in a span of fifty-two years, and that having fulfilled this, if he was still alive, their son the legitimate successor had needs come into the government; and if he died before fifty-two years, the republic had to rule until they were completed."[192]

Based on such information, as supplied by early indigenous chroniclers like Alva Ixtlilxóchitl, it seems reasonable to suppose that the power of the divine fire that resided in the breast of hombres-dioses and rulers alike lasted for a period of fifty-two years—lasted, that is, for a century.

Hombres-dioses come and go as the cycles are completed. "Call the Sun for me," intones Quetzalcoatl, who, on setting out for Tlapallan, abandons his precious stones and the instruments of his office.[193] He goes off to the heavens and the world of the dead,[194] in obedience not only to the course of years that marks his own time but also to the track taken by the stars. Thus was a text, brought out in Spanish translation by León-Portilla,[195] able to affirm that Quetzalcoatl had not been born but, instead, had simply returned: "Then our prince Acxitl, Quetzalcoatl, was born, there in Tula. But in truth he was not born, because he had only returned in order to make his appearance there. As the elders note, it is not known from exactly where he returned." What is at work is the god's force returning in its prescribed time, to the hearts of men, and it goes on in what for some could have been considered a prolongation that stretched for century after century. Huitzilopochtli is once again born of Coatlicue "in addition to the other times that he had been born, because since he was a god he did and could do what he wished."[196]

The fire returns to repose in new hombres-dioses, and the gods return to ratify the pact when the heavens rumble. They accept the offering that the pueblo makes, and, in consequence, Huitzilopochtli himself lights the new fire for the Mexica. At a certain point, however, the people attain a level of stability such that their sacred bundles no longer need to speak to them, or the god finally says, bidding them farewell, that he will return when the times truly demand it of him[197] or when the end of the world approaches.[198] The god also steals away when the date arrives, that fate has appointed, on which his pueblo comes to the end of its power;[199] but in this case he warns of a return that will implicitly bring vengeance and destruction with it.[200] Hence, Topiltzin Meconetzin can be secure in the knowledge, can trust that his descendants will punish the kings who have deposed him.[201] This kind of return carries the full weight of the life of the astral gods, in whom the return ignites a drama in the immense expanse of the heavens.

It is possible that a date exists, hidden deeply away, well removed from ordinary human cognizance, on which it is believed that the entire pueblo will suffer its demise. The gravity of this date far exceeds those known periods of vital importance that recur in each century. It follows that calculations of this nature are the concern of and are reserved for a select group of priests. What Coatlicue, the mother of Huitzilopochtli, says—in the language of metaphor—to the Mexica emissaries dispatched by Motecuhzoma Ilhuicamina seems intended to offer certain indications. These emissaries, as noted earlier, had gone beyond the gates of the supernatural world to bring the message of their lord to the mythical place of origin, from where their pueblo had set out. The goddess averred that her son had asked her for two pairs of sandals for his outward journey and two pairs for his return, when he came back, once and for all, to be at her side, when the fate of the Mexica shall come to an end.[202] Could the period of Mexica rule, then, be measured in the time that elapsed between Huitzilopochtli's first and last pairs of sandals? Thus, the lives of men are established and turn anew on an immense wheel. The vanquished pueblo, as though groaning under an enormous weight of conscience, promises its return. Quetzalcoatl had set off in the company of his family line, in whose same company he vowed to return.[203] He would carry out and fulfill the vengeance of Topiltzin Meconetzin and of all those whom the sorcerers had driven from their capitals. When the band of Spaniards arrived in the year *ce ácatl* (1519), it could indeed have entailed the return of the deposed ruling god and his company of hombres-dioses. When Hernán Cortés was near the city-state of Tlaxcallan, he was asked by the Indians of Tlaxcala, "If you are one of the gods that consumes blood and flesh, consume these indians, and we will bring you more, and if you are a benevolent god, behold here incense and feathers; and if you are a man, behold here fowls and cherries."[204]

When, amid tremendous misgivings on the part of the native priests, the white-skinned Europeans reached Mexico-Tenochtitlan, the idea seemed to hold sway that they were the beings who had been prophesied to return. According to the Nahuas, Motecuhzoma Xocoyotzin said to Cortés,

> O our lord, thou hast suffered fatigue; thou hast spent thyself. Thou hast arrived on earth; thou has come to thy noble city of Mexico. Thou hast come to occupy thy noble mat and seat, which for a little time I have guarded and watched for thee. For thy governors [of times past] have gone—the rulers Itzcoatl, Moctezuma the Elder, Axayacatl, Tizoc, Ahuizotl—who, not very long ago, came to guard [thy mat and seat] for thee and to govern the city of Mexico. Under their protection the common folk came here. Could they, perchance, now find their descendants, those left behind? O, that one of them might be a witness to marvel that to me now hath befallen what I see, who am the only descendant of our lords. For I dream not, nor start from my sleep, nor see this as in a trance. I do not dream that I see thee and look into thy face. Lo, I have been troubled for a long time. I have gazed into the unknown whence thou has come—the place of mystery. And thou hast come among clouds, among mists. For the rulers [of old] have gone, saying that thou wouldst come to instruct thy city, [that] thou wouldst descend to thy mat and seat; that thou wouldst return. And now it is fulfilled: thou hast returned; thou hast suffered fatigue; thou hast spent thyself. Arrive now in thy land; Rest, lord; visit thy palace [that] thou mayest rest thy body. Let our lords arrive in the land.[205]

And Cortés, in the second letter that he wrote to King Charles, reports that Motecuhzoma further said to him,

> For a long time we have known from the writings of our ancestors that neither I, nor any of those who dwell in this land, are natives of it; but foreigners who came from very distant parts; and likewise we know that a chieftan [*sic*], of whom they were all

vassals, brought our people to this region. And he returned to his native land and after many years came again, by which time all those who had remained were married to native women and had built villages and raised children. And when he wished to lead them away again they would not go nor even admit him as their chief; and so he departed. And we have always held that those who descended from him would come and conquer this land and take us away as their vassals. So because of the place from which you claim to come, namely, from where the sun rises, and the things you tell us of the great lord or king who sent you here, we believe and are certain that he is our natural lord, especially as you say that he has known of us for some time.[206]

And just as Ce Acatl Topiltzin had relinquished power to the sorcerers, so this same Motecuhzoma, who in defeat handed power over to Cortés, will one day return and establish a new capital of the Republic in Huitziltépec (present-day Guerrero)—according to the confident assertion, expressed in terms that perhaps date back a great many years, of a woman in that small town. On the next day, all eyes will behold the pueblo's church, miraculously reconstructed.[207]

After their actions and labors on earth, the hombres-dioses pass over to the worlds of the gods, where everlasting life awaits them. They are at once in the worlds of the gods while also still very near their pueblo, for it is the mountain, the dwelling place of the tutelary god, wherein the body of the ruler finds a home. According to the Tzotziles of Larráinzar, the mountains were vehicles through which to communicate with heaven. William Holland has noted, on the theme of the mountains and the Tzotzil, "In the past, the dead were buried under the floor of their own hut, so that even in death they could be close to their family. The remains of members of the elite were buried in caves within the sacred mountains of their ancestors; according to what was believed, their spirits ascended to the heavens where they settled at the side of the gods. Once in heaven, men's spirits changed into gods for their descendants."[208]

These beliefs of the Tzotzil sound remarkably similar to those of the ancient Nahua. Among the latter, in Tlaxcallan, it was also believed that whereas the men of the pueblo turned into weasels and beetles after death, the lords made themselves into mist and clouds[209]—that is, they journeyed to the dwelling place of Tlaloc as auxiliaries of the gods of water. This belief can explain an observation of Motolinía's: "They name all of their dead *teutl fulano* (teutl somebody), which means god or saint."[210]

We have seen that on the eve of his death, Huitzilopochtli went off to the sacred mountain of Culhuacatépec, where he encountered the gods.[211] Tecpatzin, too, died on a mountain, known by the name Tecpayo.[212] In the Mayan world, the four hombres-dioses of the Quiché went to die on the mountain called Hacavitz.[213] In some cases, the personage is said to have gone himself into the mountain. Interestingly, a parallel to this storyline surrounded the medieval German monarch Frederick II (1194–1250), who not only believed himself divine because of his inborn nature but, popular legend had it, would also one day emerge to reclaim his throne after awaking from his sleep under a mountain.[214] Quetzalcoatl, who in Fray Diego Durán's history is called Topiltzin, journeyed to the seashore, but after reaching the coast managed, through the utterance of words alone, to open a mountain that he proceeded to enter and make his dwelling place.[215] According to the document known as the *Origen de los mexicanos*, Huemac either hung himself in a mountain cave or went into it in order never to emerge.[216] In the Mixtec pueblo of Icxitlan, Malinaltecuhtli climbed to the top of a mountain, where he died, after which his body passed through into what would be his dwelling place.[217] Gagavitz was buried in the mountain of Paroxoné, where the dawn shone before the Cakchiquel people.[218] It was from his mountain that the venerated nephew of King Zaachiylla watched over the lands of the Zapotec monarch.[219] The Mexica averred that their ancestors had gone to the cave of water.[220] Finally, according to the findings of Pablo González Casanova, even as late as the 1920s, the Catholic priest of Tepoztlán used to bless the mountain because it was believed that in the absence of the blessing, the deity Tepoztecatl would emerge in the form of hurricanes that would damage the pueblo.[221]

Among the celebrated personages who dwell, never dying, in the mountains are Topiltzin, Meconetzin, Nezahualcoyotl, Nezahualpilli, and Moquihuix, who are all found inside the mountain of Xicco.[222] In the case of Topiltzin, nothing needs to be said to justify the fact, since he is the hombre-dios writ large, the hombre-dios whose very name conveys the general idea. Nezahualcoyotl counseled that when the time came there should be no word of his death, and the pueblo believed from the outset that he had gone to be with the gods,[223] doubtless because of his "charmed" and invincible character and the aureole that surrounded him as a descendant of "the greatest gods in the world": Tezcatlipoca, Huitzilopochtli, Mixcohuatl, Huemac, Nauhyotl, and others.[224] Nezahualpilli descended from the same gods and was famed as a prophet.[225] With respect to Moquihuix, also an Aculhua,[226] some compelling reason existed that helped contribute to the belief that he had not died, even though a great many histories recorded that he had.[227] Tzutzumatzin, with his relatives Tezozomoc, Chimalpopoca, and Maxtla, becomes a lord of mountains;[228] Matlalcueye becomes a mountain range in Tlaxcala;[229] and Quetzalcoatl buries his father, Mixcoatl, inside of a temple called Mixcoatépec—"the mountain of Mixcoatl."[230] Similarly, an old man, who represents Mictlantecuhtli,[231] was placed in a pyramid; and four children sacrificed to Tlaloc were each put in a cave,[232] where, according to popular belief, they lived very happily, enjoying the delights of Tlalocan, like all the rest who were dedicated to this deity.[233]

Under the fear that gripped him of the world's imminent end, and of the downfall of the Mexica wrought by men who rode strange animals, were covered with metal, and now had Tenochtitlan directly in their sights, Motecuhzoma Xocoyotzin reflected madly on the futility of his own physical presence and, were his movements not hindered by night watchmen and men in the city who had been warned by the gods of the sovereign's intentions, he would have gone to stay in Cincalco. This was a "very pleasant and joyful place, where men lived forever without dying, and that according to what he had been told it was a place of clear crystalline waters, a place of great fertility where all kinds of food flourished and there was the freshness of roses and flowers."[234] The king made the necessary overtures to the mysterious cave dwellers whose eyes and mouth were as small as the point of a stick,[235] and they told him that to gain entrance to that place he could not eat anything other than *huahtli* (amaranth), mixed in water and taken hot, and that he must refrain from any contact with his many wives.[236] Fate decreed otherwise, however, and Motecuhzoma Xocoyotzin, the great Motecuhzoma whose power had made him famous across Mesoamerica but whose misfortune would be recounted throughout the world, continued living from day to day, eaten away by doubt and questions, as the men clothed in metal drew ever closer to his city.

The bodies of kings reposed, like relics that attracted power, in the most sacred places. As Sahagún's informants related to him, as contained in a text translated by León-Portilla, Teotihuacan was the site where the dream of death preceded the arrival of a dawn amid birds and the sound of their trilling: "According to what they said: 'When we die, it is not true that we die, because we live, we are revived. Be happy for this.' Thus did they address themselves to the dead person when he died. If he was a man, they spoke to him, recited to him, with a pheasant's name, how to be divine, [and] with an owl's name if she was a woman, they said to them: 'Awaken, the sky is reddening now, now the dawn has broken, now the pheasants with their color like flames [and] the sparrows the color of fire, are singing, now the butterflies are fluttering.' That is why the elders have said, whoever has died has become a god. They have said 'there he became a god, meaning that he died.'"[237]

The similarity of this dawn to the primordial dawn of pueblos is readily apparent. The site where the Mixtec kings came to rest was known as Chacaltongo;[238] for the Zapotec sovereigns, there were two counterpart places, Yooba (Mitla) and Zeetoba.[239] The force that Tetzauhteotl possessed and commanded would persist with his people, even after the chieftain's death, if his remains were conserved:

> And nonetheless, although you [Huitzilopochtli] will die, so that your spirit is together with and close to us, you for this reason as our leader, will truly not move away, the god of wonder, certain inside your bones, inside your skull, there, for cer-

tain there, will the spirit be put, because of you, similarly will it speak ... Command thusly [to your men] that when your spirit comes to an end, when you have died, that they encase your body in a stone urn; your bones will be cast in there for four years, until they rot and your flesh turns into earth; ... later in a cover of cloth, in a bundle, they will put you in the upper part of the temple, your bundle will be seated in a fine and peaceful place, the covering of your bones.[240]

Is this urn perhaps like the stone coffer that Quetzalcoatl ordered hewn for himself? When the work had been done, the Toltec priest spent four days lying down in it; then he got to his feet and with his page by his side made his way to Tlillan Tlapallan, to the burning ground.[241] This detail may allow us to assume that the trek toward Tlapallan is made, symbolically, when Quetzalcoatl has died.

In the Mayan world, too, bones—among them the ornamented half skulls of the lords Cocom—serve as an instrument, a medium of communication.[242] As in the case of precious stones that were worshipped as relics, bones produced fright in those who discovered them, a reaction observed by the conquistadores when, digging through some terrain, they found vessels containing the bones of a "giant,"—the remains, clearly, of Pleistocene-era mammals—that terrified the native laborers.[243] The bones of those whom Fray Francisco Núñez de la Vega called "*nahualistas*" were deposited in caves and made the object of offerings.[244] Bishop Landa relates that the ashes of the bodies of Mayan lords were placed in vases or in hollow statues.[245]

Mummified cadavers, like that of a Cora ruler, in whose body it was believed the pueblo's god used to speak, were employed in the mountainous areas of Nayarit to resolve people's problems,[246] and people in the Zapotec pueblo of Coatlán kept the cadaver of their chieftain, Petela.[247] Many sources refer to the practice that existed of worshipping human remains—so many, in fact, that it would be tedious to list them.[248]

The worship of semiprecious stones was particularly important in the Oaxacan region.[249] It could be expected in some cases that such adoration derived from the belief that the stone itself was the very body of the hombre-dios. This transference took place, for example, with the already mentioned Pinopiaa, who upon dying and after the shattering sound of a heavenly thunderclap, turned into an enormous *chalchiuite* (semiprecious green stone).[250] Following the same process in the Nahua world, the Quetzalcoatl of Coatépec-Chalco was transformed into the stone that he subsequently entered and through which he spoke to the pueblo.[251] In like fashion, offerings and sacrifices were made to the sacred bundles—the *tlaquimilolli*,[252] inside of which the corporal remains of hombres-dioses, or of objects that had belonged to them, were placed. On occasion, these were the objects that conferred political power on the hombre-dios or that garnered the respect of pueblos for him, as in the case of the *pizom-gagal* (sacred bundle) left by Balam Quitze to the Quiché.[253] Other such objects were the representations of hombres-dioses, among them Kabul, the hand of the Mayan Itzmat,[254] and the statues of dead lords that, according to Francisco Cervantes de Salazar, were placed next to the images of the gods.[255]

Deceased hombres-dioses were exceedingly close to the gods, and it is not out of line to think that their figures went on accumulating, one over another, like simple adhesions to those of the numens and that, paralleling the steady draining away of their individuality, the process of simplification fed into the fusing of historical tales and accounts. The Tollans followed the same pattern of blending and fusing, from the very greatest Tollan to its more humble counterpart in Hidalgo. They kept expanding and becoming ever richer with the immense light that was projected from a mythical place along the Sun's path. This magnification made Tula Xicocotitlan seem very poor in the eyes of any who expected the sprawling urban center of the vassals who were called *tlancuacemilhuique*, who expected the great city of astounding prosperity, of the crops of cacao, of enormous pumpkins and corncobs that had to be carried enfolded within one's arms, of the stalks of amaranth that could support a man's weight, like tree trunks; of the cotton in its bright array of different colors; of the tropical birds; of the gold, silver, and precious stones; of the city where men were so rich that they heated their baths with corncobs. But against this magnified Tollan, Teotihuacan and Chololan also appeared small. Tollan, the Tollan of the great civilizer, of the prodigious priest, was repeated and replayed—together with its priest—many times. Tollan and Quetzalcoatl—the entombed albino, perhaps, protected from the sun's rays, who, by means of a drug, communicated with the god—were the dispensers of power in a world in which the passage of time governed the rhythm of the blow of the planter's stick on clods of earth. Both were part of a heaven and a god. And surrounding many pueblos, many *calpulli* submerged in the content of their beliefs, was the technique to dominate the gods and the cycles of time.

## NOTES

1. Muñoz Camargo, *Historia de Tlaxcala*, 41; Mendieta, *Historia eclesiástica*, 1:98; and Román y Zamora, *Repúblicas*, 1:55–56.

2. Motolinía, *Memoriales*, 13; Mendieta, *Historia eclesiástica*, 1:98–99; Sahagún, *Historia general*; and Muñoz Camargo, *Historia de Tlaxcala*, 41.

3. Mendieta, *Historia eclesiástica*, 1:98–99; and Román y Zamora, *Repúblicas*, 1:55–56.

4. Sahagún, *Historia general*, 1:63; and Mendieta, *Historia eclesiástica*, 1:98–99.

5. Sahagún, *Historia general*, 1:66.

6. Ibid., 49.
7. Ibid., 47.
8. Ibid., 70.
9. *Florentine Codex*, 9:79.
10. Muñoz Camargo, *Historia de Tlaxcala*, 5–6.
11. Sahagún, *Historia general*, 1:64.
12. Torquemada, *Los veinte*, 2:20.
13. Ibid., 2:42.
14. *Códice Telleriano-Remensis*, part 2, plate i.
15. Lizana, *Historia de Yucatán*, folio 13v and 14r.
16. Herrera, *Historia general*, 3:176.
17. Muñoz Camargo, *Historia de Tlaxcala*, 5–6.
18. Sahagún, *Historia general*, 1:90.
19. Seler, "Uitzilopochtli," 395.
20. Armillas, "La serpiente emplumada," 168.
21. Carrasco, *Los otomíes*, 143.
22. Jiménez Moreno, *Notas sobre historia antigua*, 19.
23. Bernal, "Huitzilopochtli vivo."
24. G[onzález] de Lesur, "El dios Huitzilopochtli."
25. Reyes, "Los dioses tribales," 37.
26. *Relaciones de Yucatán*, 1:51–52.
27. *Códice Ramírez*, 25.
28. Mendieta, *Historia eclesiástica*, 1:90.
29. Hernández, *Antigüedades de la Nueva España*, 118.
30. Serna says Teotécpatl, but the name is referred to as that of a calendrical sign. Ce Técpatl is Huitzilopochtli's name.
31. *Codex Mexicanus*, plate xxxviii.
32. Alvarado Tezozómoc, *Crónica mexicáyotl*, 41.
33. Sahagún, "Primeros memoriales," folio 60r, 131.
34. León-Portilla, "Religión de los nicaraos," 62.
35. Boturini, *Idea de una nueva historia*, 166.
36. Durán, *Historia de las Indias*, 1:23
37. Thompson, *Grandeza y decadencia*, 123.
38. *Anales de Cuauhtitlán*, 8.
39. G[onzález] de Lesur, "El dios Huitzilopochtli," 182.
40. Acatonale's name suggests a shared kinship with Quetzalcoatl. It means "the possessor of the sign *ácatl*" or—stated differently—that someone with this name could also be called Ce Acatl.
41. *Mapa de Sigüenza*.

42. Durán, *Historia de las Indias*, 1:222.
43. *Historia de los mexicanos por sus pinturas*, 214.
44. Chimalpahin, *Memorial*, folio 21v.
45. Ibid., folio 36v.
46. Chimalpahin, *Relaciones*, 56.
47. Ibid.
48. *La historia de Tlatelolco*, 33.
49. Alvarado Tezozómoc, *Crónica mexicáyotl*, 70.
50. Castillo, *Fragmentos*, 83: "inic zaepan oquimixiptlati in tlacatecolotl Tetzauhteotl, inic za itoca omochiuh Huitzilopochtli."
51. Ibid., 59.
52. "Canto a Huitzilopochtli" and "Canto al Guerrero del Sur," in Garibay K., *Veinte himnos sacros*, 29, 31, 40–41.
53. *La historia de Tlatelolco*, 32.
54. Alvarado Tezozómoc, *Crónica mexicáyotl*, 23.
55. Chimalpahin, *Memorial*, folio 22r.
56. Chimalpahin, *Relaciones*, 64.
57. Tello, *Crónica*, book II, vol. 1:35.
58. For example, Huitzilopochtli in the form of an eagle, according to Cristóbal del Castillo, 87 and *Codex Mexicanus*, xviii–xix.
59. See, for example, Alvarado Tezozómoc, *Crónica mexicáyotl*, 70–72.
60. León y Gama, *Descripción histórica*, part 2, 31.
61. Brinton, "Toltecs," 96.
62. Krickeberg, *Las antiguas culturas*, 202.
63. León-Portilla, "Quetzalcoatl," 131.
64. Piña Chan, *Arqueología y tradición*, 78.
65. Castillo, *Fragmentos*, 84.
66. Chimalpahin, *Relaciones*, 63.
67. González Obregón, *Procesos de indios*, 75.
68. Berlin and Rendón, *Historia tolteca-chichimeca*, 68.
69. *La historia de Tlatelolco*, 33.
70. *Anales de Cuauhtitlán*, 7.
71. *Título de los señores*, 227.
72. *Anales de Cuauhtitlán*, 12.
73. Chimalpahin, *Relaciones*, 64.
74. Castillo, *Fragmentos*, 87.
75. *Título de los señores*, 218–21.
76. López Austin, "Cuarenta clases," 95–96.
77. Castillo, *Fragmentos*, 59.

78. Schultze-Jena, *Wahrsagerei, Himmelskunde und Kalender der alten Azteken. Quellenwerke zur alten Geschichte Amerikas*, vol. 4 (Stuttgart: 1950): 350, cited by Broda de Casas, "Tlacaxipehualiztli," 243n147.
79. Garibay K., *Veinte himnos sacros*, 177–78.
80. Broda de Casas, "Tlacaxipehualiztli," 243.
81. Hvidtfeldt, *Teotl and ixiptlatli*, 78–80.
82. Molina, *Vocabulario*, folio 150r.
83. Lehmann, *Una elegía tolteca*, 48.
84. Garibay K., *Veinte himnos sacros*, 94.
85. Chimalpahin, *Memorial*, folio 22r.
86. Ibid.
87. Ibid., folio 28r.
88. *Florentine Codex* (translated by Dibble and Anderson), 1:19.
89. See the words *demonio*, *tener*, and *endemoniado* in Molina, *Vocabulario*.
90. See the word *quinehuac* in Siméon, *Dictionnaire*.
91. Garibay K., "Paralipómenos," 234, 245n49.
92. The text, it must be acknowledged, is very confusing, but this seems to be the sense of it. See *Origen de los mexicanos*, 261.
93. Libro de Daniel, 14:22–30.
94. Chimalpahin, *Relaciones*, 54–55. Alvarado Tezozómoc, in his *Crónica mexicáyotl*, 54–55, declares that the one who fought against Copil was Huitzilopochtli himself, who handed over the heart of the defeated Copil to Cuauhtlequetzqui.
95. Gutierre Tibón believed that this second name was intimately related to the image of the eagle devouring the serpent. See his "Mito y magia," 677.
96. Chimalpahin, *Relaciones*, 55.
97. Sahagún, *Historia general*, 1:325.
98. Ibid, 75.
99. Hvidtfeldt, *Teotl and ixiptlatli*.
100. Krickeberg, "Mesoamérica," 38.
101. *Título de los señores*, 220.
102. *Memorial de Sololá*, 88.
103. Lizana, *Historia de Yucatán*, folio 41r.
104. Alvarado Tezozómoc, *Crónica mexicana*, 227.
105. Durán, *Historia de las Indias*, 1:217.
106. Muñoz Camargo, *Historia de Tlaxcala*, 198.
107. Durán, *Historia de las Indias*, 2:199.
108. Ibid., 172.
109. Ibid., 106–7.
110. Motolinía, *Memoriales*, 307.

111. López de Gómara, *Historia general*, 2:388; and Alva Ixtlilxóchitl, *Obras históricas*, 1:190.

112. Alva Ixtlilxóchitl, in *Obras históricas*, 2:185, remarks on the custom of storing weapons in the lofts of the temples.

113. Spence, *Gods of Mexico*, 42–43; and Nowotny, "Restos de especulaciones," 418–19.

114. Vogel, *American Indian Medicine*, 27.

115. López Austín, *Augurios y abusiones*, 142–45. See my notes 90 and 91.

116. Castillo, *Fragmentos*, 19.

117. *Relaciones geográficas de la Diócesis de México*, 45.

118. Sahagún, *Historia general*, 1:274.

119. León-Portilla, *La filosofía*, 320–21.

120. Motolinía, *Memoriales*, 78; Durán, *Historia de las Indias*, 2:173; and Motolinía, *Historia de los indios*, 174.

121. Sahagún, *Historia general*, 1:334.

122. Landa, *Relación de la cosas de Yucatán*, 101.

123. Burgoa, *Geográfica descripción*, 2:329–30.

124. *La historia de Tlatelolco*, 36–37.

125. Madsen, *Virgin's Children*, 195.

126. Castillo, *Fragmentos*, 90.

127. Durán, *Historia de las Indias*, 1:389.

128. González Obregón, *Procesos de indios*, 55.

129. *Historia de la nación Mexicana*, 39–41.

130. *Historia de los mexicanos por sus pinturas*, 221.

131. *Título de los señores*, 218.

132. *Título de los señores*, 220; and *Anales de Cuauhtitlán*, 12, in the case of Huemac and the representatives of Tezcatlipoca. It was from that point that Huemac ceded his power.

133. Durán, *Historia de las Indias*, 2:172.

134. Cervantes de Salazar, *Crónica*, 1:68.

135. Castillo, *Fragmentos*, 92.

136. Ibid., 92–93.

137. *Anales de Cuauhtitlán*, 11.

138. Ibid., 8.

139. *Relaciones geográficas de la Diócesis de México*, 45.

140. *El conquistador*, 36–37.

141. González Obregón, *Procesos de indios*, 64.

142. *Proceso de Yanhuitlán*, cited by Dahlgren de Jordán, *La Mixteca*, 293.

143. González Obregón, *Procesos de indios*, 58.

144. Ibid., 67.

145. *Anales de Cuauhtitlán*, 12.

146. Ibid., 7.

147. Ibid., 5–6.
148. Ibid., 14.
149. Chimalpahin, *Relaciones*, 55–56.
150. *La historia de Tlatelolco*, 32.
151. Chimalpahin, *Relaciones*, 77.
152. Alvarado Tezozómoc, *Crónica mexicáyotl*, 109.
153. "Códice Carolino," 35.
154. *Códice Ramírez*, 93.
155. Riva Palacio, *El virreinato*, 201.
156. Chimalpahin, *Relaciones*, 56.
157. González Obregón, *Procesos de indios*, 58.
158. *Título de los señores*, 226.
159. Alvarado Tezozómoc, *Crónica mexicana*, 380.
160. *Memorial de Sololá*, 87–92.
161. *Anales de Cuauhtitlán*, 13.
162. Chimalpahin, *Relaciones*, 226–27.
163. *Códice Ramírez*, 92–93.
164. Alvarado Tezozómoc, *Crónica mexicana*, 380–81.
165. Durán, *Historia de las Indias*, 1:385.
166. *Códice Ramírez*, 31.
167. Popol Vuh, 149–50.
168. *Título de los señores*, 228–29.
169. *La historia de Tlatelolco*, 35.
170. *Anales de Cuauhtitlán*, 40.
171. Alvarado Tezozómoc, *Crónica mexicana*, 9 and Alvarado Tezozómoc, *Crónica mexicáyotl*, 14.
172. Durán, *Historia de las Indias*, 1:393.
173. Berlin and Rendón, *Historia tolteca-chichimeca*, 69.
174. Durán, *Historia de las Indias*, 1:205–6.
175. *Anales de Cuauhtitlán*, 12.
176. Córdova, *Arte del idioma*, 215.
177. Alvarado Tezozómoc, *Crónica mexicana*, 384.
178. The text says *tlacaztalmicoa*. See *Memoriales con escolios*, 178.
179. Alva Ixtlilxóchitl, *Obras históricas*, 1:49.
180. Torquemada, *Los veinte*, 2:150–51.
181. *Relaciones geográficas de la Diócesis de Tlaxcala*, 164.
182. Fuentes y Guzmán, *Recordación florida*, 1:17; 3:69–70.
183. Castillo, *Fragmentos*, 98.
184. *Anales de Cuauhtitlán*, 9.

185. *Relaciones de Yucatán*, 1:77.
186. Muñoz Camargo, *Historia de Tlaxcala*, 243–44.
187. Alva Ixtlilxóchitl, *Obras históricas*, 1:44.
188. *Leyenda de los Soles*, 122.
189. Castillo, *Fragmentos*, 88.
190. Alvarado Tezozómoc, *Crónica mexicáyotl*, 36–37.
191. Chimalpahin, *Relaciones*, 56.
192. Alva Ixtlilxóchitl, *Obras históricas*, 1:30–31.
193. Sahagún, *Historia general*, 290; and Chimalpahin, *Relaciones*, 62.
194. Alvarado Tezozómoc, *Crónica mexicana*, 524.
195. León-Portilla, *Quetzalcoatl*, 26.
196. *Historia de los mexicanos por sus pinturas*, 220–21.
197. Ramussio, in Fernández de Oviedo y Valdés, *Historia general y natural*, 10:103–4.
198. Sahagún, *Historia general*, 3:208–9.
199. Durán, *Historia de las Indias*, 1:225.
200. Ibid., 229.
201. Alva Ixtlilxóchitl, *Obras históricas*, 1:54.
202. Durán, *Historia de las Indias*, 1:225.
203. Chimalpahin, *Relaciones*, 12.
204. Tapia, "Relación," 48.
205. Translator's note: The translation of this passage is taken largely from the version found in Dibble and Anderson's *Florentine Codex*, 12:42. López Austin uses Garibay K.'s translation of the passage.
206. Cortés, *Letters*, 85–86. (Translator's note: I have used Anthony Pagden's translation of the passage, which differs only stylistically from the version used by López Austin.)
207. Weitlaner, Velásquez, and Carrasco, "Huitziltépec," 61.
208. Holland, *Medicina maya*, 115.
209. Mendieta, *Historia eclesiástica*, 1:105.
210. Motolinía, *Memoriales*, 39.
211. Castillo, *Fragmentos*, 91.
212. Chimalpahin, *Memorial*, folio 52v.
213. Popol Vuh, 140–41.
214. Eliade, *El mito del eterno retorno*, 194.
215. Durán, *Historia de las Indias*, 2:75.
216. *Origen de los mexicanos*, 263.
217. *Relaciones geográficas de la Diócesis de Tlaxcala*, 74.
218. *Memorial de Sololá*, 87.
219. Burgoa, *Geográfica descripción*, 2:242.
220. Sahagún, *Historia general*, 2:160.

221. González Casanova, "El cielo legendario," 63.
222. Alva Ixtlilxóchitl, *Obras históricas*, 1:55–56.
223. Torquemada, *Los veinte*, 1:174.
224. Alva Ixtlilxóchitl, *Obras históricas*, 1:205, 264.
225. Durán, *Historia de las Indias*, 1:398.
226. Alvarado Tezozómoc, *Crónica mexicáyotl*, 111.
227. To the point of affirming, according to the *Códice Cozcatzin*, that his remains had been scattered. See McAfee and Barlow, "La guerra entre Tlatelolco," 197.
228. Alvarado Tezozómoc, *Crónica mexicana*, 380.
229. Las Casas, *Apologética*, 1:643.
230. *Leyenda de los Soles*, 125.
231. Gómez de Orozco, "Costumbres, fiestas," 45.
232. Motolinía, *Memoriales*, 67.
233. Torquemada, *Los veinte*, 2:151.
234. Durán, *Historia de las Indias*, 1:518.
235. Alvarado Tezozómoc, *Crónica mexicana*, 506.
236. Durán, *Historia de las Indias*, 1:520.
237. León-Portilla, *La filosofía*, 298–99.
238. Dahlgren de Jordán, *La Mixteca*, 271–72.
239. Burgoa, *Geográfica descripción*, 2:64–65.
240. Castillo, *Fragmentos*, 92.
241. *Anales de Cuauhtitlán*, 11.
242. Landa, *Relación de las cosas de Yucatán*, 59.
243. López de Cogolludo, *Historia de Yucatán*, 188.
244. Núñez de la Vega, *Constituciones*, libro segundo, 134.
245. Landa, *Relación de las cosas de Yucatán*, 59.
246. Tello, *Crónica*, book II, vol. 1:42.
247. Herrera, *Historia general*, 4:172–73.
248. For example, González Obregón, *Procesos de indios*, 202; Muñoz Camargo, *Historia de Tlaxcala*, 243–44; and Román y Zamora, *Repúblicas*, 2:138–39.
249. A simple example of which was the enormous stone of Yoyna Xiñuho, a pueblo described in the account of Cuzcatlán, *Relaciones geográficas de la Diócesis de Tlaxcala*, 66–67.
250. Burgoa, *Geográfica descripción*, 2:330.
251. *Relaciones geográficas de la Diócesis de México*, 45.
252. This practice was followed among the Mixtec. Dahlgren de Jordán, *La Mixteca*, 293.
253. *Popol Vuh*, 140–41.
254. Lizana, *Historia*, folio 14r.
255. Cervantes de Salazar, *Crónica*, 1:40.

# 9

## The Life of the Man-God

The indigenous inhabitants of Mesoamerica sought in the course of the heavenly bodies above direction and guidance for their own movement and actions on earth. Archetypes, once divined, revealed formulas and schemes that dictated the proper course and conduct of human affairs. One of the most valuable elements underlying the native conception of the cosmos—elementary numbers—also served as a basic pillar in the organization of society. In his study of the mid-sixteenth-century Nahua text and pictorial manuscript, *Historia tolteca-chichimeca*, Paul Kirchhoff observed a feature that recurred throughout the work—the appearance of significant, revelatory numbers in references that were made to social and political relations: dual government, founded on the cosmic oppositions symbolized by the eagle and the jaguar; the value of the number four; seven tribes that undertake a migration journey; four chieftains who lead each migrant group; two children for each couple, with each child invariably possessing two names, one of which had a calendrical character, and so on.[1] To this complex, one could add, with respect to the political organization of Mexico-Tenochtitlan, two supreme rulers—the *tlatoani* and the *cihuacóatl*—two supreme priests, two supreme military leaders, two supreme legal functionaries, thirteen supreme judges, and the city subdivided into four administrative districts. The numerological guidelines were rigid and in their observance obeyed a world of gods; although in their own world the gods, too, perhaps obeyed, in like fashion, a structure that was laid out for them and determined their position and field of action. Fortune was also guided and traced out—for the future, through auguries and omens; for the past, through history. Our problem, however—the study of men in their appearance as Ce Acatl Topiltzin Quetzalcoatl—is rooted in the time frame of the present, his present.

To begin with, one must establish as a premise and governing principle that the connection between myth and history is real and cannot be doubted. Brinton, Seler, Preuss, Spence, and Kelly have all shown this to be the case, even if at the same time they eliminate, or virtually eliminate, the connection as a lived reality. Yet we cannot overlook or forget it. Standing alone, solely in himself, Ce Acatl Topiltzin Quetzalcoatl can perhaps be denied, but not if others are joined with him—other figures whose lives could for similar reasons fall into the skeptical school of interpretation, figures about whom there are incontrovertible historical data, demonstrating that they truly lived, all of them ruling as kings, all appearing in the final years preceding the Spanish conquest, all living lives that have been adequately documented, albeit more as men than as hombres-dioses: Tepetecuhtli, Moquihuix, Nezahualcoyotl, Nezahualpilli, Tezozomoc, Maxtla, Chimalpopoca, Tzutzumatzin. That the myth is the controlling factor can be deduced from the persuasive argument made by Brinton—namely, when an extraordinary story is recounted by various communities separated by language and location, the probability that it is not legend but myth is exceptionally high, and it should therefore be interpreted as such.[2] Working from this hypothesis, Brinton proceeded to document the great geographical reach of the myth of the white hero of daylight.

How do three basic elements—the particular historical event, the myth, and the wider historical record—all come together? Whether offered implicitly or explicitly, the answers given by scholars of the Mesoamerican cultures have differed considerably. They vary above all in trying to explain the occurrence of Huitzilopochtli's birth in Coatépec, a Huitzilopochtli who is already armed and in combat against his sister and brothers. Some authors, among them Wigberto Jiménez Moreno, who at one time held this opinion, have thought that this moment in the Mexica migration was the critical point that marked the end of the myth and the beginning of an account based on historical events. Yet one must note that there is no hard and fast distinction, either before or after Huitzilopochtli's birth in Coatépec, between the myth and the historical occurrence; and so it is incumbent upon us to search for an answer that will explain the cause of this intertwining of myth and history. At first glance, there appear to be three possible solutions:

a. The legend arises from some extraordinary event, possibly a military victory of signal importance. Instead of being recorded in its actual historical dimension, the event takes on epic-like overtones in which the heroes acquire divine attributes.

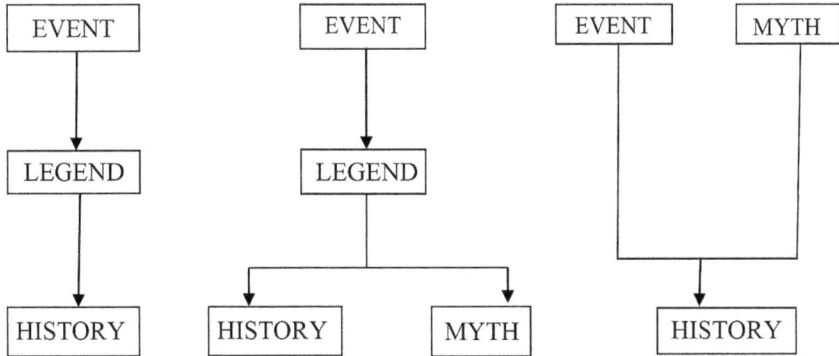

FIGURE 9.1. Myth, legend, and history: Three possible relationships

b. The event sparks the legend and, in turn, the legend spawns two divergent readings: the mythical, which in this case can be solar (i.e., Huitzilopochtli appearing as the sun), and the historical, whose rich array of extraordinary elements makes it difficult to distinguish events with clarity.

c. A myth exists that functions as an archetype. The event, which comes a good deal later, is merged with it so as to be recorded in history as not just a lived event but as a myth that is relived.

With specific reference to this third explanation, there is an interesting case that could be seen as offering parallel elements:

Dieudonné de Gozon, third Grand Master of the knights of St. John of Rhodes, has remained famous for having slain the dragon of Malpasso. Legend, as was natural, bestowed on him the attributes of Saint George, famed for his victorious fight with the monster. Needless to say, the documents of de Gozon's period make no reference to any such combat, and it does not begin to be mentioned until some *two centuries* after the hero's birth. In other words: by the simple fact that he was regarded as a hero, de Gozon was identified with a category, an archetype, which, entirely disregarding his real, [*historical*] exploits, equipped him with a mythical biography from which it was *impossible* to omit combat with a reptilian monster.[3]

The three solutions adumbrated above can be expressed diagrammatically (see figure 9.1):

Before committing to one of these, we must first analyze some of the defining characteristics of the biographies of hombres-dioses, beginning with their progenitors, their conception, and their intrauterine life.

In the first instance, the hombres-dioses who are mentioned most frequently, in terms of their ancestry, are Quetzalcoatl, Xelhua, Tenuch, Ulmecatl, Xicalancatl, Otomitl, Mixtecatl, and Huemac. Their progenitors are abbreviated in number:[4] their fathers total six (Iztacmixcoatl, Mixcoatl, Mixcoatl Camaxtle, Camaxtle, Totepeuh, and Citlalatonac); and their mothers, when they are mentioned, which is not always the case, are Coatlicue, Chimalma, and Ilancueitl. As a second point, which the reader will perhaps have noted, the progenitors—with two apparent exceptions, Totepeuh and Ilancueitl—bear the names of gods; although Totepeuh is mentioned as a god, as "our father Totepeuh," in the *Historia tolteca-chichimeca*[5] and there are good reasons to associate Ilancueitl with the goddess Cihuacoatl. Third, the names indicate groups that refer to the same divinity: Iztacmixcoatl is the god of the Milky Way; Mixcoatl is the name of the same deity. Camaxtle is identified as Mixcoatl in the *Historia de los mexicanos por sus pinturas*,[6] and Citlalatonac is mentioned in the Códice Vaticano Latino as the Way of Saint James or the Milky Way.[7] With respect to mothers, Coatlicue as well as Chimalma and Cihuacoatl—in the event that Ilancueitl is this goddess—are either the same or are different aspects of mother earth. The mythical character of the progenitors is unquestionably present in some sources, such as the *Historia de los mexicanos por sus pinturas*;[8] and what is narrated in one of the references that the *Leyenda de los Soles* makes to the sexual act is nothing but myth, since the coupling of the two personages is preceded by a pair of encounters in which the woman, Chimalma, presents herself naked before Mixcoatl, places her shield on the ground, and, on a series of occasions, evades four arrows that fly past both sides of her head and between her legs.[9] Nonetheless, a possibly historical Totepeuh appears on occasion: as ruler of Culhuacan, as father of Huemac,[10] or as a Totepeuh of Tollan, whose posthumous son was Quetzalcoatl.[11]

In short, the cited originators of pueblos have the heavens as their father and the earth as their mother.

Conception frequently takes place without direct physical contact. Huitzilopochtli was the offspring solely of his mother, who was impregnated upon inserting into her womb white eagle down that fell from heaven. Chimalma, sweeping as Coatlicue, became pregnant by placing a *chalchihuite* (semiprecious green stone) in her womb[12] or by receiving the heavenly breath of Citlalatonac.[13] Tepozteco was born when his mother introduced into her womb a little bird that disappeared[14] or a small image of a green stone that she found that likewise disappeared and was the origin of the hero.[15] Guatezuma, that strange king of Mexico whom Ramussio mentions, was the son of a virgin who dreamed that Orchilobos had sexual relations with her.[16] Quetzalcoatl was born the posthumous son of Totepeuh, but his conception was not the result of any physical contact since Totepeuh died in the year *chicuace ácatl* and Quetzalcoatl was born in the year *ce ácatl*,[17] or eight years later.

TABLE 9.1. Progenitors and their male offspring

| Father | Mother | Son |
| --- | --- | --- |
| Iztac-Mixcoatl-Camaxtle | Coatlicue | Quetzalcoatl |
| Iztac-Mixcoatl-Camaxtle | Chimalma | Quetzalcoatl |
| Iztac-Mixcoatl-Camaxtle | Ilancueitl | Xelhua |
| Iztac-Mixcoatl-Camaxtle | Ilancueitl | Tenuch |
| Iztac-Mixcoatl-Camaxtle | Ilancueitl | Ulmecatl |
| Iztac-Mixcoatl-Camaxtle | Ilancueitl | Xicalancatl |
| Iztac-Mixcoatl-Camaxtle | Ilancueitl | Otomitl |
| Iztac-Mixcoatl-Camaxtle | Ilancueitl | Mixtecatl |
| Iztac-Mixcoatl-Camaxtle | Name not specified | Mixtecatl |
| Iztac-Mixcoatl-Camaxtle | Name not specified | Quetzalcoatl |
| Citlalatonac | Name not specified | Quetzalcoatl |
| Totepeuh | Name not specified | Quetzalcoatl |
| Totepeuh | Name not specified | Huemac |

Motecuhzoma Ilhuicamina—and here perhaps we are confronting a myth that is projected onto the life of an ordinary man, albeit one who is notable—was also conceived miraculously, by means of a precious stone that his father, Huitzilihuitl, shot in an arrow at his mother, Miahuaxihuitl.[18]

Inside the womb, life is also no ordinary matter. Fray Bernardino de Sahagún's informants mentioned in a very general way, with reference to a wizard, astrologer, and the one who wards off hail, that "he disappeared four times in his mother's womb, as if she were not pregnant, and then he appeared."[19] This phenomenon seems to be directly related to what the Nahua said about the planet Venus: "These people called the star Venus *citlalpol, uei citlalin*, great star; and said that when it comes out in the east it makes four charges four times, in three [of these] it shines but little, and hides again, in the fourth it comes out in all its brightness, and moves along its course; and they say that its light seems like that of the moon."[20]

Vague references suggest that the matter of the pregnancy attendant upon the hombres-dioses, and their subsequent birth, is like the four appearances of Venus: in one version of the story, Quetzalcoatl was born after a period of labor that lasted four days, resulting in the death of his mother,[21] and Nezahualpilli was already invested with supernatural power—in exactly what way is not clear—while still inside his mother's womb.[22]

History presents us with two alternative possibilities: either the names of the fathers of hombres-dioses were assigned to them at a later date, after their sons had at some point attained this status; or the requirement had already been established that, say, an hombre-dios Totepeuh should be followed by his son, Huemac or Quetzalcoatl, as an hombre-dios. For now, I cannot shed any further light on the question.

In any case, let us set aside for the moment the problems associated with the birth of hombres-dioses and turn to the substance of their lives. Much attention has been focused on the penitent, chaste, and solitary life of the priest Quetzalcoatl, as one entailing a truly exceptional form of existence. But how truly exceptional, or radically different, was it? From what was reported and has come down about the conduct and performance of many other hombres-dioses, it seems clear that their lives followed very similar strictures and guidelines.

Quetzalcoatl is the inventor of self-sacrifice;[23] he is the perfect embodiment of the penitent.[24] The symbols of penitence and of fasting houses are bound up with him.[25] His dwelling places—one made of corals, another of seashells, another of quetzal feathers, and still another of wooden planks, the last one his fasting house in Tollantzinco, where it is said he lived in darkness—are famous.[26] He was the priest who performed penance for all of Tollan.[27] The story is also told that, together with the priestess Quetzalpetlatl, he would come down in the night to the *acequia* (canal, or irrigation ditch), Xippacoyan, where the two performed self-sacrifices using thorns.[28] Quetzalcoatl was forever holed up in his cells, not allowing others to see him,[29] and it appears that one of his ways of doing penance was to lie on the ground, although this deduction is not ironclad.[30]

There is little in this pattern of conduct that is unique to Quetzalcoatl, when it is compared with the lives of other hombres-dioses, some belonging to distant lands and to very different cultures. The Quiché hombres-dioses similarly practiced self-sacrifice by making blood offerings to their god Tohil,[31] and Chalchiuhtlicue, of Coyohuacan, was accustomed to ingesting bitter water as a form of penance.[32] Iztactototl, Mixcoatl's representative in Cuauhtitlan, and Xiuhtlacuilolxochitzin, who used to invoke Itzpapalotl, lived in thatched houses.[33] The wizard-soothsayer of the itztlacozauhques amaquemes lived atop the summit of Amaqueme, and Cuauhuitzatzin, the founder of Chiconcóac, was performing penance inside a cave on the eve of discovering the divine sign that would indicate to him his pueblo's new place of settlement.[34] In Guatemala, the high priest, who at times was also the supreme ruler, had the custom of spending entire months shut away, adhering to a diet of roasted dry corn and some fruit; he could not ingest anything that had touched fire, nor did he converse with anyone. His dwelling place was a tiny hut made of a thatch of green leaves that was situated in a forested area, where he gave himself over to self-sacrifice.[35] The Totonaca priests, intermediaries dedicated to the Sun's consort, also lived lives characterized by chastity, self-sacrifice, a strict diet, and solitude.³⁶ The Caxcanes were accustomed to locking themselves into their houses, drinking *tenéxyetl* (a mixture made using a tobacco plant with hallucinogenic properties) until they were intoxicated, and then, lost in a trance, making their way to the river in the hope of speaking to their god.³⁷ To conserve the divine fire in them, the Quiché hombres-dioses, as noted earlier, practiced sexual continence,³⁸ and Gagavitz, the Cakchiquel, could not have carnal relations with his wife, Qomakaa. When together while bathing, they extended their genital organs, seeking a way for the semen to penetrate without having to touch each other.³⁹ The prohibition against this form of contact, which was feared by so many hombres-dioses as causing the loss of their divine force, is doubtless analogous to the fear that drove them to avoid drinking pulque. When the sorcerers approached Quetzalcoatl to induce him into transgressing his rules of conduct, they said that they would give him pulque so that his observance of penance should cease.⁴⁰ Perhaps out of a fear of the sun's light, the prophet Chilam Balam would not show himself in public,⁴¹ in similar fashion to Tezcatlipoca's representative in Tetzcoco, who would go into seclusion before the break of day.⁴² This practice is quite interesting when compared to one of the last tales gathered in: Quetzalcoatl was constructing a stone bridge to cross the sea; dawn broke and, with his power now lost, he went out over the salty waters. His interrupted edifice remained as the mountain range of San Martín.⁴³ Finally, a notice exists, the veracity of which is questioned by Alfredo Barrera Vásquez, that Chilam Balam found himself flat upon the ground inside of his temple.⁴⁴

Unquestionably, it is not his priestly attributes that best characterize the Toltec Quetzalcoatl, who, from his place of reclusion, in solitude, cut off, fearful of the sun's light, containing within himself—as if he were a receptacle—the vitality of his people, was obliged first and foremost to protect his community.

It is unnecessary to reemphasize the connection that exists between the myth and the lives of hombres-dioses, since I have made it a leitmotif of this book. Yet it does need to be underscored that, in some sources, the only element that seems to be present is the myth itself. Stories of Quetzalcoatl exist in which the human factor is entirely missing,⁴⁵ or in which the things of heaven play an overbearing role.⁴⁶ The completely inexplicable also turns up, such as the existence of the mountain from which issues a great cry—like that which so astonished Sahagún in Xochimilco⁴⁷— calling men to the service of Quetzalcoatl. Or the exercises of ascending and descending, of sliding up and down mountainsides, while seated, that are attributed to Quetzalcoatl in sources as different as the *Relación de Coatepec-Chalco*⁴⁸ and the *Historia general* of Sahagún.⁴⁹ It is myth, like the many tales of Tollan's downfall, or the stories of its phantasmagorical giants, its malodorous dead whom no one can transport or drag off, the generalized drunkenness that leads the Toltecs into unconscious death, the multitudes who trample on and crush each other, the men who willingly offer themselves in sacrifice holding their paper flags in their hands, the wizards who set homunculi dancing in the palm of their hand, the birds that fly transfixed as arrows shoot past them, the mountainside of Zacatépec in flames, the rains that fall as stones . . . It is myth, like the pilgrimage of Quetzalcoatl and the ball game (*pelota*) session in which Huemac defeats the rain gods.[50] And that is why there is singing in religious hymns to Coatépec, which to the naked eye seems solely to be a geographic entity, proclaiming that in him the Sun is born.[51] Myth, like the story of Mixtecatl, who with his arrows bloodies the day star in the western sky.[52]

The myth likewise gives uniformity, primarily within popular tradition, to a life that could—with the exception of interpretations that really bore in—be regarded as anecdotal. The hands, buttocks, and feet that are imprinted on the rocks impart special cachet to the pueblos through which the pilgrim passes, across lands that are now more than just the simple Mesoamerican landscape,[53] in testimony to an ancient American current in which men uphold and pass on a stable, rich, and shared tradition. Another deed that was integral to this ubiquitous and continuous personage whom the pueblo retains in its memory is that one day he endowed the valleys, mountains, and rivers with their names,[54] like the first light that keeps on uncovering everything, revealing everything. It is the inaugural, the bellwether hagiography that drapes (and will drape) the same clothing over different bodies.

A mythical life, the anecdotal working of wonders, and similar priestly habits and practices could lead people to believe that the unrepeatable occurrence of the existence of the Quequetzalcoah mattered little. Nonetheless, it has clearly been shown that the diverse range of exploits, together with the homogeneity of the myth, could unleash a historiographical chaos such as no other biography has done in the long centuries of our tradition. For the occurrence also stamped its own imprint. The problem is to know how it does this, how this comes about.

There were hombres-dioses (and *mujeres-diosas*) whose lives in that state were ephemeral. The story was recounted of a daughter of Achitometl, lord of Culhuacan during the period in which the Mexica were prowling around the lake zone, whom the latter asked to be the mother or grandmother of their patron god, Huitzilopochtli.[55] She became a goddess for a brief moment, and only for that moment, because the role that the Mexica designed for her condemned her to be sacrificed and flayed. The Culhua lord had accepted the offer and handed his daughter over to the newly settled people, thinking that she would be worshipped and revered by them, as thus far they had behaved in a submissive fashion. Unaware of the fate that had befallen his maiden daughter, he attended the ceremony to which he was invited, only to look on with horror at the priest who was dressed in his daughter's skin. He took out his justifiable fury on the Mexica, but his daughter remained a goddess.

Like her, though as part of the normal practice of the rite and not as a spectacular historical showpiece, there were many others who, throughout the twenty-day periods, or "months," of the year, briefly represented the divinities and departed with them after dying. Special attire, names, and ritual acts joined, in these men, present time with the divine and, above all, mythical time of the life of the gods. On many occasions, the performance of a ritualized violent death demanded persons with physical abnormalities or some particular condition of life: the already-mentioned albinos;[56] women who were nearing the age of forty-five and who represented the goddess Toci;[57] or the two noble youths, from the lineage of Tezcacoatl, of different ages,[58] who had to be immolated in a ceremony that was held annually. They not only represented the gods but were also taken as such themselves. As a general rule, the prisoners and captives of war were considered to be children of the Sun and needed to be guarded and treated with full respect.[59] The remains of some of these prisoners were kept in stone boxes and valued as relics,[60] in similar fashion to what was done with the remains of hombres-dioses.

Members of the priestly class were in charge of other, very brief representations that invoked and venerated the gods. The gods Ixtlilton and Nappatecuhtli, for example, participated in ceremonies through the bodies of men—priests—who in their office were dedicated to religion;[61] and the elder who fasted over a period of eighty days and emerged attired in the garments of Camaxtle, to have a volley of arrows shot over his head in an apparent symbolic sacrifice, was also a priest.[62]

Those chosen to die on the sacrificial stone, after representing a particular divinity, might spend twenty, forty, or eighty days, or a year, or even four years doing so before they were put to death. Every four years, Titlacahuan,[63] Quetzalcoatl,[64] and Xiuhtecuhtli[65] were represented in different cities, after having endured varying lapses as true numens on earth. Captives of war were chosen on the basis of exceptional physical condition that mandated the complete absence of any scars or other blemishes or defects. They were even given special beverages that, as their guards could mark, caused them to slim down when they had put on too much weight. At times, a lesser representative, Tlacahuepan, who did not enjoy such widespread worship, could be named together with and would accompany the principal representative, Titlacahuan.[66] For the remainder of their now consecrated lives, these men wandered through their cities listening to pleas and requests, holding in their arms the children presented by their mothers and receiving honors even from the sovereign rulers, though always under strict guard so they could not escape, while being kept during the night in wooden cages. Their life was marked by the hallmarks of the gods' own lives: Xilonen—the woman who represented Xilonen—frequented weddings, feasts, and markets;[67] and in Tenochtitlan the aforementioned Titlacahuan entered into marriage with four women, each of whom bore the name of a goddess.⁶⁸ On certain occasions, conduct was regulated in the simplest, most direct way: nothing more than the copulation of a male and female slave before they were sacrificed in the *veintena*, or month, of *etzalcualiztli*.⁶⁹ As a rule, the final days and hours of the soon to be sacrificed were guided and dictated by a lengthy ritual, and if by chance fortune interceded, a way had to be found to ensure that this interruption did not produce unwanted or adverse consequences. In the days preceding the sacrifice, the *neyolmaxitiliztli*, or "satisfaction of the doubt," was carried out. This was a ritual act that entailed recording the date on which the god's representative had to depart this world. It was obvious that the sacrificial ceremony (at least in the emotions that it provoked in those destined for sacrifice) contravened the ease and happiness of the honors and pleasures that it offered. To forestall sadness, which was seen as the unwanted product of contingent circumstance, a remedy was always available—a ritual drink, a brew made with the water poured over the bloody knives that had been used in a sacrifice, or excessive amounts of pulque—preparations to which drugs of one type or another must also have been added.⁷⁰ The divine force, which could perhaps escape with the expression of grief and anguish, was retained through the contentment induced by the magic potion.

Given the force and range of the miraculous exploits attributed to hombredioses, we might well think that the formulaic acts of the priesthood and of those who were marked for ritual death and considered for a brief time to be numens, were hardly sufficient to equate with all that men-gods had done across their entire lives. Nonetheless, one must factor in that some penitents whose lives appeared to lack anything of special note came to be worshipped after their death. According to what is recounted in Mayan sources, the mere recollection that some virginal young women died was enough for them to become the object of worship and for images to be made of them.⁷¹

Moreover, the unduly regulated life was not restricted to priests and the sacrificed but, instead, characterized the conduct and practice of entire communities. The Tlappanecas, for example, owed their name to Tlappan, "Place of the Red," and they worshipped Totec Tlatlauhqui Texcatlipoca—that is, Our Lord Tezcatlipoca [the] Red. Their priests dressed in red, and everyone in the pueblo painted their skin this color.⁷² The Coyohuaques wore metal nose rings in honor of Tezcatlipoca, who had established the practice.⁷³ The Matlatzincas, or the "[people] originating in the Place of the Venerable Sling," stripped the kernels of corn off the cobs, which they beat with sticks, after placing them inside of nets; they hauled the corn in nets and used a type of slingshot—*temátlatl*, or, rendered etymologically, "sling for [hurling] stones"—as a main weapon from childhood on; and they sacrificed their captives by stuffing them inside of nets, in which they pressed them down until achieving their purpose.⁷⁴ And the Teotlixcas, whose name means "those from the

Place Facing the Sun," always walked—or so a prime source states—with their face to the Sun.[75] To repeat then, these are patterns of regimented behavior that involve entire groups of people, not just individuals. What could the highly regulated life of some singular beings matter, important as they might be, if the security of the community as a whole also depended on such collective ritualized observance?

The regimented ways of high priests among the Zapotec shed considerable light on the life of Quetzalcoatl. In his *Geográfica descripción*, Burgoa writes, "these priests never married, nor communicated with women, only on certain solemn occasions that they celebrated with lots of drink and intoxication were unwed ladies brought to them, and if one of them happened to conceive, they kept her apart until she delivered, because if a male was born he was brought up to succeed into the priesthood, which fell to the son or closest relative, and he was never chosen or elected."[76]

This situation led Seler to aver that the system of succession within the highest rank of the Zapotec priesthood confirmed that priests were looked upon as living images of the Toltec god, the incarnation of Quetzalcoatl.[77] Based on Seler's opinion, Laurette Séjourné claims that these priests were considered reincarnations of Quetzalcoatl and that they carried out a ritual that evoked certain memorable instances in the life of the priest. She reinforces the argument by recalling that the end of the rule of Huemac, Quetzalcoatl's successor, was due to his having carnal relations with the so-called "devilresses"; and she further maintains that Sahagún doubtless confused one of these priests who came after the original Quetzalcoatl with the true Quetzalcoatl of Teotihuacan.[78]

A similar line is found in the *Relación de Tilantongo*, which mentions the prohibition against imbibing alcohol and having sexual relations that is placed on the supreme priest of this Mixtec community, but it adds that "to make him desist from the priesthood and that he might not practice it, they made him drink wine and contract marriage."[79] Barbro Dahlgren de Jordán, it seems to me, is quite correct in stating that a connection exists between this set of events, or transgression, and the destitution that Ce Acatl suffers in Tollan because of the sin he commits.[80] The fact is that priests, whether Mixtec, Nahua,[81] or of any other people, were sentenced to death for becoming intoxicated or having sexual relations. Why was there an exception made in this case? It undoubtedly involves a ritual that, among other things, granted the possibility of passing on the position through inheritance.

In and of itself, by virtue of its own requirement, the conservation of the divine fire meant that the god's representative, even if the god he represented was that of fertility, as in the case of Quetzalcoatl, had necessarily to lead a chaste life. This demand notwithstanding, and in fulfillment of the myth itself, hombres-dioses were able to engage in a sexual act that possessed particular ritualistic characteristics. It should be recalled that some sources mention certain mythical sexual relations that can be linked to this type of ritual conduct on the part of priests and hombresdioses. Indeed, the performance of the sexual act by the gods acquires great importance in some myths. For example, the Códice Magliabechiano narrates that while washing himself, Quetzalcoatl masturbated; the gods turned his semen into a bat that tore off a piece of the vagina of the goddess Xochiquetzal.[82] Although it was heard of and recorded only recently, there is a story, a myth, about two brothers that is perhaps more closely connected to the life of the Quequetzalcoah. As a result of having sexual relations, the older brother forfeits the right of primogeniture as well as his greater standing relative to his younger brother. The myth serves to explain the course followed by both the Morning and the Evening Star.[83] Vague mention is also made to a situation involving Tezcatlipoca *before he falls into sin*, when he still has both of his feet,[84] a possible reference, in the same way, to the course of the stars. In some myths, then, a crucial moment seems to exist in which the impulse toward, or the arrest or repeated pattern of, or the change in a cosmic process is marked by the representation of a divine sexual act, a transgression in certain cases.

Why must it be believed that only an isolated ritual act is at work? The story is told of a priest named Texpolcatl who, in the time of Topiltzin Meconetzin, made a vow of chastity and lived in the temple of the god Ce Acatl. He had a love affair with a Toltec priestess who gave birth to an infant boy. This boy and his descendants proceeded to inherit the position of great priests. Moreover, two brothers, great sorcerers named, respectively, Tezcatlipoca and Tlatlauhqui Tezcatlipoca, were identified as the provocateurs of these illicit relations.[85]

Why must it be believed that the matter revolves around the attempt to imitate an original priest Quetzalcoatl? From where, in turn, does he extract the pattern or model of conduct? It is not the transgression of an original priest but rather the comportment of a god in the myth, ritually repeated on earth.

In addition, we are in the presence of events that should not be confined exclusively to isolated ritual moments. Two testimonies exist in history, two testimonies that, in relation to a ritualized *life*, offer us on the one hand fulfillment and on the other frustration, as I will expound below in the case of Huemac.

According to Alfredo Barrera Vásquez, Suyuá, Suiuá, or Suivá is the Mayan name for a place from which different Mesoamerican communities were said to have originated—a place, furthermore, that at times bears a relationship to Tollan and Chicomóztoc.[86] There is an esoteric language, recorded in the books of Chilam Balam, that refers exclusively to the formulas used by the supreme ruler to request a serving of food or of tobacco from his inferiors, whose loyalty in these instances he put to the test. The language of Suyuá is unquestionably beautiful but also falls disappointingly short or seems inadequate when something so thoroughly prosaic—the request for food—is offered as the solution to a riddle charged with metaphors.

This has caused some Mayanists to think that what we know about this esoteric language is only the record of the bare bone remains of an exceedingly interesting system of riddles and verbal puzzles that at one time covered a much more extensive field. Yet that explanation seems off base because the texts themselves mention that there is an appropriate time in which to request meals by means of riddles: "From the seashore the Heart of the Mountain will take his sustenance, will defeat the katún of droughts and vomiting of blood, the katún who puts an end to joy and gladness and brings the request for food by means of enigmas and riddles."[87]

This is all entirely too mysterious and complex. For now, we need concern ourselves with only a single element or case, a riddle that says, "My son, bring to me here an old woman who takes care of corn fields, who has the black body and the buttocks of seven palms of the hand; I wish to gaze at her."[88]

Perhaps misled by the expectation that a question or riddle framed in sacred language will yield a correspondingly deep and revealing answer or solution, our reaction may be one of disappointment that what the Mayan lord desires is simply a serving of pumpkin. Such disappointment, however, would be misplaced, because in this context the saucer filled with pumpkin is just that—a saucer filled with pumpkin and no more. It is not the Mayan lord's desires that are of interest, but the enormous buttocks of the woman. We are confronted with an enigma the significance of which still lies beyond our understanding, but an enigma that we can relate, outside the Mayan world, to the Tollan of the altiplano of central Mexico, to Huemac and to the life of the hombres-dioses. We know with certainty that in the altiplano, the priest Huemac asked his subjects to bring to him a woman with similarly sized buttocks.

In two cases there is a reference to the woman who is physically marked out by the gods. The first story relates that when Tlilcoatzin, the king of Tollan, died, the city's government continued in the hands of his widow, Coacueye, a mujer-diosa who may have owed her position as woman-goddess to her gargantuan backside. She married a priest from Xicócoc and still later wed Huemac.[89]

The second story takes a different turn. A boy who must have been Huemac was discovered in Tollan—the same Tollan we are to surmise? Grown into young adulthood, he ordered that a woman with buttocks that spanned four palms of the hand be brought to him, and the Nonohualcas set off in search of her. The woman whom they produced, however, failed to measure that size; she was rejected, and the young man asked for another who would satisfy the request. The subject people rose up in rebellion, and the hombre-dios fled, under persecution, until he reached a cave called Cincalco, where he met his death from the arrows that were shot at him.[90]

In the first case, Huemac's participation was sought for the celebration of a marriage that took place between a hombre-dios and a mujer-diosa. In the second, the true woman did not even appear, but evidently this Huemac also had a ritual need for one of them. He had to undergo a rite that the Nonohualcos—not the Toltec subjects but the peasants—perhaps did not understand or were not disposed to fulfill. These diverse episodes, in which attempts are made to fulfill schemes that are similar in nature, also illustrate that there was more to the picture than just sporadic rites, more than just the need to reincarnate a celebrated, admired personage. The hombres-dioses fulfill on earth an obligatory passage that is established in the divine world before the beginning of this time, earthly time. Their lives are guided by a set regimen.

How many downfalls could Tollan sustain? Possibly, one each century, when the critical year *ce ácatl* fulfilled its function. Tollan "ran its course," Quetzalcoatl either died or set off for some other precinct; another of Tollan's lives was begun, and other hombres-dioses continued as Quetzalcoatl. If on one or more occasions the ritual downfall by chance corresponded to the real downfall, the ritual downfall, with its cyclical arrival a fait accompli, doubtless contributed greatly toward getting the journey underway, a decision spurred on by both the pueblo's desperation over what had been lost during the period of bad omen and its hope for what could be promised to it. So could it be for one Tollan after another, and so could one and another Aztlan come into being, with the distinction, however, that Tollan could exist, could be Tollan, when the community that called it by that name lived in it, whereas Aztlan was given its name at the time that the pilgrimage commenced. Aztlan, the place left behind.

Coatépec could likewise have been both mythical and real. This was the place where the personages who came from the *calpulli* called Huitznáhuac, and who were in charge of the cult of Huitzilopochtli[91] during the festival of Toxcatl, were Huitzilopuchtli born anew. Once these personages assumed and became the masters of their role, the great rite was carried out in which the lord of the sun, recently arrived, scarcely born, grasped the turquoise serpent, rolled the head of his lunar sister Coyolxauhqui beyond the mountains, and killed the four hundred Huitznahuas—who could have been fewer in number, given the economic situation of the migrants. These four hundred, or fewer, were also hombres-dioses, although for some hours only, and they remained as relics for the people of a settlement called Cuzco.[92]

Only the rigid life of such worthy men can explain the search for evolutionary formulas that, as we shall see, become multiplied during the sedentary periods that pueblos experienced. A stable existence demanded new ritual ways through which the lives of personages deemed of great value for society could be saved.

The existence of the type of god whom Adolf Jensen calls a *dema* may be one of the causes underlying the need for the enactment of violent ritual death. He takes this name from the Marind-anim of New Guinea, noting that one of their most important characteristics is to take some defining action at the end of original, or mythical, time, which produces the order of human time.[93] Luis Reyes has noted the presence of this type of god in the region of Mexico's central plateau, citing examples such as Mayahuel, dismembered by those strange beings, called *tzitzimime*, who frequently appear in the myths. Ehecatl Quetzalcoatl buried the bones of the goddess Mayahuel, and the maguey plants were born from pieces of them. Cinteotl is also a *dema*, and, according to another myth, after he burrowed down beneath the earth, cotton came from his hair, *huauhtzontli* (a type of vegetable) from one of his ears, chia from his nose, sweet potatoes from his fingers, corn from his fingernails, and different types of fruit from the rest of his body.[94] The course of time, the mythical beginning of one of its cyclical turnings, obligated men to carry through with a revivifying ritual death, that of the rains, of the vegetation, or of the corn . . . The hombres-dioses, tied indissolubly to the ritual rules and norms marked by time, had not only to commence their functions on a date that was predetermined but, it is believed, had also—at least in certain cases and during certain epochs—to conclude their functions by carrying out the ultimate rite, their own suicide.

In this connection, a particular Huemac was said to have killed himself inside a cave.[95] Tecpatzin, as noted earlier, died in Tecpayo on a key date: the time of the new fire.[96] According to Spinden, because Quetzalcoatl's death came in the form of a ritual suicide, he was able to calculate the exact hour and date called for, and then carry it out in strict conformity with those calculations.[97] Huitzilopochtli proceeds to announce that he is going to die on the occurrence of the next day of *miquiztli*,[98] and Nezahualpilli bids his farewell, announcing that he is withdrawing from the world.[99] In the place called Cíncoc, Huemac killed "his people's idol, that bore the name Ce Coatl and that he offered as a victim," in the year *ce técpatl*.[100] The hombre-dios in Tzotzompan, a savage, hairy man, died the victim of sacrifice.[101] Many other examples could be added to these, among them (as cited earlier) the extremely interesting case of the three hombres-dioses in the Mayan zone, all of whom disappeared on the consecrated mountain at the same time, following which their three sons returned, bearing the names of their vanished fathers. If we recall what Alva Ixtlilxóchitl said concerning the Toltec kings—that they held onto power for a maximum of fifty-two years—and compare this with the actions surrounding the tragic end of their lives, then it should not surprise us (as it did José Fernández Ramírez) that Alva Ixtlilxóchitl's text relates, though rather obscurely, "[the Toltecs] had a custom; and it was that their kings should not govern for more than fifty-two years, as I have already stated, and so, before [their] time, the fifty-two years fulfilled, their life was taken from them, because they all died as young men."[102]

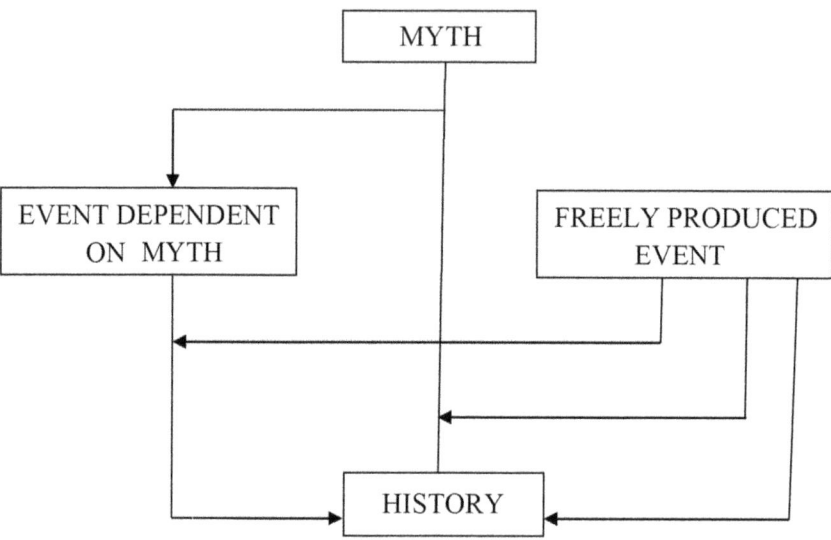

**FIGURE 9.2.** Pathways taken by myth in helping shape historical narrative

How was it possible to conceive of the plurality of an apparently singular personage when, together with the quite distinct episodes of a life, circumstances existed that seemed unrepeatable? Unrepeatable, that is, if all determination were left to chance. But in Mesoamerica the narration of the occurrence not only modifies the myth, so that both are interwoven into history, it also rules over events, predetermines them, struggles to annul chance and to convert life—at least a certain type of life—into a rite. Rites and profane life intermix in history, in that history that is an instrument of men who search for a place to locate themselves on earth.

This reality goes beyond the framework of the three schemes proposed at the beginning of the chapter. Hence, I propose a fourth, in which the myth precedes two types of recordable occurrences: on the one hand, the type that is freely produced; on the other, the type that is guided by a myth. Both generate a narrative that will enrich the storyline of history. The narrative of the event that is dependent on myth will doubtless be augmented by the narrative that derives from the event that is not so encumbered and, consequently, will lend the former a patina of verisimilitude. For its part, the myth in some cases will influence the narrative of the freely produced event. The interplay of this dynamic is diagrammed in figure 9.2.

All of these permutations will flow into history, into a stream of history in which the similarities and dissimilarities in the biographies of parallel personages, and in the stories of the migrations, and of the events that befall city-states will result—as all the particular versions get woven together—in a chaos in which it is not possible for one thing to be placed over another until a definition clearly emerges, either of the interests of those whose function it was to construct the historical record, or of several interrelated things: the purposes they had in mind in constructing it, its quality and effectiveness as an instrument, the material that nourished it, the processes of synthesis and of censorship that it underwent, and the systems employed to safeguard tradition. In sum, not only are we dealing with material that is quite different from the material that historians "normally" work with, but the very life that produced this history followed a course, or courses, that at best we can understand only with great difficulty. They were the courses of rituals that filtered into and intermixed with the events of ordinary, everyday existence; that directed, modified, clashed with, triumphed over, or brought it to an end.

## NOTES

1. Kirchhoff, "La Historia tolteca-chichimeca," xxxiv–xxxviii.
2. Brinton, "American Hero-Myths," vii–viii.
3. Eliade, *El mito*, 44. (Translator's note: The italicizations are López Austin's.)
4. Mention of these hombres-dioses, and of their parents, is found principally in Muñoz Camargo, *Historia de Tlaxcala*, 40; Burgoa, *Geográfica descripción*, 1:370; Motolinía, *Memoriales*, 10, 12; López de Gómara, *Historia general*, 2:379; *Leyenda de los Soles*, 122; Chimalpahin, "Memorial," folio 17r; Mendieta, *Historia eclesiástica*, 1:89; and *Historia de México*, 112.
5. From a photostatic copy published in *Historia tolteca-chichimeca* in the *Corpus Codicum Americanorum*, 43.
6. *Historia de los mexicanos por sus pinturas*, 216.
7. *Códice Vaticano Latino*, plate viii.
8. *Historia de los mexicanos por sus pinturas*, 217.
9. *Leyenda de los Soles*, 124.
10. Chimalpahin, "Memorial," folio 17r–17v.
11. *Anales de Cuauhtitlán*, 7.
12. Torquemada, *Los veinte*, 2:80.
13. *Códice Vaticano Latino*, plate xvii.
14. González Casanova, "El cielo legendario," 59.
15. Tibón, El héroe Tepozteco," 452.
16. Fernández de Oviedo y Valdés, *Historia general y natural*, 10:104.
17. *Anales de Cuauhtitlán*, 7.
18. Alvarado Tezozómoc, *Crónica mexicáyotl*, 94–95.
19. The text of Sahagún's informants was translated by Garibay K., in "Paralipómenos," 167.
20. Sahagún, *Historia general*, 1:263.

21. *Leyenda de los Soles*, 124.
22. Alva Ixtlilxóchitl, *Obras históricas*, 1:330.
23. *Códice Vaticano Latino*, plate ix.
24. *Códice Telleriano-Remensis*, part 1, plate vi.
25. *Códice Vaticano Latino*, plate ix.
26. *Anales de Cuauhtitlán*, 7–8.
27. Torquemada, *Los veinte*, 2:50.
28. Sahagún, *Historia general*, 1:279; and *Anales de Cuauhtitlán*, 10.
29. Durán, *Historia de las Indias*, 2:73.
30. Sahagún, *Historia general*, 1:278.
31. *Popol Vuh*, 116
32. Chimalpahin, *Relaciones*, 154.
33. *Anales de Cuauhtitlán*, 31, 7.
34. Chimalpahin, *Relaciones*, 134, 202–3.
35. Román y Zamora, *Repúblicas*, 1:192–93.
36. Las Casas, *Apologética historia*, 1:641–42.
37. "Relación de Nuchistlán," 66.
38. *Título de los señores*, 220.
39. *Memorial de Sololá*, 85.
40. *Anales de Cuauhtitlán*, 9.
41. *El libro de los libros de Chilam Balam*, 95.
42. Pomar, *Relación de Texcoco*, 11.
43. García de León, "El dueño del maíz," 357.
44. *El libro de los libros de Chilam Balam*, 95.
45. *Historia de México*, 112–16; and *Leyenda de los Soles*, 124–25.
46. *Códice Vaticano Latino*, plate viii.
47. Torquemada, *Los veinte*, 2:48.
48. *Relaciones geográficas de la Diócesis de México*, 45.
49. Sahagún, *Historia general*, 1:291.
50. *Leyenda de los Soles*, 126–27.
51. Garibay K., *Veinte himnos sacros*, 78.
52. Burgoa, *Geográfica descripción*, 1:369–71.
53. Metraux, "El dios supremo," 14.
54. For the Nahua Quetzalcoatl, see Sahagún, *Historia general*, 1:291; and for the Maya region, *Relaciones de Yucatán*, which abounds in such references.
55. Durán, *Historia de las Indias*, 1:33.
56. Alva Ixtlilxóchitl, *Obras históricas*, 1:49.
57. Durán, *Historia de las Indias*, 2:187.
58. Ibid., vol. 2: 195–96.

59. Ibid., 1:173.
60. Gómez de Orozco, "Costumbres, fiestas," 43.
61. Sahagún, *Historia general*, 1:62, 70–71.
62. Durán, *Historia de las Indias*, 2:129.
63. *Códice Ramírez*, 137–38.
64. Ibid., 157–58.
65. Las Casas, *Apologética*, 2:192.
66. Sahagún, *Historia general*, 1:159–60.
67. Durán, *Historia de las Indias*, 2:172.
68. Sahagún, *Historia general*, 1:154.
69. Motolinía, *Memoriales*, 63–64.
70. Sahagún, *Historia general*, 1:122–23; *Códice Ramírez*, 157–58; and Durán, *Historia de las Indias*, 2:120–21.
71. Lizana, *Historia de Yucatán*, folio 39v–40r.
72. Sahagún, *Historia general*, 3:205
73. Chimalpahin, *Relaciones*, 154.
74. Sahagún, *Historia general*, 3:199.
75. Chimalpahin, *Relaciones*, 169.
76. Burgoa, *Geográfica descripción*, 2:125.
77. Seler, "Wall Paintings of Mitla," 275–76.
78. Séjourné, "Teotihuacán, la ciudad sagrada," 203–4.
79. *Relaciones geográficas de la Diócesis de Oaxaca*, 74.
80. Dahlgren de Jordán, *La Mixteca*, 303.
81. Cervantes, "Descripción de Teotzacualco," 175–76; Aznar de Cozar, "Relación del pueblo de Instlauaca," 137; and López de Gómara, *Historia general*, 2:423.
82. *Códice Magliabechiano*, folio 61v.
83. Preuss, "El concepto de la Estrella," 382, among the present-day Nahua of Durango. The author also compares their notions to the beliefs of the Cora and the myth of Quetzalcoatl.
84. *Códice Telleriano-Remensis*, part 1, plate ix.
85. Alva Ixtlilxóchitl, *Obras históricas*, 1:47.
86. Barrera Vásquez, "Glosario," in *Códice de Calkiní*, 118–19.
87. *El libro de los libros de Chilam Balam*, 82.
88. Ibid., 142.
89. *Anales de Cuauhtitlán*, 12.
90. Berlin and Rendón, *Historia tolteca-chichimeca*, 68–69.
91. So van Zantwijk believes. See his "Principios organizadores," 200.
92. *Historia de los mexicanos por sus pinturas*, 221.
93. Jensen, *Mito y culto*, 110

94. Reyes, "Los dioses tribales," 36.
95. *Anales de Cuauhtitlán*, 4; and *Origen de los mexicanos*, 263.
96. Chimalpahin, "Memorial," folio 52v.
97. Spinden, "New Light on Quetzalcoatl."
98. Castillo, *Fragmentos*, 92.
99. Alvarado Tezozómoc, *Crónica mexicana*, 485.
100. *Anales de Cuauhtitlán*, 14.
101. *Relaciones geográficas de la Diócesis de Tlaxcala*, 164.
102. Alva Ixtlilxóchitl, *Obras históricas*, 1:79.

# 10

## The History of the Man-God

The portrait that I have sketched of the *hombre-dios* has been formed out of the bits and pieces, the accumulated remnants, of myriad, centuries-old tales and accounts. There is really no other way of bringing the picture into focus. The cultural nature of man underlies and dictates the process, and like so many before me, I am impelled to look for historical explanations. Who, across this long span of centuries, has the hombre-dios been and what form has he taken? To search for every element of his existence would take us beyond the horizon of the visible. For now, it is more than adequate simply to inquire into the origin of this ensemble of elements; and for that, we must deem it valid to set down, hypothetically, the social, economic, and political conditions of an era whose historical records have not survived to our day.

Within this ensemble, this complex of elements, the hombres-dioses lead pueblos that, paradoxically, retain their organized family structures and lineages. They are members of a specialized class and, as such, form part of an immense Mesoamerican world of religious beliefs.

Since there is no documented history of either the end of the Classic or the beginning of the Postclassic period on which to fall back, it is necessary to establish our historical bearings and points of reference on the basis of simple logical inference and deduction. The description and analysis that follows is only hypothetical. Any other hypothesis that attempts to address the problems posed by the life of the hombre-dios may also be considered perfectly valid. From this jumping-off point I move on to a period that is semi-documented, and from there, to one that is comparatively well documented.

In the great cities of the Classic period, there could have been rulers who maintained an intimate connection with the divinities, a connection manifested through images, male offspring, representatives, those who were gods themselves—in short, through all of the forms and representations that government of a theocratic type could entail. Nevertheless, the origin of our hombres-dioses appears to have been more humble. Of course, this likelihood does not mean that the great rulers may not also have come from similarly humble backgrounds, but the line followed by those under study here does not seem to have passed directly through them.

We should envision Mesoamerica in the Classic period as being a very heterogeneous world in which the more highly civilized communities could not entirely forestall or block the constant penetration into their territories of less civilized or "barbarian" peoples crossing through the northern frontier. The distance that these two groups kept, or tried to keep, between each other steadily decreased, until the time arrived in which past wariness dissolved, and the treaties that the two sides had sporadically concluded were turned into more or less open relationships of mutual benefit.

Ángel Palerm refers to the existence of key areas, areas that were the axes of interrelationships in which recently arrived segments of the population doubtless had their own specific role to play:

> The term key area is applied to a special locale of concentrated power, primarily of an economic and demographic character. The most developed forms of urbanism and the greatest densities and massing of population are found in it, sustained by the most efficient systems for exploiting communications, transport, and use of the land. The key area appears, in the first instance, as the product of the complex interaction of a fixed natural environment, the technologies in use, and forms of social-political organization. It arises in the second instance as the center of a network of economic and allied relationships, with other dependent areas. This combination of key and dependent areas constitutes what we call a symbiotic zone.[1]

The newly arrived settlers from the wild could draw certain advantages from their proximity to more civilized communities. Their villages, now positioned directly on the fringe of the great cities, might perhaps be relieved of the constant bellicose frictions that were the norm of daily life in the most northerly zones. If their work as simple peasant farmers happened to yield some surplus, then the extra crop would be secure from bands of wandering thieves, whose marauding and violent incursions would not be tolerated by the villagers' powerful neighbors. In addition, they could now engage in commercial transactions, which they viewed as advantageous to their interests. Their agricultural products would easily find a market, in return for which they would receive goods that they were incapable of producing. Moreover, the time that they devoted to nonagricultural work would now be more productive for them than it had been before they resettled near the large urban centers. They would fulfill specific work orders, giving them a sense of reward that they had perhaps not known or experienced in the past. In some cases, possibly, the products they turned out may have resulted from training and apprenticing that they received from those who requested these items. In a word, they entered into and joined the network of economic relationships prevailing in the central urban complexes, and they became members of the dependent areas. The first great benefit to them was the almost complete jettisoning of the random character of their life, which had before been grounded more or less exclusively in an agriculture subject to the vicissitudes and cycles of nature. In the wake of this benefit would come the advantages of forming part, albeit in a position far down the rung, of a world of high culture. The great cities looked upon them sympathetically because of their function as a buffer against the trouble caused by incursions of hostile groups from the north.

Within this broad framework, the possibility that the civilized city-dwelling population and its more rough-hewn neighbors managed to find common ground in the realm of religious belief can also be entertained as a hypothetical. Such convergence could have played out on an elementary level, arising both from what the two populations had in common, out of their similar origins as incipient peasant agriculturalists who create the first complex elements of polytheism—with a pointed focus on water and the sun—and from the remnants of still earlier periods that were present in the religion practiced by the civilized groups. The religion of the latter was unquestionably quite different, its richness and complexity expressed and given tangible form in great sanctuaries and temples, sumptuous festivals, an opulent and hierarchical priesthood, cultural advancements realized on both the practical-administrative and artistic-esoteric levels, and complex techniques infused with magic for dominating nature—all of which was built upon and facilitated by the exertions of thousands upon thousands of peasants working the land. But at bottom the two currents of religious thought not only did not directly clash but, through their adherents, may have left some imprint on each other. Of much greater weight, however, was the deep admiration felt by those in the outlying settlements for the lavish rituals practiced by the people of the cities.

In this way, then, the centers of power managed to become agents of homogenization. What had been simply a participation in the worship of religious cults of equal origin and a degree of cultural influence not grounded in any sort of systematic contact was transformed into a full-fledged affirmation of a community of faith. On a lesser scale, the religious complexity of the more cultured pueblos began to be assimilated by the less cultured. Two things—the ineluctable need for a heart, for a central driving force, that all beings had and the initial impulse on the part of humans to personify the heart—gave a particular protector deity to each community. It may be that the participation of the pueblos, expanding by degrees in a very wide network of cultural relations, gave a fixed position to this deity in the pantheon. Thus, in this fashion, each pueblo would be able to locate itself within the order of the symbiotic zone as a whole. At the same time, each group would acquire a location for its god as well as a tradition of which that god had been a part, from the beginning of time—that god who had endowed the group with the specialized form of labor that it had only just obtained in its new state and condition.

The acquisition of a specialized craft permitted these groups to pass over the threshold into a great market economy. In referring to a city of the Classic period, Julio Olivé wrote,

> Economically, we can speak of the regional specialization of work, driven by ecological and cultural factors, within a community that begins to acquire extra-local dimensions, integrating cultural regions. The great centers have full-time specialists who carry out sumptuary work; they require great quantities of agricultural provisions, and the primary materials needed to execute their crafts, which [in turn] spurs commerce and makes the establishment of mercantile channels a necessity.[2]

Beyond the confines of the city, the rude villagers who had come down from the north represented the solution to a set of problems encountered by the civilized city dwellers. They could take charge, without having to live within the area of the local dominant city, of all of the activities that the city's inhabitants found distasteful or preferred to avoid, activities that were almost always linked to geographic regions that furnished needed raw materials. Furthermore, while they maintained their presence in the fields and in agricultural labor generally, they also acquired a needed craft or specialized form of work. On occasion, their specialization might be agriculture itself—for example, when a type of cultivation was the first link in a chain of production, such as the cultivation of the agave plant followed by its use for making pulque or when the particular conditions of the area under cultivation required special knowledge and techniques, as in the case of the *chinampas* (the shallow lake beds that were used to grow certain crops). This dynamic explains how and why an entire pueblo, though its inhabitants were not given to chronic drunkenness, should have as its protector the god of intoxicating drink—pulque—and that it should devote itself to producing a beverage that could not tolerate a prolonged lapse of time between the beginning of its fermentation and its eventual consumption. Because the pulque—the product of a process that took very little time—would soon go bad, it had to enter the market and be sold quickly. These pulque-producing communities had necessarily to depend, if they were to succeed within the market economy, on the immediate receipt by large urban zones of the product of their labors. This situation also explains why, if they were later dislodged from their position in the balanced Classic world, they would find themselves living in areas that no longer matched the required level of pulque production, thus leaving them as the bearers of a tradition that, in many aspects, had become useless to them.

The groups of outlying communities seem to have remained politically autonomous. If their attachment to the urban complex had taken hold spontaneously, and their dependence on it was such as to oblige them to be purchasers and sellers within a single market, what need was there, on the part of the ruling dominant center, to organize and impose a high-flown system of government that would only offend the sensibilities of people who still believed themselves to be free? Yet their subjection, though not apparent on the surface, was nonetheless a reality; hence, a potential problem for the more powerful urban centers—that of forging closer relations with people who perhaps were seen to be ethnically inferior—could be thrust aside. The one-time barbarians preserved their own structure of family lines and lineages, a structure on which many centuries later, in times of recorded history, they would capitalize to limit the exploitation visited on them by state political power. A strong possibility exists that, even in the great cities themselves, the system of political organization was founded on the subsistence of collections of core groups that were organized along family lines, over which the machinery of state control exercised its will, as took place during the Postclassic period. Much later, in the final years of the Postclassic, the history is clear: the state sought to undermine the political foundation of these *calpulli*, with the purpose of extending and tightening central control over the capital city, Mexico-Tenochtitlan, during the despotic rule of Motecuhzoma Xocoyotzin.

Both the religious character of large-scale structures and edifices and the abundant representations of priests indicate that in the Classic period religion was the principal integrating force within society.[3] Initially, it may have been exclusively over their own urban people that the dominant group of the civilized centers exercised magical-religious-calendrical power and authority. As the dependent areas grew more extensive with the arrival of new groups, however, those recently settled on the fringe must have been greatly impressed by these same ritual techniques and ways of prophesying future events and fortunes, good or ill. In a more or less spontaneous fashion, the outlying villagers could have been drawn to the acceptance and acquisition of these divinatory practices and techniques, with the result that the cord of subjection was wrapped one notch tighter. Under these circumstances and conditions, the creation and stationing of a military force was not needed. If such a force was needed to take care of *external* problems, there were dependent pueblos that specialized in the art of war—and persisted in doing so into the historical era—that were led, of course, by military experts belonging to the dominant centers.

Sometime later, disaster struck. Many words have been spilled in trying to explain the crisis that engulfed the Classic period urban centers. The theories—some put forward and defended more robustly, some less—that have been propounded include, as the main agent, a spreading decadence, the appearance of epidemics or radical climate change, the exhaustion of the land, earthquakes or other physical calamities, the influence of superstition or religious beliefs, the pressure of wars both external and internal as well as uprisings and revolutions.[4] In this connection, a problem that dates to a later time, the revolt of the nonohualcas, who abandoned the lands that they cultivated because they were no longer willing to work for the Toltecs, has been projected back onto the Classic period.[5] This line of reasoning seems plausible, since a state of affairs that had held in the absence of military subjection could have unraveled for a lack of symbiosis. It is perfectly imaginable that the world of the Classic period continued receiving a steady inflow of barbarian peoples and that for a certain span of time it also maintained the capacity to assimilate them as dependents. But because the men of the cities wanted to draw a strict line between themselves and those whom they viewed as inferior, they steered away from incorporating these outliers beyond the minimum that was needed to assure the success of commercial transactions. Naturally, the day arrived when the avarice of the powerful grew out of all proportion to the advantages realized by the dependent groups, and the subject population, perhaps sufficiently developed by then to obtain its own goods for subsistence, no longer secured from their more civilized urban counterparts any benefits that could not safely be renounced. The once-advantageous symbiosis had become parasitical; the civilized city dwellers had lost their capacity to arrange things for themselves and satisfy their needs without the participation of outlying village groups, and the rebellion, which need not have been bloody, since the movement of peoples could evade armed conflict, spread like a stain, and the Classic world fell apart. Armillas has stated that no abrupt transformation of the social structure took place.[6] Some centers remained, composed now of those who were the inheritors of what had been a monumental epoch. Between the catastrophe and the subsequent reconstruction a considerable period of time must have elapsed, a time of painful anguish for the civilized survivors, sunk in misery and chaos, and of a more or less normal life for the oppressed, who paid only a small price for their refusal to remain any longer in a dependent state. By the same token, however, the rebel groups were incapable of taking a truly evolutionary step. The best that they could manage was to begin a slow process of reconstruction that, unsurprisingly, took some rather odd twists and turns. The culture of the Classic period was not entirely obliterated, as many of its savants entered into the service of the victorious parties, but it lacked an economic and political foundation; consequently, many of the cultural attainments of that era disappeared. The ensuing disequilibrium led to a state in which the migrations seem to have been considered the virtual norm, and two important elements of the myth were perhaps fortified during this epoch: that of the birth of the pueblos as occurring in a place that would not hold them permanently and that of the need to undertake the search for their promised place of settlement.

The lack of great centers with a consumer population caused the remnant elements of villages that had evolved a specialized craft to gather together in new cities in which the heterogeneity of the *calpulli* might promote an interchange of goods that commerce along the path of the migrations could not completely satisfy. The tutelary gods of the villages came to be those of the *calpulli*—social units that were particularly suitable for the migratory way of life— and the dispersion of peoples unquestionably precipitated a distinct evolution in the name, the attributes, and the manner of worshipping these divinities.

I believe that this scenario rather than the hypothetical confrontation between two conjectured social classes—the military and the priesthood—is the more likely one. To begin with, the idea that the defining events of the Late Classic period revolved around a struggle for supremacy between these two social classes does not rest on anything solid. In the Postclassic period—and logic would argue that this was also true in the Classic period—priests and warriors formed part of a single dominant group, to which administrative authorities also belonged. On many occasions, the three functions were carried out by the same individual. There is no reason why militarism should be seen, even from the standpoint of logical inference, as a stage that comes after theocracy. Rather, it is more correct to see it as a state designed to serve a transitory purpose, in which the expectation is to subject first by force of arms those who, at a later point, endeavoring to avoid tensions, frictions, the loss of men, and discontent in general, will submit to authority through the more hypocritical avenues of religion and social and political institutions deemed "eternal" in nature. The militarism of the Postclassic period is simply the result of the immediate organizing capacities of those who, now enjoying a favorable position, strove to recover a modicum of the glories of the past. The tendency of the new rulers was to supplant militaristic authority with strong and respected institutions, like those that had earlier guaranteed an exceptional degree of social and political harmony.

As bands of rebellious groups broke away and dispersed, those select men who were accustomed—because it was their function in life—to speak with the protector god undoubtedly played a prominent role. Moreover, they would not lead and direct their community as simple human beings; to assure that the end point of the journey would be crowned by a happier life for all in the group, a greater force, a force beyond the mere human, was needed. For now (in this hypothetical reconstruction of the Late Classic and Early Postclassic worlds) it was they, and they alone who, by possessing the god's force in their heart, spoke through him and conveyed his word to their pueblo. Leadership and political command must have been very heterogeneous, but the force of the gods undoubtedly fired the spirit of warrior daring, with the result that in a good many cases the positions of hombre-dios and of chief leader of the group coincided. At other times, the group was led by a collegial body, in which the hombres-dioses occupied an important position. It should be understood that such plural leadership came about, for the most part, when several migrant groups joined together, particularly when they passed through hostile territories and needed to assemble and wield greater military force.

The plurality of hombres-dioses and of other principal figures—all of whom were leaders of different groups that came together during the journey—doubtless produced problems when the time arrived to found permanent settlements. A simple comparison of forces would have likely determined who the general god of the new site would be and who would become his representative. When two groups were both very powerful, the ensuing government was possibly divided, so that, in turn, two places were consecrated as protector mountains. This same division must have occurred in cities in which a dominant group imposed itself over a population that continued to be sizeable. For example, in addition to its great, water-filled pyramid of Quetzalcoatl, Cholollan was home to the far more ancient worship of Tlachihualtepetl, dedicated to the gods of water.[7] This type of accommodation or arrangement could give rise to dual governments. Bernardino de Sahagún appears to confirm this situation in the case of Tollan, before which he simultaneously places Quetzalcoatl and Huemac.[8] Other cases are more obscure since, while they unquestionably involve two rulers, it is impossible to know whether the particular institutional structure demanded this, as it did in the governments led by consorts, when each consort, as the result of being either an hombre-dios or mujer-diosa, occupied his or her place. Two examples of this situation are the governments of Huactli and Xiuhtlacuilolxochitzin and of Cuauhtli and Coacueye.[9]

What is crystal clear is that in many of the newly founded pueblos, hombres-dioses became the rulers, and their descendants—in some cases the fading of their mysticism is readily apparent—continued through dynastic succession to hold this position. Among the numerous communities that could be cited as followers of this practice are the Cakchiquel;[10] the Maya of Tiquinbalón, governed by Erbalam;[11]

the Nahua of Ehecatlan, governed by Ehecatl; or the Totonaca of Tutulla, ruled over by Tutul and his descendants.[12]

The dispersion of power resulting in the simple leadership of chieftains and hombres-dioses undoubtedly awakened the desire, among those who had belonged to or had lived near the major centers of power, to promote a new paradigm of rule. The surviving cults of those urban complexes were certainly highly valued, but their value now manifested itself differently. Now they were appreciated not as the objects of worship constitutive of numerous groups but as individual cults that became incorporated into the strongest villages. Others, by contrast, could perhaps continue in their old integrative form within smaller settlements, distinguished, as a matter of pride, from the rest, from those possibly called Chichimecas at that juncture—from men, that is, who came from outside and beneath the old Mesoamerican tradition.

The newly empowered and the priests and savants in their service were not able peaceably to reunite those men who had proved themselves capable of sustaining an independent life. It was perhaps at this moment that the concept arose of Tollan as a conquering city of the newly dominant who succeeded in extending their reach and control by force of arms. Actions of this type could accentuate the military characteristics of the god Quetzalcoatl, who has now taken the form of Tlahuizcalpantecuhtli, the warrior of dawn. And in Mayan lands the conquerors of Quetzalcoatl, who crush their opposition, impose political dominion, and invent human sacrifice, make their appearance.[13] The run of violence brought about a current of religious thinking, and after it flowered and took root, there was a belief that peace and tranquility were possible. The warrior caste became ardent worshippers of order and peace, and each great city that received the name of Tollan could assure itself of the loyalty of the groups it ruled, when their kings came forward, professing religious devotion, to submit themselves to the authority of only one hombre-dios, a superior hombre-dios, Quetzalcoatl, Nacxit. Due to this turn of events, Cholollan, for example, was transformed into the foundational site of religion in the region of the central plateau[14] and the cultural centers of Kukulcan arose in Yucatán:

> It is the opinion among the Indians that a great lord named Cuculcán reigned with the yzaes who settled Chichenizá, and that the truth of this is shown in the main edifice, which is called Cuculcán; and they say that he came from out of the west and that they differ about whether he made his way in before or after the yzaes or with them, and they say that he was of comely appearance and had neither wife nor children; and that after his return he was taken as a god in México and called Cezalcuati and that he was also taken as a god in Yucatán because he was a great republican, and that this was perceived in the seat of authority that he instituted

in Yucatán after the death of the lords, to ease the dissension that their deaths had brought about in the land.

[And] that this Cuculcán returned to settle another city, dealing with the native lords of the land, that he and they might come (to the city) and that all matters and transactions might come through and [be handled] there; and that for this [to be so] they chose a very good seat of authority eight leagues further into the land where Mérida now lies, and fifteen or sixteen leagues from the sea; and that they encircled it with a very wide wall of dry stone of some quarter of a league, leaving only two narrow doors and the wall not too high, and in the middle of this enclosure they built their temples; and that they called the largest one, which is like the one in Chicheniza, Cuculcán . . . and that inside this enclosure they built houses for the lords, among whom alone the lands were parceled out, allotting pueblos to each one according to the antiquity of his lineage and his personal stature.[15]

Among the new settlements, those that were of greatest size and occupied a leading position became jurisdictional centers, and important matters of a legal nature had to be brought before them. This status held for Chollolan, where the *tlachtac* and the *achtac* were accepted as supreme judges,[16] and also applied to Yucatán, where the mythical Nacxit, in addition to being "the sole supreme judge of all the kingdoms," dispensed the emblems and insignias that were necessary for the hombres-dioses to become, magically and with a much augmented divine power, the rulers of their pueblos.[17] Step by step, all of these events and processes became increasingly grounded in religious justification. The tendency to give greater weight to the worship of a supreme god, such as characterized the Toltecs, quite possibly sprang from this development.[18] The pueblos that were under the influence of the new great centers and had reckoned each one of their protector numens to be somewhat distanced from a hierarchical order, now had to confront—with their outlook shaped, first and foremost, by the presence of foreign arms, the alternative—that a superior order did exist, presided over by the god of heaven, the creator of the world, and of the gods, men, animals, and all things. Next to him, very close—much closer than any of the other gods—was now found Quetzalcoatl, who was given a role second to none: creating humankind. In this way, the god Quetzalcoatl became and went on being a kind of captain of the particular creators of pueblos, and all had to subordinate themselves to him.

A lineage could be derived from each hombre-dios whose godly connection was to Quetzalcoatl. According to Juan Bautista Pomar, the historical accounts and chronicles served fundamentally to establish and validate the line of descent.[19] All of the native lords, right to the eve of the Spanish conquest, said of themselves that they were descendants of Quetzalcoatl.[20] Four disciples of Ce Acatl ruled in

Cholollan.[21] Much further away, in the region of Oaxaca, Mixtecatl also inaugurated his family line of kings, and every pueblo that for some reason had lost its rulers followed the practice of coming before him.[22] Tollan was the dispenser of power, furnishing both sons who were the founding heads of lineages and sacred bundles with divine fire. The city also confirmed hombres-dioses in their power; the latter in many cases had to have their nasal septum perforated to demonstrate the rights that had been delegated to them, from the heavens and on the earth, through Quetzalcoatl. The world was reconstructed, and everyone within it desired a return to normality—or almost everyone, because the members of one-time dependent pueblos had been able to savor what their independence brought them.

Quetzalcoatl came to be more the source and the symbol of power than power itself. Many of the biographies of him reveal him to us as the mystic locked up in his house made of wooden planks. A reasonable supposition is that all around him, with the strong Chichimeca on one side and a body of cultivated persons in reciprocal service to them on the other, a new set of high-level administrators had been formed—military leaders, priests, engineers, judges—who also held themselves up as being part of an elite corps of specialists, as persons wise in the ways of power, to whom the ignorant would have to appeal. To the religious pretext was thus added that of government. Furthermore, the level at which government then operated indeed made these men indispensable when *calpulli* sought to integrate themselves into settlements that offered something more than so-called "military government."

Tollan's name as heralding the great city that dispensed power disappeared. The great centers of population that were called by that name, that had flourished at one time and been able to reorganize their world, came to be ineffective. Those that followed in their wake lacked the name but still maintained the pretension of command. What happened to the Tollans? Possibly, a proliferation of centers took place; and, with all of them laying claim to and enjoying the same rights, each could have presented itself as possessor of the lineage of the sacred fire of Quetzalcoatl and of the fitness to command. Each, therefore, wanted to live as an independent entity, with the result that the recourse to arms and military conflict again came to be employed with relative frequency. This development loomed large, along with the element of the political, which endeavored to achieve a new type of equilibrium. The powerful states that commanded and dispensed power and exercised a greater or lesser degree of dominance across extensive zones planned and created alliances that were oftentimes triple in character. This was the state of affairs when one of the many pueblos that roamed about—the community of lake-based fisherman and hunters—inserted itself into the fray.

In falling within this scheme, the Mexica were forced to deal with the power relations that governed this world of tribal alliances. Like all communities, they had a double origin—that is, they were born in two mythical places. In the first sacred place, they were created as human beings; subsequently, they lived in a second sacred place, from which they later emerged into the world. They were guided by their *calpulteteo* (their *calpulli*'s patron gods)—Quetzalcoatl, Xomoco, Matla, Xochiquetzal, Chichitic, Centeutl, Piltzintecuhtli, Meteutli, Tezcatlipoca, Mictlantecuhtli, Tlamacazqui[23]—and at the head of all these gods, in the lead position, Huitzilopochtli. Each new group that wished to incorporate itself into the pilgrimage route had to submit to the supreme will of the dominant god.[24] And while each group composed its own story of the pilgrimage, it is nonetheless likely that these were all variations on what had been compressed into one central version of the migration. Despite the compression and whittling down, however, the collective experience of this movement and settlement of peoples also likely included an intense and difficult political life, one replete with intrigue and misdeeds. One such conflict was captured in the story of Malinalxochitl, the mujer-diosa who was abandoned because of her lack of discipline. Some divisions could not be resolved, so that it was necessary to found dual settlements—as exemplified in the case of Mexico-Tenochtitlan and Mexico-Tlatelolco.

The site eventually chosen as the place of settlement was the one that best suited the dominant family groups within the greater body, those that would extract maximum benefit from the environs tailored to their hunting, fishing, and cultivation of crops on *chinampas*. The remaining *calpulli* sensed the appeal and advantages of forming part of a larger whole. It held promise for those seeking a way to advance their interests in a population base that was large enough to provide them outlets for the products that they specialized in making. Cuauhtlequetzqui and Tenoch, two of the most important hombres-dioses, appear to have reached an agreement in deciding on the ritual and symbolic aspect of the settlement. Cuauhtlequetzqui pointedly represented Huitzilopochtli, the eagle that devoured the bird or the serpent, while Tenoch performed the same function for the stone and the nopal.[25] Were all of these representations elements of one ritual and one symbol? And if not, which god did Tenoch represent? The matter is quite opaque, since on the one hand it was always stressed that the only important numen was Huitzilopochtli, while on the other certain reports to the contrary existed that went unnoticed, among them the doubtless heterodox commentary that Mexico-Tenochtitlan's principal god was Tezcatlipoca.[26] Tlaloc, Tezcatlipoca, and Mictlantecuhtli were all unquestionably of great importance.

In the end, both priests found the eagle's sign: a shallow lake, nutrient; firm islands for the core group; cattails, reeds, an aggregation of birds' nests; schools of silvery fish. And before them appeared the vision: hands that drove rows of posts into the gummy mud to make the walls of the chinampas, sinking down poles that had been polished smooth by the chafed skin of the men who made them; paddles with rounded ends, flat as a griddle, that were used to load canoes dangerously full with silt; machete-like instruments, made of wood, stuck into seedbeds to separate the small plants growing in the black soil; willows that steadied areas of land; the sharp sounds of hard blade and flesh that broke forth with the vibrating blow of the *minacachalli* (a trident-like spear); paddles that slapped the water; nets swollen with fish; stalks of corn that sprouted—it was the miracle.

The settlement, as founded, kept its two names: one that of Huitzilopochtli—Mexi—the other that of Tenoch, in parallel fashion to the name of the leading hombre-dios and to the name corresponding to the second son of the great progenitors Iztacmixcoatl and Ilancueitl. All of the remaining protector gods were grouped around Huitzilopochtli, as subordinates, distributed among their respective *calpulli*, and, in reproduction of the important sites—*Cuauhxicalli, tlachco, tzompantli*—of the archetypal city, the settlement was built up and took shape. The government was placed under the control of Tenoch, and thus began the enterprise of an autonomous life, undertaken without requesting a group of rulers from any of the powerful neighboring communities that flanked it. Things went on like this for some years. Now split off, the Tenochca Mexica led the Culhua, and the Tlatelolca Mexica did likewise for the Tepaneca of Azcapotzalco. The moment was not propitious for the two groups to patch over and resolve their division, and each of the city-states set off on its course independently of the other under the prevailing norms of political conduct. Or, to put the case slightly differently, the rule of ordinary hombres-dioses did not find it possible to confront and master a political situation as complex as that which afflicted the central part of the lake-based region.

The beginning of the Culhua lineage in Mexico-Tenochtitlan presents serious problems of interpretation. Some sources allocate too much importance to a woman named, as the mother of the original Tenuch, Ilancueitl. It is extremely difficult to form an unclouded idea of this lineal process because there is no uniform or consistent explanation of how Acamapichtli and Ilancueitl came to be chosen as the first sovereigns of Mexico-Tenochtitlan. The one and only thing that clearly stands out is that the legitimacy of the Mexica-Tenochca dynastic line was tied to interests that were responsible, a posteriori, for the refinement of quite diverse traditions. The same role of an original *cihuacoatl*—that is, a public office the name of which corresponded to that of a feminine divinity, and that served as the immediate auxiliary of the *tlatoani*—has been attributed to Ilancueitl,[27] who would be the coadjutrix of her husband; or alternatively, it has been ascribed to him,[28] as he could also be considered the *cihuacoatl* of his wife, following which he filled the office of *tlatoani*.

In line with all members of the Culhua nobility, Acamapichtli was said to be a very remote descendant of Quetzalcoatl. Wanting their own families to reap the benefits of this lineage, all of the leaders of the various *calpulli* gave one of their daughters to the Culhua lord. The *tlatoani* who succeeded him, his son, was the grandson of Cuauhtlequetzqui and therefore partook of the fire of Huitzilopochtli. Apparently, however, having been fathered by Acamapichtli was not sufficient in itself to endow one with the requisite divine fire, so that all his sons, though born to the daughters of his vassal lords, were also treated as the offspring of Ilancueitl. This woman, a mujer-diosa to judge by her name and her stature, while barren, nevertheless "gave birth" to her husband's children. As she lay in bed, they were each brought to her to hold, as though she were the natural mother and had delivered them.[29] In this way, based on the teaching and preparation that they received in the schools administered by the Culhua nobility, the divine fire that they inherited from Acamapichtli or Ilancueitl, and the ascendancy on earth that representatives of Huitzilopochtli enjoyed, beginning with Huitzilihuitl, the descendants of Acamapichtli began to lead the Tenocha Mexica in all matters of state. More effective still, the third *tlatoani* was Chimalpopoca, a Cuecuex (perhaps the name of a lineage as well as that of a god), and grandson hombre-dios of the then most powerful and feared hombre-dios: the Tepaneca Tezozomoc of Azcapotzalco. This line of descent, however, did not continue, because another Cuecuex, Maxtla, assassinated his Tenochca nephew.

What could have been the continuing exercise of rule in Mexico-Tenochtitlan by hombres-dioses seems to have come to an end with Chimalpopoca. The political needs of the state went considerably beyond what a ruler charged with religious obligations, and possessing a mystical presence and personality, could provide. The adept administration of men of practical skills was the need of the hour, although some of the *tlatoque* of neighboring kingdoms still retained their rank and position as hombres-dioses. For the Tenochca Mexica, however, it was sufficient that a ruler possess the divine fire in his heart to the extent that he needed it, and that he maintain it through the simplest curative remedies and magical measures: bits of *quetzalilin* (a medicinal plant), flowers from the magnolia tree, the blood of wild animals, a quantity of precious stones, the flesh of a white rabbit … and all else that worked to strengthen and fortify those who carried out the duties of a public office.[30] The problem did not lie at the level of the ruler but beneath it, in the pueblo.

Itzcoatl, a *tlatoani* who retained the faculty of serving as an oracle of Huitzilopochtli,[31] as did others who followed him down to the arrival of the Spanish, issued an order that books of history should be burned. His edict has been interpreted as constituting an attempt to change the historical narrative because it failed to square with the new impulse to militaristic expansion that began at this point in his rule.[32] This reading is partially correct, above all as it relates to the change that was made to the original pact that obtained between the pueblo and its protector god. In addition, however, the book burning has been viewed as the destruction of a secular library in which the wisdom of the great, powerful states had been distilled, a library that had been passed along from one political center to another, whether as something that legitimized its inheritance of power, or whether as the simple booty of war.[33] I believe that this latter view is overly colored by the experience of the Library of Alexandria. We need to remember that the initial activity of recording historical events and processes took place within groups that belonged to a particular locale and that each *calpulli*, to satisfy its immediate needs, carried this vitally important instrument with it. Thus, for example, it can be affirmed that the Xochimilcas had journeyed alone and brought their pictographic manuscripts with them.[34] Similarly, as reported by Fuentes y Guzmán, the history of the Quiché *calpullis* in Guatemala had been recorded in a formal way.[35] To a certain extent these histories were composed to aid and fulfill the internal needs and imperatives of communities, for which a uniform storyline was of little moment. That the versions of one pueblo versus another, or of multiple pueblos, did not correlate was therefore immaterial. Each looked on things from its own perspective, "and since Mexican history[36] treats not of alien deeds but of its own, it overlooks those that do not touch upon it."[37]

> Since I am sure that if I went to Tacuba to ask about their glorious deeds the people there would tell me that they had been greater than Motecuhzoma's. This situation has tied my hands and has made it impossible to fulfill my desire to write a history of each city, state, and town. There is no village, small as it may be, that does not take credit for all the grandeur of Motecuhzoma. All of these towns claim that they were exempt from tribute, had royal insignia, and were the victors in war. I speak from experience because in a certain town in the Marquesado I asked about their power and preeminence in ancient times and they exaggerated to such an extent, raising this superiority to the skies, that before they reached the stars with their tales I was forced, with soft words, to get them to admit that they had been subjects of and had paid tribute to Nezahualpilli of Tezcoco, who had subjected them in a fair war."[38]

In this context, it is useful to recall what León y Gama related (see page 118) regarding the priests who were in charge of carrying the history that recorded the origin of the gods and of the times in which the captains and leaders, who would be transformed into those gods,[39] had been born. Particularly relevant on this score is some brief text, that I have transcribed and translated below, that explains the conduct of Itzcoatl:

> amo monequi mocha tlacatl quimatiz in tlilli, in tlapalli. In itconi, in tlamamaloni ahuilquizaz, auh inin zan nahualmaniz in tlalli. Ic miec, mopic in iztlacayotl, ihuan miequintin neteutiloque.[40]

(It is unnecessary that everyone knows the black ink, the red ink [the books]. The one that is borne, the one that is carried on one's back [the pueblo] will be harmed, and the land will be naught but intrigues. Because many lies have been invented and many have been worshipped as gods.)

Nothing is concealed or even merely suggestive in Itzcoatl's words. On the contrary, he declares forthrightly that difficulties are caused when the pueblo knows its history, when it stands in possession of it. If this condition is allowed, intrigue and discord will break out and the pueblo will not be ruled, as it rightly should be, by the group that holds power—by men, coming from Culhuacan, who struggle just to make their subjects pleased with their rulership. The force of the *calpulli* was substantial, and it was these very books, as instruments that created awareness and, through their guidelines, directed historical-ritual conduct, that could serve as the foundation for movements to break away from the imperial center and reclaim independence. It was not the history of a remote past that posed a threat, because that was perfectly consonant with the purposes for which the pueblo was established. The outline and content of that history fed into the stream of the wider Mesoamerican world—its origin, its account of the birth of humankind, and its protector gods. All that had to be done with the history from ancient times was to change the terms of the pact that governed the relationship between rulers and gods. Rather, what brought harm, or could potentially do so, was the history of the *calpulli* that the current elders of the community possessed and would pass down. And more harmful still was the historical tradition that served, in some measure both as a memorial and as the object of a rite, to install hombres-dioses. The latter may have proliferated when three principal groups—lake-based fishermen, hunters, and peasants who grew crops—saw themselves being mobilized and armed for a fight that they considered alien to their interests. It was the Culhua nobility who wanted to wage war, not the people; and the voice of rebellion was again trumpeted by those who carried the pueblo's god in their heart and his words on their lips. These individuals, the ones who "were falsely worshipped as gods," were the men who must disappear so that the intrigue and plotting might cease and "the one who carried [the sacred bundle] on his back, the one who bore it," would leave off from doing so. The intrigues that distanced Mexico-Tenochtitlan from its majesty and glory, the glory that war and conquest had fathered, and not the peace favored by the population of lacustrine fisherman and peasants, had to be ended. To put an end to the hombres-dioses it was necessary to cancel out or shrink the historical memory of the *calpulli*. Subsequently, additional steps needed to be taken; these men had to be brought together and absorbed within some institutionalized framework. The force exerted by young men, whose qualities marked them as future hombres-dioses, had to be annulled. Born and raised as they were among the subject population, they represented the possibility of a new dangerous leadership. The simplest way to annul their power was by co-opting them, so that they responded to and cultivated the interests of the nobles, whether through placing them ahead of the *macehualtin* (commoners) and permitting them to discharge fiscal, administrative, and judicial responsibilities that were typically given to the *tetecuhtin* (nobles) for brave conduct in war, or giving them a status that was completely distinct from that of commoners, by granting them hierarchical offices, including the highest positions within the priesthood, when—should the political tides shift—matters of religion and their own affinity for the same could result in their serving at the head of a rebellious *calpulli*. Bernardino de Sahagún pointedly addressed himself to this process of co-optation and absorption:

> The one who had distinguished his way of life and observed the precepts of the priests of the idols, he was the one chosen as the high priest, the ruler or lord and all the nobles selected him, and they gave him the name of Quetzalcoatl; and there were two high priests ... and these two high priests were equal in station, although they were of low rank, and their father, their mother, were the poorest of the poor, the reason they were chosen to be high priests was because they carried out well the way of life, the precepts of the priests who served the idols in the monastery of the *calmécac*.
> 
> And for this reason, they gave one the name Quetzalcoatl, or the name Totec tlamacazqui, and the other was named Tlaloc tlamacazqui; and in the choice lineage was not considered, only practices and precepts and a good life, whether the high priests had these, whether they lived chastely and observed the practices of the priests of the idols: the one who was righteous, humble, and tranquil, who considered others, [and was] constant, and modest, and firm, tender in his practices, and compassionate of others, a friend to all and devout and god-fearing.[41]

The nobles (*pipiltin*) looked for the most distinguished students attending the *telpochcalli* (schools that largely taught practical and military skills) and, "as a prize," transferred them to one of their own schools, the *calmécac*. The pueblo, which considered this to be an honor, was unaware of the great price that it paid by allowing its most talented sons to be siphoned off by the nobles. The existence of hombres-dioses in the old sense contravened the prevailing political-military interests. Their responsibilities were now taken up by the kings, and—emblematic of this reordering—Motecuhzoma Ilhuicamina ordered that all of the *tlatoque* should be worshipped. They were enjoined to abstain even from showing themselves in public[42] and, employing the divine fire they possessed within them, they became the ones who furnished the protection that the city as a whole required. If his ancestor, Itzcoatl, had "centralized" history by burning the codices and beginning the construction of an official history, then he proceeded to centralize in the kings—without the need to transform them into mystical penitents—the power to protect their subjects.

The protector god could also be appropriated by the nobles, who descended from the daughter of Cuauhtlequetzqui. Motecuhzoma Ilhuicamina could now provide assurance that Huitzilopochtli was their god, although he still identified the Mexica as villains and traitors.[43] With their god, the *pipiltin* military forces could begin the great militarized expansion that both Alfonso Caso and Miguel León-Portilla characterized as impelled by warrior-like mysticism.[44] History reverted to the very moment in which the Mexica had departed their ancestral homeland and began their migration, to the time they made their pact with Tetzauhteotl. Cristóbal del Castillo paints a picture for us that is wholly military in character: the god promises to bestow riches and dominion in exchange for the hearts of the conquered pueblos.[45] This, unquestionably, is the official version of the historical narrative that was precipitated in the change wrought by Itzcoatl. The promise that was made leaves no room for doubt:

> And the teomamas called to their older brother, who led them and was king of the mexicanos, [and] whose name was that of Chalchiuhtlatonac, and Huitzilopochtli said to Chalchiuhtlatonac: "come, o Chalchiuhtlatonac, and with care and deliberation arrange all that is needed so that you lead the many people who will set off with you; and may each one of the seven *calpulli* inherit those whom they shall catch here, those who had fallen nearby the spiny cactus; of the strongest and sturdiest of the mexicanos, since the natives will be innumerable, because we will go forth to [make] settlements, and we shall conquer the natives who are settled in the universe; and I therefore tell you in all truth that I will make you lords, kings of all that there is everywhere in the world; and when you are kings, there you shall have countless, interminable, an infinite number of vassals, who shall pay you tribute, give you countless, very fine precious stones, gold, quetzal feathers, emeralds, corals, amethysts, that you shall wear most exquisitely, as well as different feathers, [of] the blue *cotinga*, the red flamingo, the *tzinitzcan*, all of the precious feathers, and the cacao of varied colors, and the poly-chromatic cotton; and all of it shall you see, since verily this is my task and for this was I sent here.[46]

The myth of the donation of the instruments of office gets distorted so that no longer will the *átlatl* be used to propel the spear that wounds ducks with its three-pointed head but, instead, will be the weapon for spears that are thrown against enemy warriors. In time, the Mexica will aspire to dedicate themselves to no other calling than that of war: "and thus little by little [the city of Mexico-Tenochtitlan] was rebuilt [after the flood caused by the waters of the Acuecuéxatl], because every day the mexicanos said that they did not know how to do it, that it was not their craft or charge, but instead to conquer, to cut flint, to make knives and to bend poles into place for arrows and spears, and for the moment this was what all of the mexican people waited for."[47]

The Mexica did no more than imitate those stonecutters and builders who had returned to being specialists in all the arts and crafts and later resumed fulfilling the offices and duties of priests and administrators. Just as the Toltecs before them had altered course, so they, too, moved from lacustrine activities to those organized around military conflict through no more than changing a contract and switching to a throwing weapon. Their god, Huitzilopochtli, transformed his invention: as the god who bestowed types of work and specialized crafts, he now became the one who had granted knowledge of human sacrifice and of war to men.[48] This development does not mean, as historians during the immediate post-conquest period wrongly concluded, that sacrifices and wars had been introduced by the Mexica. On the contrary, their origins lay much further back. At the beginning of human time, a *dema*-type god had made an invention, the substance of which he gifted to one of the pueblos: its members would be specialists in the military arts, in conquest, and in nourishing the gods with blood and the hearts of men.

In line with these developments, Quetzalcoatl began gradually to be replaced. According to later versions of the pueblo's history, the dynasty, from Acamapichtli down, had been founded by Huitzilopochtli.[49] The substitution of Huitzilopochtli for Quetzalcoatl may help explain why so many different versions appeared concerning the origin of the first *tlatoani*, whom some sources claim was the son of a Mexica. In addition, it came to be said that Acamapichtli was as esteemed as Topiltzin Quetzalcoatl, of whom only a vague recollection remained.[50] Something similar was attempted in the allied domain of Aculhuacan, where an effort was made to trace all of the lineages of the existing kings back to Xolotl.[51]

Motecuhzoma Xocoyotzin hatched a wonderful plan centered around a similar type of replacement, and one day he called for Tzompantecuhtli to tell him about it. The old Toltec source of power could be dispensed with if power now resided, as it did, in the hands of those whose dwelling place lay in the center of the lake. He confided to the nobleman,

> It has seemed necessary to me that Huitzilopochtli's house be of solid gold, and that inside it be of chalchicuites and of rich quetzalli feathers . . . thus it will be necessary [to have] the world's tribute; because our god will be in need of it. What do you think? Tzompanteuctli responded, saying: 'our Lord and King, it is not so. Be advised that with this you shall hasten the downfall of your pueblo and you will offend the Heavens that we see above us. Understand that the one who is here now

does not have to be our god; that he is coming, that the master of everything and creator of all creatures is going to arrive . . .' Upon hearing [these words], Motecuhzoma became enraged and said to Tzompantecutli: 'Be off with you and be revolted by your words.' In this way Tzompantecutli and all his children perished.[52]

It was not enough for Mexico-Tenochtitlan to be one of the most feared and respected of the powerful city-states; it aspired to be "the heart of the entire earth."[53] To be the heart on such a scale it was necessary that its tutelary god be transformed from protector of the city into protector of the world. It began to be revered everywhere, in the festival of *coailhuitl*,[54] until the religious worship of all of Mexico-Tenochtitlan's subject pueblos was reshaped by their Tenochca conquerors.[55] While there is scant evidence that the claim is true, the complete subjection of Nezahualcoyotl was attributed by the Mexica to Huitzilopochtli, as the supreme god.[56] The historians of Motecuhzoma have doubtless been guilty of exaggeration, but what is not in doubt is that the Tetzcocano monarch was forced to erect an enormous temple in his capital in honor of the numen of his powerful ally, Mexico-Tenochtitlan.

A notable change seems to have come over the memory and recollection of Quetzalcoatl. There is evidence that human sacrifices took place in Tula Xicocotitlan,[57] although these are judged to have occurred during the final years of the city's history. As has been seen, the Yucatecan Ru Ralcan or Kukulcan distinguished himself as a conqueror and inventor of human sacrifice, as Huitzilopochtli would later be. In Tenochtitlan, in the temple called Ilhuicatitlan, human sacrifices were carried out to honor the Morning Star.[58] Every fourth year, a young captive who represented Quetzalcoatl was sacrificed in Cholollan, a city that—as many traditions held—came down directly from Ce Acatl. The priests who cut open the chests of captives bore the names Topiltzin and Quetzalcoatl.[59] Alva Ixtlilxóchitl, defending the absence of sacrifices in Tollan, states that annually only five or six young maidens were offered to Tlaloc and just one adult male to Tonacatecuhtli.[60] From where, then, does the tradition arise of an absence of sacrifices in Tollan to Quetzalcoatl? The question is difficult to answer. The myth may have assured that the blood of men was not needed for the movement of the stars until the Sun began its course. This would give to the heavenly personage, at least during one of the stages of the narration of the myth, the role of a god who had no relation to human sacrifice—and in human sacrifice the beginning of a forceful push in the astral process that coincided with the movement of the heavens. The application of this principle to the life of the Toltecs could have been forgotten during the first years of the Toltec political-military expansion, when the use of force was required, and upheld in a later period as the basis of their form of government, when it became feasible to impose rule through the instruments of stable political institutions and religious ideology. The principle could also have been sustained, and with greater force still, by all those communities that later opposed the militaristic course pursued by people like the Tepaneca and the Mexica. And even for the Tepaneca and Mexica, to invoke a way of life that ran contrary to one replete with sacrifices and war, which was precisely the life that their god, Huitzilopochtli, had aided with his invention, was not absolutely wrong-headed.

At bottom, the Mexica, too, wanted the cost of rule to be less. In time, as the centuries passed, a weariness of war as the modus vivendi of life set in, and the attempt to spread the worship of Huitzilopochtli as the prime leader and that of his sons as modern Toltecs, creators of ruling nuclei of government, augured—as was evident to all—a changed life. At the very least, a consciousness that the world was going to change is apparent in the words that Motecuhzoma Xocoyotzin directed to Quetzalacxoyatl: "And it is true that [before], the countryside was reddened and the clouds gave off smoke and the day was dun-colored, dark in all of its parts: people died in the defense of this honor, and the elders carried it out: now we take pleasure in it with hands not stained by blood, without [it] costing us the spilling of Mexican blood: now, as you well know, the Mexicanos will not lord it over the entire world?"[61]

The era of peaceful, religious rule was purportedly to begin when other conquerors arrived, the said sons of Ce Acatl, the men outfitted in metal. What was to be done, what action taken, in the face of them? Motecuhzoma Xocoyotzin must have looked on with horror when the one he had tried to expel, to banish, came back. Rather than act like a Mexica warrior, Motecuhzoma chose to act like a refined, peace-loving Culhua. It was the stark awareness of a return to believing in the transitory seat of Quetzalcoatl.

I earlier stated that one of the ways of stifling and doing away with the hombres-dioses of the Tenochca *calpulli* was to harness them institutionally. Before examining just how they and their power were suppressed and annulled, it will be useful to observe what occurred outside the Mexica capital, where a similar process of curtailment and absorption was also necessary.

The government presided over by a mystical hombre-dios, a government limited in its actions and operations by time, space, and strict regulation of its conduct, subject to overly fallible rules of succession and frequently at odds in its very character with the delivery of effective rule, came to produce figures who were truly ornamental, repositories of the pueblo's fortune in terms purely of their magical-religious activities, or—alternatively—this government simply moved aside, to give a freer hand to those who were effectively running the affairs of state. A fair number of city-states had embraced the second option and were ruled by *tlatoque* who, simultaneously to being receptacles of the divine fire, were celebrated for their upright life and their supernatural attributes, among which was the possibility of foretelling the future. Some of these figures, as is the case with Nezahualcoyotl, were famed for being inventors as well as oracles; Nezahualcoyotl was especially renowned in this regard, for having invented not only crafts and laws but also human sacrifice and the practice of ingesting the flesh of the sacrificed.[62]

In other cases, the function of serving as the pueblo's protector and oracle of the gods had been delegated to the priests who occupied the highest positions in the priestly hierarchy. Mentioned in this regard are the Zapotecs, who, as has already been noted,[63] maintained special days that involved the performance of a ritual sexual act as a way of assuring themselves of successor hombres-dioses and priest-leaders. At other times, as occurred among the Nicarao, the ruler underwent penance for a year, during which time other headmen[64] fulfilled, uninterruptedly, the function of holding the divine fire in their hearts; or, as practiced by the Mixtec, the king was apparently replaced by very young male relatives—youths of five or six years of age—when he went into a period of seclusion.[65] Common to all of these cases was a development that advanced by degrees, whereby the individuals who were most valuable to society were liberated from undertaking certain functions and involving themselves in difficult situations; such service and entanglements were instead delegated to the devout, to priests, to relatives, or to the prisoners of war. Needless to say, one of the hardest functions to perform was that of submitting to violent ritual death. There are vague reports that some priests enacted the role of god and died in the act of representing him,[66] and the custom of carrying out the symbolic ritual death of an elder priest has already been noted. The general rule, however, was to use physically able warrior captives, whose bodies were free of imperfections and scars, as the victims of such sacrifice.

The routine and practices that governed entrance into the priesthood and its highly regulated life were relaxed; among the Mixtec[67] and the Tehuacanos,[68] men remained in the priesthood for fifteen and four years, respectively. The performance of special functions, such as participating in certain ceremonies or discharging oracular duties, were parceled out to different classes of priests—for example, the chanes and the chilanes among the Yucatecan Maya.[69] All in all, however, hombres-dioses who were celebrated for their wisdom and powers and who were free of this institutionalized system of control could still crop up virtually anywhere.

Without converting himself into an hombre-dios—at least the evidence does not indicate categorically that he did so—the *tlatoani* in Mexico-Tenochtitlan clearly inherited many of the functions of the hombre-dios. In the first instance, he was the bearer of a fire that turned him into the heart of the city—*ca zan ce in tlatoani, in iyollo altépetl*[70]—and, like all the great leaders of the most powerful city-states, he served as the representative not only of his pueblo's god but of all heavenly divinity. In Sahagún's words,

Although you are our friend and fellow man, son and brother, we are not your equal nor do we consider you as a man, because you have the person and the image and discourse and familiarity of our lord God, who speaks and instructs within you, and speaks through your mouth, and your mouth is his, and your tongue is his tongue, and your face is his face, and your ears, and [he] graced you with his authority, gave you fang-like teeth and finger nails so that you might be feared and held in reverence.[71]

Francisco Cervantes de Salazar asserts that one of these leaders, Motecuhzoma Xocoyotzin, remained constantly in touch with a god who appeared to him as a terrifying figure,[72] and Diego Durán describes the fear that gripped the ruler's subjects at the idea of seeing his face: "I would like to recount here what I was told by an Indian whom I had asked about the physiognomy, stature, and manner of Montezuma, he responded: Father, I have not to lie to you nor tell you what I do not know: I never laid eyes on his face. Asking him the reason why, he said that if he should dare to look at him then he should also die, like all the rest who had dared to look at him."[73]

In the face of these and similar testimonies, why am I so resistant to affirming categorically that these leaders, these men, are indeed hombres-dioses? There are several reasons. First, because despite their power, they were reprehended when they attacked some of these personages. Second, because Motecuhzoma, despite his supernatural powers and his conversations with the god, was unable to enter Cincalco directly but, instead, had to supplicate Huemac, promising him that he would not seek admittance in his capacity as a sovereign, like the Toltec, but as a servant; and Huemac responded that he had to observe a proper diet and also abstain from the pleasures of sexual intercourse. Third, because these leaders always consulted soothsayers, who included *tlatoque* allies who indeed were hombres-dioses, such as Nezahualpilli, as well as those who were simply men of the pueblo, such as the Xochilmilcan Quilaztli. In short, because upon dying they did not make their way to privileged worlds, but—as is reiterated in so many poems—to the place of the dead shared by the general run of men. They were not turned into clouds, like the Tlaxcaltecans; rather, the flesh came off their bodies in Ximoayan.

The formula by which violent ritual death was enacted enjoyed wide acceptance. It is not specified exactly when, but there were youths in Tenochtitlan who were treated as representatives of the god and had to be sacrificed—the more important one to Titlacahuan and the less important one to Huitzilopochtli, the latter referred to under the name of Tlacahuepan.[74] In addition, each year at the time of the festival known as *tlacaxipehualiztli*, a sacrificial prisoner of war was furnished by each *calpulli* as a representative of various gods: Xipe Totec, the Sun, Huitzilopochtli, Quetzalcoatl, Macuilxochitl, Chililico, Tlacahuepan, Ixtliltzin, and Mayahuel.[75]

The required participation of the god(s) in particular festivals meant that his representative could be him transitorily. One such case, as we have already seen, was that of Ixtlilton—to which can be added that of the men who bore the flayed skin of the sacrificed; the power that this function gave them enabled them to bless the children presented to them by their mothers.⁷⁶

Finally, we reach the issue of the institutionalization of people who could become dangerous. One such person was possibly the priest Ome Tochtzin, who, in Tenochtitlan, had been granted the highly important functions of song master and leader of the ceremony of the *teooctli*, or "sacred pulque."⁷⁷ The others in this category had landed in a sad condition: in each temple there was a *mocexiuhzauhqui*, a young man who was pulled out of the community, to serve as the hombre-dios of the temple, where he lived chastely and in a state of penance. The *mocexiuhzauhqui*'s term lasted *one year*, after which he was quietly reintegrated into his *calpulli* without having implemented a single political act. And which young men could aspire to play such a role? The mystics of little moment, the rueful transgressors of the pueblo's sexual norms, the pursuers of a cheap fame. When Motecuhzoma Xocoyotzin, alarmed and discombobulated by the heavenly signs of misfortune, questioned the living image of Huitzilopochtli, the boy answered, "that he was a poor ignorant young man and that he had no grasp of the things of heaven, because he was neither astrologist, nor wizard, nor fortune teller; that the astrologers and soothsayers and those who knew of nocturnal things should be called in and that they be asked, that that was their skill and office."⁷⁸

Into such a state had the saviors of the pueblo fallen! Nevertheless, some hombres dioses arose spontaneously, from outside the institutional framework, and the texts refer to one who took on the role of Huitzilopochtli:

> He who emerges like a god, some say, presents himself like that god, for example, Huitzilopochtli, whose attire is the same as that of Huitzilopochtli; clothed in the same way that this god clothed himself, painted himself with blue stripes; dressed himself in all of the garments of this god.
>
> And they saw him as a true and worthy personage, they called him such a personage, and they bade him eat, and at times even gave him clothes. No longer did they view the ravines, the mountains, or the rain and the wind with fear. He who sees him is the first to believe fully in him; where the living image of the god commands him to go, there will he go. Some have died because of him, [and] some have healed.⁷⁹

Among the hombres-dioses who managed to cross the sad bridge from the pre-Hispanic to the early colonial world, we have glimpses—from recollections that were set down—of men who acquitted themselves with honor and dignity, such as that of the intoxicated Chalca who represented Tezcatlipoca and disappeared, before the frightened emissaries of Motecuhzoma Xocoyotzin, after reproaching the Tenochca for their blundering and cowardly measures in the face of the invasion of the white-skinned interlopers.[80] One of the living images—one who had perhaps operated within the institutionalized framework—received a wound on the nose during the massacre that Alvarado unleashed in the *templo mayor* during the festival of *Tóxcatl*.[81] This hombre-dios was possibly Tlapaltecatl Opochtli, the one who wore the disguise of a quetzal-feathered owl and brandished the sacred weapon with the intention of dying in the fight with the Christians but remained alive after causing a superstitious panic to break out within the enemy ranks.[82] Another such figure was Ometochtli of Tlaxcallan, who came to an unfortunate end in 1524 when he was stoned to death by a group of Christian children, whose act first caused horror (albeit hypocritical horror) and then an indulgent acceptance among their missionary friar teachers.[83] Likewise worthy of mention were the brothers Martín Ocelotl and Andrés Mixcoatl, staunch enemies of the friars, the first of whom was exiled to Spain and who died with everyone else on board when their ship sunk en route. Among the Cakchiquel, an hombre-dios who served as the representative of Thunder led his people in their flight from the city of Sololá on August 26, 1524, after the fortune hunting Pedro de Alvarado had demanded a large quantity of gold from them.[84] With their weapons in hand, and these proved much less effective than they imagined would be the case, all these and many more such figures faced off against the more powerfully equipped foreign invaders.

And in time, as the centuries passed, living echoes of the hombres-dioses sprang up. In one instance, the Great Thunderclap; in another, the instigator of a revolt that found aid in the talking box; in still another, the rebel who piously makes his way into the Christian temple, takes the crown and cloak of the holy image, declaring, before marching off into battle, that he represents the saint or the virgin. Tomorrow perhaps, or perhaps in time that has already past, in one or in twenty places, men who believe they speak on behalf of their god and carry him in their heart continue at the head of movements that aim at liberation.

## NOTES

1. Palerm, *Introducción a la teoría*, 263.
2. Olivé Negrete, *Estructura y dinámica*, 112.
3. Armillas, "Tecnología, formaciones," 26.
4. Olivé Negrete, *Estructura y dinámica*, 112–15.
5. Olivé Negrete and Barba, "Sobre la desintegración," 69.
6. Armillas, "Tecnología, formaciones," 28.
7. Rojas, "Descripción de Cholula," 162–63.

8. Sahagún, *Historia general*, 1:281.
9. *Anales de Cuauhtitlán*, 7, 12.
10. *Memorial de Sololá*, 87–92.
11. *Relaciones de Yucatán*, 2:160.
12. *Relaciones geográficas de la Diócesis de Tlaxcala*, 140, 169–70.
13. *Relaciones de Yucatán*, 1:78–79 and 1:255, to cite just two examples.
14. Las Casas, *Apologética*, 1:262.
15. Landa, *Relación de las cosas de Yucatán*, 12–13.
16. Rojas, "Descripción de Cholula," 164.
17. See, for example, Popol Vuh, 142.
18. Sahagún, *Historia general*, 3:187–88.
19. Pomar, "Relación de Texcoco," 6.
20. Sahagún, *Historia general*, 2:118–19.
21. Román y Zamora, *Repúblicas*, 1:293.
22. Burgoa, *Geográfica descripción*, 1:369–71.
23. Alvarado Tezozómoc, *Crónica mexicana*, 8.
24. Chimalpahin, *Relaciones*, 66.
25. Ibid., 55.
26. Mendieta, *Historia eclesiástica*, 1:86.
27. Van Zantwijk, "Principios organizadores," 214.
28. So José Corona Núñez judges it, in his commentary to the *Códice Mendocino*, 8, plate ii.
29. Durán, *Historia de las Indias*, 1:49–50.
30. Cruz, *Libellus*, folio 39v, 193.
31. Chimalpahin, *Relaciones*, 196.
32. Garibay K., *Historia de la literatura*, 1:22–23; León-Portilla, *La filosofía*, 243–48.
33. Séjourné, *El universo de Quetzalcoatl*, 12–13; and Florescano, "*Tula-Teotihuacan*," 228.
34. *La historia de Tlatelolco*, 76.
35. Fuentes y Guzmán, *Recordación florida*, 2:391.
36. I.e., the history of the Mexica.
37. Durán, *Historia de las Indias*, 1:398.
38. Translator's note: This rendition is taken primarily from Doris Heyden's translation of Durán's *Historia de las Indias*, published as *The History of the Indies of New Spain* (Norman: University of Oklahoma Press, 1994): 465.
39. León y Gama, *Descripción histórica*, 2nd part, 31.
40. *Códice Matritense*, vol. 8, folio 192v.
41. Sahagún, *Historia general*, 1:307–8.
42. Durán, *Historia de las Indias*, 1:214.
43. Alvarado Tezozómoc, *Crónica mexicana*, 171.
44. Caso, *El pueblo del Sol*, 121; and León-Portilla, "Itzcóatl, creador de una cosmovisión."

45. Castillo, *Fragmentos*, 85–86.
46. Alvarado Tezozómoc, *Crónica mexicáyotl*, 23–24.
47. Alvarado Tezozómoc, *Crónica mexicana*, 388.
48. Las Casas, *Apologética historia*, 1:643–44; and Castillo, *Fragmentos*, 88.
49. Alvarado Tezozómoc, *Crónica mexicana*, 155–57.
50. *Origen de los mexicanos*, 270.
51. Alva Ixtlilxóchitl, *Obras históricas*, 2:41–42.
52. *Anales de Cuauhtitlán*, 61.
53. Durán, *Historia de las Indias*, 1:552.
54. *Códice Ramírez*, 134.
55. So affirms Carrasco, basing it on the *Relación de Atlitlalacyan*, in *Los otomíes*, 155.
56. Durán, *Historia de las Indias*, 1:27.
57. Acosta, "Interpretación de algunos," 101–2.
58. Sahagún, *Historia general*, 1:237.
59. Pomar, "Relación de Texcoco," 17; Durán, *Historia de las Indias*, 2:92–93; and Herrera, *Historia general de los hechos*, 4:123.
60. Alva Ixtlilxóchitl, *Obras históricas*, 1:39–40.
61. Alvarado Tezozómoc, *Crónica mexicana*, 490.
62. *Historia de México*, 91, 99–100.
63. Burgoa, *Geográfica descripción*, 2:121–25; and Villegas, "Relación de los pueblos de Tecuicuilco," 126–27.
64. Fernández de Oviedo y Valdés, *Historia general y natural*, 11:84–85.
65. Aznar de Cozar, "Relación del pueblo de Instlahuaca," 37.
66. Hernández, *Antigüedades de la Nueva España*, 176–77.
67. Aznar de Cosar, "Relación del pueblo de Çacatepeque."
68. Motolinía, *Memoriales*, 72–73.
69. Landa, *Relación de las cosas de Yucatán*, 49.
70. *Florentine Codex*, 6:110, "because the tlatoani is but one, the heart of the pueblo."
71. Sahagún, *Historia general*, 2:95.
72. Cervantes de Salazar, *Crónica de Nueva España*, 2:8.
73. Durán, *Historia de las Indias*, 1:421–22.
74. Sahagún, *Historia general*, 1:159–60.
75. Durán, *Historia de las Indias*, 2:149.
76. Ibid., 153.
77. Sahagún, *Historia general*, 1:249.
78. Durán, *Historia de las Indias*, 1:489–90.
79. As furnished by Sahagún's indigenous informants and translated by Garibay K., in "Paralipómenos," 237.
80. Florentine Codex, as translated by Garibay K., in Sahagún, *Historia general*, 4:102–3.

81. *Historia de la Nación Mexicana*, 56.
82. Florentine Codex, as translated by Garibay K., in Sahagún, *Historia general*, 4:158–59.
83. Motolinía, *Historia de los indios*, 174–75.
84. *Memorial de Sololá*, 129.

# Epilogue

For centuries, the attempt to construct the biography, to know the full picture, of the life of Ce Acatl Topiltzin Quetzalcoatl has caused historians no end of perplexity, and now I have reached the end of my own search for the cause of that perplexity. I believe that I have partially discovered the elusive cause, in perceiving that his mystery was also the mystery of others: that his life, guided by a myth, was virtually the same as the life of others; and that his history, the history of many, was moved by the living force that moves all of history—a community of people, nameless and faceless, that is brought forth on earth.

The reader will understand that within the pages of this book, within its truths, there is a littering of errors, and under its covering, within its fastenings, there are loose ends. In a case such as this, working with the materials and sources that remain, that is only to be expected, and those who look for final arguments and proofs must inevitably concede the point. To place the problem in its proper context, I needed to imagine a life that endured for centuries, and this, naturally, lay at the opposite extreme of offering data that met every test of valid detail. Others will correct me where I am wrong, as I will endeavor, in the same way, to clear up mistakes. It is the law under which we all operate.

# Bibliography

Acosta, Jorge R. "Interpretación de algunos de los datos obtenidos en Tula, relativos a la época tolteca." *Revista Mexicana de Estudios Antropológicos* 14, 2nd part (1956–57): 75–110.

Acosta, Joseph de. *Historia natural y moral de las Indias en la que trata de las cosas notables del cielo, elementos, metales, plantas y animales dellas, y los ritos y ceremonias, leyes y gobierno de los indios*. 2nd ed. Edited by Edmundo O'Gorman. Biblioteca Americana, Serie de Cronistas de Indias, 38. Mexico City: Fondo de Cultura Económica, 1962.

Acosta Saignes, Miguel. *Los pochteca: Ubicación de los mercaderes en la estructura social tenocha*. Acta Antropológica I. Mexico City: Acta Antropológica, 1945.

Acosta Saignes, Miguel. "Migraciones de los mexica." Reprint from the *Memorias de la Academia de la Historia* (Mexico) 5, no. 2 (1946): 34–42. (Tlatelolco a través de los tiempos, 7).

Alva Ixtlilxóchitl, Fernando de. Introduction to *Obras históricas*, by Alfredo Chavero. With prologue by J. Ignacio Dávila Garibi. 2 vols. Mexico City: Editora Nacional, 1952.

Alvarado Tezozómoc, Hernando. *Crónica mexicana*. Edited by Manuel Orozco y Berra. Mexico City: Editorial Leyenda, 1944.

Alvarado Tezozómoc, Hernando. *Crónica mexicáyotl*. Translated by Adrián León. Mexico City: Universidad Nacional Autónoma de México, Instituto de Historia/Instituto Nacional de Antropología e Historia, 1949.

*Anales de Cuauhtitlán*. In the *Códice Chimalpopoca*. Translated by Primo Feliciano Velázquez. Primera serie, 1: 118, 145–64, and facsimiles. Mexico City: Instituto de Historia, 1945.

Armillas, Pedro. "La serpiente emplumada, Quetzalcóatl y Tláloc." *Cuadernos Americanos* 6, vol. 31, no. 1 (January–February 1947): 161–78.

Armillas, Pedro. "Tecnología, formaciones socioeconómicas y religión en Mesoamérica." In *The Civilizations of Ancient America: Selected Papers of the XXIXth International Congress of Americanists*, edited by Sol Tax. Chicago: University of Chicago Press, 1951.

Armillas, Pedro. "Teotihuacán, Tula y los toltecas: Las culturas post-arcaicas y preaztecas del centro de México: Excavaciones y estudios (1922–1950)." *Runa: Archivo para las Ciencias del Hombre* (Buenos Aires) 8, parts 1–2 (1950): 37–70.

Aznar de Cozar, Andrés. "Relación del pueblo de Çacatepeque que está encomendado en Rafael De Trejo vezino de la ciudad de México, sufragáneo al corregimiento de Instlauaca." *Revista Mexicana de Estudios Históricos* 2, no. 6 (November–December 1928): 159–63.

Aznar de Cozar, Andrés. "Relación del pueblo de Instlauaca que está puesto en corregimiento con la jurisdicción del pueblo de Tecomastlahuala." *Revista Mexicana de Estudios Históricos* 2, no. 6 (November–December 1928): 135–42.

Aznar de Cozar, Andrés. "Relación del pueblo de Puctla que está puesto en la Corona Real y es de la Jurisdicción del Corregimiento del pueblo de Instlauaca." *Revista Mexicana de Estudios Históricos* 2, no. 6 (November–December 1928): 156–9.

Bandelier, A.F. *Report of an Archeological Tour in Mexico, in 1881*. American Series 2. Boston: Archaeological Institute of America, 1884.

Barlow, Robert. "El Códice Azcatitlan." *Journal de la Société des Américanistes*. New Series 38 (1949): 101–35.

Benavente o Motolinía, fray Toribio. *Historia de los indios de la Nueva España: Relación de los ritos antiguos, idolatrías y sacrificios de los indios de la Nueva España, y de la maravillosa conversión que Dios en ellos ha obrado*. Edited with notes by Edmundo O'Gorman. Sepan Cuantos, 129. Mexico City: Editorial Porrúa, 1959.

Benavente o Motolinía, fray Toribio. *Memoriales o Libro de las cosas de la Nueva España y de los naturales de ella*. Edited with notes by Edmundo O'Gorman. Serie de Historiadores y Cronistas de Indias, 2. Mexico: Universidad Nacional Autónoma de México, Instituto de Investigaciones Históricas, 1971.

Berlin, Heinrich, and Silva Rendón. *Historia tolteca-chichimeca: Anales de Quauhtinchan*. With a historical-sociological study by Paul Kirchhoff. Fuentes para la Historia de México, 1. Mexico: Antigua Librería Robredo de José Porrúa e Hijos, 1947.

Berlin, Isaiah. *The Power of Ideas*. Edited by Henry Hardy. Princeton, NJ: Princeton University Press, 2000.

Bernal, Ignacio. "Huitzilopochtli vivo." *Cuadernos Americanos* 96, no. 6 (November–December 1957): 127–52.

Borunda, Ignacio. "Clave general de geroglíficos americanos." In *Bibliografía mexicana del Siglo XVIII*, edited by Nicolás León, 3:195–351. 6 vols. Mexico: Imprenta de la viuda de Francisco Díaz de León, 1906.

Boturini Benaduci, Lorenzo. *Idea de una nueva historia general de la América Septentrional*. Biblioteca Histórica de la Iberia, 6. Mexico: Imprenta de I. Escalante y Cía, 1871.

Brackelwelda, Othón E. de. "Apuntes para un estudio sobre el cristianismo en América en los Tiempos anteriores a los descubrimientos de Cristóbal Colón." *Boletín de la Sociedad de Geografía y Estadística de la República Mexicana*. 4th ed. Vol. 2, nos. 8, 9, and 10 (1893): 606–32.

Brasseur de Bourbourg, LÁbbé. [Charles Étienne] *Histoire des nations civilisées du Mexique et de l'Ámerique-Centrale, durant les siècles antérieurs a Christophe Colomb, écrite aux anciennes archives des indigènes*. 4 vols. Paris: Arthus Bertrand, 1857–1859.

Brinton, Daniel G. *American Hero-Myths: A Study in the Native Religions of the Western Continent*. Series in American Studies. New York: Johnson Reprint Corporation, 1970.

Brinton, Daniel G. "The Sacred Names in Quiche Mythology." In *Essays of an Americanist*, ed. Daniel G. Brinton. Series in American Studies, 104–29. New York: Johnson Reprint Corporation, 1970.

Brinton, Daniel G. "The Toltecs and their Fabulous Empire." In *Essays of an Americanist*, ed. Daniel G. Brinton, 83–100. Series in American Studies. New York: Johnson Reprint Corporation, 1970.

Briones, Montoya, and José de Jesús. *Atla: Etnografía de un pueblo náhuatl*. Mexico: Instituto Nacional de Antropología e Historia, Departamento de Investigaciones Antropológicas, 1964.

Broda de Casas, Johanna. "Tlacaxipeualiztli: A Reconstruction of an Aztec Calendar Festival From 16th Century Sources." *Revista Española de Antropología Americana* 5 (1970): 197–274.

Burgoa, fray Francisco de. *Geográfica descripción*. Publicaciones del Archivo General la Nación, 15–16. 2 vols. Mexico City: Secretaría de Gobernación, Archivo General de la Nación.

Calvino, Italo. "Why Read the Classics?" Translated by Martin McLaughlin. New York: Pantheon Books, 1999.

Carrasco, Davíd, and Scott Sessions. *Cave, City, and Eagle's Nest: An Interpretive Journey through the Mapa de Cuauhtinchan No. 2*. Albuquerque: University of New Mexico Press, 2007.

Carrasco Pizanna, Pedro. *Los otomíes: Cultura e historia prehispánicas de los pueblos mesoamericanos de habla otomiana*. Primera serie, 15. Mexico: Universidad Nacional Autónoma De México, Instituto de Historia/Instituto Nacional de Antropología e Historia, 1950.

Carrasco Pizanna, Pedro. "Quetzalcóatl, dios de Coatepec de los Costales, Gro." *Tlalocan* 2, no. 1 (1945): 89–91.

Carrión, Jorge. "La ruta psicológica de Quetzalcóatl." *Cuadernos Americanos*, no. 5 (September–October 1949): 98–112.

Caso, Alfonso. "El águila y el nopal." *Memorias de la Academia Mexicana de la Historia* 5, no. 2 (April–June 1946): 93–104.

Caso, Alfonso. "El complejo arqueológico de Tula y las grandes culturas indígenas de México." *Revista Mexicana de Estudios Antropológicos* 5, nos. 2–3: 85–96.

Caso, Alfonso. *El pueblo del Sol*. Mexico City: Fondo de Cultura Económica, 1953.

Caso, Alfonso. "Quetzalcóatl." *Humanismo: Revista Mensual de Cultura* 30 (April–June 1955): 31–4.

Castillo, Cristóbol del. *Fragmentos de la obra general sobre historia de los mexicanos*. Translated by Francisco del Paso y Troncoso. Ciudad Juárez: Editorial Erandi, 1966. Reimpression of the 1908 edition.

Castillo, F., and M. Víctor. *Estructura económica de la sociedad mexica*. Serie de Cultura Náhuatl, Monografías, 13. Mexico City: Universidad Nacional Autónoma de México, Instituto de Investigaciones Históricas, 1972.

Ceballos Novelo, R[oque] J[acinto]. "Quetzalcóatl. Los dos templos que sucesivamente tuvo en Cholula, Estado de Puebla." *Anales del Museo Nacional de Arqueología, Historia y Etnografía*, 5th ed., vol. 1 (1934): 257–65.

Cervantes, Hernando de. "Descripción de Teotzacualco y de Amoltepeque." *Revista Mexicana de Estudios Históricos* 1, no. 6 (November–December 1927): 174–78.

Cervantes de Salazar, Francisco. *Crónica de Nueva España*. 3 vols. Madrid: Est. Fot. de Hausdr y Menet, 1914–1936.

Chadwick, Robert. "Native Pre-Aztec History of Central Mexico." In *Archaeology of Northern Mesoamerica*, edited by Gordon F. Ekholm and Ignacio Bernal, 474–504. Handbook of Middle American Indians, vol. 11, part 2. New Orleans: Middle American Research Institute, Tulane University, 1971.

Charnay, Désiré. "La Civilisation Toltèque." *Revue d'Ethnographie* (Paris) 4, no. 4 (Juillet-Août 1885): 281–305.

Chavero, Alfredo. "Explicación del Códice Geroglífico de Mr. Aubin." Appendix to *Historia de las Indias de Nueva España e islas de Tierra Firme*, vol. 2, by fray Diego Durán. Mexico City: Editora Nacional, 1951.

Chavero, Alfredo. *México a través de los siglos volume 1: Historia antigua y de la conquista*, edited by Vicente Riva Palacio et al. Mexico: Publicaciones Herrerías, n.d.

Chaves, Gabriel de. "Relación de la Provincia de Meztitland, hecha por———, alcalde mayor de esta provincia por S. M., del orden del Virey de Nueva-España." In *Colección de Documentos Inéditos relativos al descubrimiento, conquista y organización de las antiguas posesiones españoles de América y Oceanía sacados de los archivos del reino, y muy especialmente del de Indias por Luis Torres de Mendoza*, edited by Luis Torres de Mendoza, 4: 530–55. Madrid: Imprenta de Frías y Compañía, 1865.

Chimalpahin, Domingo. "Memorial breve acerca de la fundación de la ciudad de Culhuacan." In *Diferentes Historias originales de los reynos de Culhuacan y México, y de otras provincias*, in *Corpus Codicum Americanorum Medii Aevi*, edited by Ernst Mengin, 3: 40–142. Havniae: Sumptibus Einar Muksgaard, 1949.

Chimalpahin, Domingo. *Relaciones originales de Chalco-Amaquemecan*. Translated by Silvia Rendón, with preface by Ángel María Garibay K. Biblioteca Americana Serie de Literatura Indígena. Mexico City: Fondo de Cultura Economica, 1965.

Clavijero, Francisco Javier. *Historia antigua de México*, edited by Mariano Cuevas. Sepan Cuantos, 29. 2nd ed. Mexico: Editorial Porrúa, 1964.

*Codex Magliabechiano*. Cl. XIII. (B.R. 232) Biblioteca Nazionale Centrale di Firenze. Fac. ed., with a study by Ferdinand Anders. Codices Selecti. Phototypice impressi, 22. Graz: Akademische Druck–u. Verlagsanstalt, 1970.

*Codex Mexicanus*. Bibliothèque Nationale de Paris. Nos. 23–24. Paris: Société des Américanistes, 1952.

*Códice Azcatitlan*. Paris: Société des Americanistes, 1949.

*Códice Boturini*; or, *Tira de la Peregrinación*; or, *Tira del Museo*. In *Antigüedades de México*, by Lord Kingsborough, 2: 7–29.

"Códice Carolino." Introduction by Ángel María Garibay K. *Estudios de Cultura Náhuatl* 7 (1967): 11–58.

*Códice de Calkiní*. Version of Alfredo Barrera Vásquez. Biblioteca Campechana, 4. Campeche: Gobierno del Estado, 1957.

*Códice Matritense de la Real Academia de la Historia*. Facsimile edition produced by Francisco del Paso Troncoso. vol. 8. Madrid: Fototipia de Hauser y Menet, 1907.

*Códice Mendocino*; or, *Colección Mendoza*. In *Antigüedades de México*, by Lord Kingsborough, 1: 1–150.

*Códice Ramírez: Relación del origen de los indios que habitan esta Nueva España, según sus historias*. With accompanying study by Manuel Orozco y Berra. Mexico City: Editorial Leyenda, 1944.

*Códice Telleriano-Remensis*. In *Antigüedades de México*, by Lord Kingsborough, 1: 151–338. Copy of the compilation by fray Pedro de los Ríos.

*Códice Vaticano Latino 3738*; or, *Códice Vaticano Ríos* or *Códice Ríos*. In *Antigüedades de México*, by Lord Kingsborough, 3: 7–314. Copy of the compilation of fray Pedro de los Ríos.

*Códice Xólotl*. Introduction by Rafael García Granados, study by Charles E. Dibble. Primera serie 22. Mexico City: Universidad Nacional Autónoma de México, Instituto de Historia, 1951.

Córdova, Fray Juan de. *Arte del idioma zapoteco*. Introduction by Nicolás León. Morelia: Imprenta del Gobierno, 1886.

Cortés, Hernán. *Cartas de relación de la conquista de Méjico. Colección Austral, 547*. Buenos Aires: Espasa-Calpe Argentina, 1945.

Cortés, Hernán. *Letters from Mexico*. Translated and edited by Anthony Pagden, with an introduction by J. H. Elliott. New Haven: Yale University Press, 1986.

"Costumbres, fiestas, enterramientos y diversas formas de proceder de los indios de Nueva España." Published by Federico Gómez de Orozco. *Tlalocan* 2, no. 1 (1945): 37–63.

Cruz, Martín de la. *Libellus de medicinalibus Indorum herbis: Manuscrito azteca de 1552, según traducción latina de Juan Badiano.* Mexico City: Instituto Mexicano del Seguro Social, 1964.

Dahlgren de Jordán, Barbro. *La Mixteca: Su cultura e historia prehispánicas.* Cultura Mexicana 11. Mexico: Imprenta Universitaria, 1954.

de la Rea, Fray Alonso. *Crónica de la Orden de N. Seráfico P.S. San Francisco, Provincia de San Pedro y San Pablo de Mechoacan de la Nueva España.* Mexico City: Imprenta de J. R. Barbedillo y G.a, 1882.

de la Vega, Núñez, and Fray Francisco. *Constituciones Diocesanas del Obispado de Chiappa.* Rome: Nueva Imprenta y Formación de Caracteres de Caietano Zenobi, 1702.

Díaz Infante, Fernando. *Quetzalcóatl: Ensayo piscoanalítico del mito nahua.* Jalapa: Universidad Veracruzana, 1963.

[Duarte, Manuel]. *Pluma rica: Nuevo fénix de América.* In *El apóstol Santo Tomás en el Nuevo Mundo. Colección de noticias y memorias relativas a la predicación del Evangelio en América antes de su descubrimiento por los españoles.* Collected and arranged by José F. Ramírez. Vol. 3 of *Bibliografía mexicana del siglo XVIII*, by Nicolás León. Mexico City: Imprenta de la viuda de Francisco Díaz de León:, 1902–1908.

Durán, fray Diego. *Historia de las Indias de Nueva España e islas de Tierra Firme.* Edited by José F. Ramírez. 2 vols. and atlas. Mexico City: Editora Nacional, 1951.

Durán, fray Diego. *The History of the Indies of New Spain.* Translated, annotated, and with an introduction by Doris Heyden. Norman: University of Oklahoma Press, 1994.

El conquistador anónimo. *Relación de algunas cosas de la Nueva España y de la gran ciudad de Temestitan: Escrita por un compañero de Hernán Cortés.* Prologue and notes by León Díaz Cárdenas. Mexico City: Editorial América, 1941.

Eliade, Mircea. *El mito del eterno retorno: Arquetipos y repetición.* Translated by Ricardo Anaya. 2nd ed. Colección Piragua. Buenos Aires: Emecé Editores, 1968.

Eliade, Mircea. *Mito y realidad.* Translated by Luis Gil. Madrid: Ediciones Guadarrama, 1968.

Eliade, Mircea. *Myth and Reality.* Translated by Willard R. Trask. New York: Harper and Row, 1975.

Eliade, Mircea. *The Myth of the Eternal Return.* Translated by Willard R. Trask. Bollinger Series, 46. New York: Bollinger Foundation, Pantheon Books, 1954.

*El libro de los libros de Chilam Balam.* 2nd ed. Translated, with introduction and notes by Alfredo Barrera Vásquez and Silvia Rendón. Colección Popular, 42. Mexico: Fondo de Cultura Econónimca, 1963.

Fernández de Oviedo y Valdés, Gonzalo. *Historia general y natural de las Indias, Islas y Tierra-Firme del Mar Océano.* 14 vols. Prologue by J. Natalicio González and notes by José Amador de Los Ríos. Asunción: Editorial Guaranía, 1944–1945.

*Florentine Codex: General History of the Things of New Spain, Fray Bernardino de Sahagún.* Translated from Aztec into English, with notes and illustrations by Charles E. Dibble and Arthur J. O. Anderson. 12 vols. Santa Fe: The School of American Research/University of Utah, 1950–1969.

Florescano, Enrique. "La serpiente emplumada, Tláloc y Quetzalcóatl." *Cuadernos Americanos* 2 (March–April 1964): 121–66.

Florescano, Enrique. "Tula-Teotihuacan, Quetzalcóatl y la Toltecáyotl." *Historia Mexicana* 8, no. 2 (October–December 1963): 193–234.

Fuentes Mares, José. *La revolución mexicana: Memorias de un espectador.* Serie Contrapuntos. Mexico City: Joaquín Mortiz, 1971.

Fuentes y Guzmán, Francisco Antonio. *Recordación florida: Discurso historial y demostración natural, material, militar y política del Reyno de Guatemala.* Prologue by J. Antonio Villacorta C., Ramón A. Salazar, and Sinforoso Aguilar. Biblioteca Goathemala, 6–8. 3 vols. Guatemala: Sociedad de Geografía e Historia, 1932–1933.

Gamio, Manuel. Introduction to *La población del Valle de Teotihuacán.* Edited by Manuel Gamio, et al. 3 vols. Mexico City: Dirección de Talleres Gráficos dependiente de la Secretaría de Educación Pública, 1922.

García, Fray Gregorio. *Origen de los indios de el Nuevo Mundo, e Indias Occidentales.* 2nd ed. Madrid: Imprenta de Francisco Martínez Abad, 1729.

García de León. "El dueño del maíz y otros relatos nahuas del sur de Veracruz." *Tlalocan* 5, no. 4 (1968): 349–57.

Garibay K., Ángel María. *Historia de la literatura náhuatl.* Biblioteca Porrúa, 1 and 5. 2 vols. Mexico City: Editorial Porrúa, 1953–1954.

Garibay K., Ángel María. "Paralipómenos de Sahagún." *Tlalocan* 2, nos. 2–3 (1946–1947): 167–74, 235–54.

Garibay K., Ángel María. *Poesía náhuatl.* Fuentes Indígenas de la Cultura Náhuatl, 4–6. 3 vols. Mexico City: Universidad Autónoma de México, Instituto de Investigaciones Históricas, 1964–1968.

Garibay K., Ángel María. *Veinte himnos sacros de los nahuas / Los recogió de los nativos Fr. Bernardino de Sahagún.* Los publica en su texto, con versión, introducción, notas de comentario y apéndices de otras fuentes, Ángel Ma. Garibay K. Fuentes indígenas de la cultura náhuatl, Informantes de Sahagún, 2. Mexico City: Universidad Nacional Autónoma de México, Instituto de Historia, 1958.

González Casanova, Pablo. "El ciclo legendario de Tepoztécatl." *Revista Mexicana de Estudios Históricos* 2, no. 1–2 (January–February 1928): 18–63.

"G[onzález] de Lesur, Yólotl. "El dios Huitzilopochtli en la peregrinación mexica: De Aztlan a Tula." *Anales del Instituto Nacional de Antropología e Historia* 19 (1968): 175–90.

González Obregón, Luis. *Procesos de indios idólatras y hechiceros*. Preliminary study by Luis González Obregón. Publicaciones del Archivo General de la Nación, 3. Mexico City: Secretaría de Relaciones Exteriores, 1912.

Guiteras Holmes, C[alixta]. *Los peligros del alma: Visión del mundo de un tzotil*. Epilogue by Sol Tax. Sección de obras de Antropología. Mexico City: Fondo de Cultura Económica, 1965.

Hedrick, B.C. "Quetzalcoatl: European or Indigene?" In *Man Across the Sea: Problems of Pre-colombian Contacts*, edited by Carrol L. Riley, et al., 255–65. Austin: University of Texas Press, 1971.

Hernández, Francisco. *Antigüedades de la Nueva España*, translated, with critical notes, by Joaquín García Pimentel. Mexico: Editorial Pedro Robredo, 1946.

Herrera, Antonio de. *Historia general de los hechos de los castellanos, en las Islas, y Tierra-Firme de el Mar Occeano*. Prologue by J. Natalicio González. 10 vols. Asunción: Editorial Guaranía, 1944–1947.

Heyerdahl, Thor. "The Bearded Gods Speak." In *The Quest for America*, edited by Geoffrey Ashe, et al., 199–238. New York: Preager, 1971.

*Historia antigua de México*. Translated by Ramón Rosales Mungía. In *Teogonía e historia de los mexicanos: Tres opúsculos del siglo XVI*, edited by Ángel Ma. Garibay K. Sepan Cuantos, 91–120. 37. Mexico: Editorial Porrúa, 1965.

*Historia de la Nación Mexicana: Códice de 1576 (Códice Aubin)*. Edited, with introduction, notes, indexes, paleography, and translation by Charles E. Dibble. Colección Chimalistac de Libros y Documentos acerca de la Nueva España, 16.

*Historia de los mexicanos por sus pinturas*. In *Relaciones de Texcoco y de la Nueva España*, edited by Juan Aautista Pomar et al., 207–40. Introduction by Joaquín García Icazbalceta. Sección de Historia, 2. Mexico: Editorial Salvador Chávez Hayhoe, 1941.

*Historia tolteca-chichimeca*. In *Corpus Codicum Americanorum Medii Aevi*, edited by Ernst Mengin, 1: xl–104.

Holland, William R. *Medicina maya en los Altos de Chiapas: Un estudio del cambio sociocultural*. Translated by Daniel Cazés. Colección de Antropología Social, 2. Mexico: Instituto Nacional Indigenista, 1963.

Huddleston, Lee Eldridge. *Origins of the American Indians: European Concepts, 1492–1729*. Latin American Monographs, 11. Austin: ILAS/University of Texas Press, 1967.

Humboldt, Alexander von. *Sitios de las cordilleras y monumentos de los pueblos indígenas de América*. Preliminary study by Fernando Márquez Miranda. Buenos Aires: Solar/Hachette, 1968.

Hvidtfeldt, Arild. *Teotl and ixiptlatli: Some Central Conceptions in Ancient Mexican Religion*. With a general introduction on cult and myth. Copenhagen: Munksgaard, 1958.

Jensen, Adolf Edegard. *Mito y culto entre pueblos primitivos*. Translated by Carlos Gerhart. Sección de Obras de Antropología. Mexico: Fondo de Cultura Económica, 1966.

Jiménez Moreno, Wigberto. "El enigma de los olmecas." *Cuadernos Americanos* 5, no. 5 (September–October 1942): 113–45.
Jiménez Moreno, Wigberto. *Notas sobre historia antigua de México*. Mexico: Ediciones de la Sociedad de Alumnos de la Escuela Nacional de Antropolgía e Historia, 1956. Unrevised student notes, mimeograph.
Jiménez Moreno, Wigberto. "Síntesis de historia pretolteca en Mesoamérica." In *Esplendor del México antiguo*, edited by Raúl Noriega et al., 2: 1019–1108. 2 vols. Mexico: Centro de Investigaciones Antropológicas de México, 1959.
Jiménez Moreno, Wigberto. "Síntesis de la historia precolonial del Valle de México." *Revista Mexicana de Estudios Antropológicos* 14, 1st part (1954–1955): 219–36.
Jiménez Moreno, Wigberto. "Tula y los toltecas según las fuentes históricas." *Revista Mexicana de Estudios Antropológicos* 5, no. 2–3 (1941): 79–84.
Katz, Friedrich. *Situación social y económica de los aztecas durante los siglos XV y XVI*. Translated by María Luisa Rodríguez Sala and Elsa Bühler. Serie de Cultura Náhuatl, Monografías, 8. Mexico: Universidad Autónoma de México, Instituto de Investigaciones Históricas, 1966.
Kelly, David H. "Quetzalcoatl and His Coyote Origins." *El México Antiguo* 8 (December 1955): 397–416.
Kelly, Isabel. "World View of a Highland Totonac Pueblo." In *Summa Anthropologica en homenaje a Roberto J. Weitlaner*. Mexico City: Instituto Nacional de Antropolgía e Historia, 1966.
Kingsborough. *Antigüedades de México*. Prologue by Agustín Ynez, interpretive study by José Corona Núñez. 4 vols. Mexico: Secretaría de Hacienda y Crédito Público, 1964–1967.
Kirchhoff, Paul. "El Imperio tolteca y su ocaso." Typescript copy of an unedited work. Copy held in the library of the Instituto de Investigaciones Históricas of UNAM, Mexico City.
Kirchhoff, Paul. "La Historia tolteca-chichimeca: Un estudio histórico-sociológico." In *Historia tolteca-chichimeca: Anales de Quauhtinchan*, ed. Heinrich Berlin and Silva Rendón, xvii–lxiv. Mexico: Antigua Librería Robredo de José Porrúa e Hijos, 1947.
Kirchhoff, Paul. "The Mexican Calendar and the Founding of Tenochtitlan Tlatelolco." *Transactions of the New York Academy of Sciences*, Series 2 12, no. 4 (February 1950): 126–32. http://dx.doi.org/10.1111/j.2164-0947.1950.tb01883.x.
Kirchhoff, Paul. "Quetzalcóatl, Huémac y el fin de Tula." *Cuadernos Americanos* 84, no. 6 (November–December 1955): 163–96.
Kirchhoff, Paul. "¿Se puede localizar Aztlan?" *Anuario de Historia* (Facultad de Filosofía y Letras, UNAM) 1 (1961): 59–68.
Krickeberg, Walter. *Las antiguas culturas mexicanas*. Translated by Sita Garst and Jasmin Reuter. Sección de Obras de Antropología. Mexico City: Fondo de Cultura Económica, 1961.

Krickeberg, Walter. "Mesoamérica." In *Pre-Columbian American Religions*, edited by Walter Krickeberg, viii–366. Translated by Stanley Davis. New York: Holt, Rinehardt, and Winston, 1969.

Lafaye, Jacques. *Quetzalóatl y Guadalupe: La formación de la conciencia nacional de México*. Translated by Ida Vitale and Fulgencio López Vidarte. Preface by Octavio Paz. 3rd Ed. Mexico City: Fondo Cultura Económica, 1999.

La historia de Tlatelolco desde los tiempos más remotos. In *Anales de Tlatelolco: Unos anales históricos de la nación mexicana y Códice de Tlatelolco*. Version prepared and annotated by Heinrich Berlin, with a summary of the *Anales* and interpretation of the *Códice* by Robert H. Barlow, 29–76. Fuentes para la Historia de México, 2. Mexico City: Antigua Librería Robredo de José Porrúa e Hijos, 1948.

Landa, Fray Diego de. *Relación de las cosas de Yucatán*. Introduction by Ángel Ma. Garibay K. 8th ed. Biblioteca Porrúa, 13. Mexico City: Editorial Porrúa, 1959.

Las Casas, Fray Bartolomé de. *Apologética historia sumaria cuanto a las cualidades, disposición, descripción, cielo y suelo destas tierras, y condiciones naturales, policías, repúblicas, manera de vivir e costumbres de las gentes destas Indias Occidentales y Meridionales cuyo imperio soberano pertenece a los Reyes de Castilla*, edited, with an introductory study, by Edmundo O'Gorman. 2 vols. Serie de Historiadores y Cronistas Indias, 1. Mexico City: Universidad Nacional Autónoma de México, Instituto de Investigaciones Históricas, 1967.

Lehmann, Walter. *Una elegía tolteca*. Edited by Wigberto Jiménez Moreno, translated by R. P. Hendrichs. Folleto no. 2. Mexico City: Sociedad México-Alemana Alejandro de Humboldt, 1941.

León, Nicolás. *Bibliografía Mexicana del siglo XVIII*. 5 vols. Mexico City: Imprenta de Díaz de León, 1902–1908.

León, Nicolás. "Causa formada al Dr. Fray Servando Teresa de Mier, por el sermón que predicó en la Colegiata de Guadalupe el 12 de diciembre de 1794." In *Bibliografía Mexicana del siglo XVIII*. Mexico City: Imprenta de Díaz de León, 1902–1908.

León-Portilla, Miguel. "El pensamiento prehispánico." In *Estudios de historia de la filosofía en México*, edited by Miguel León-Portilla, 11–72. Mexico City: Universidad Nacional Autónoma de México, Publicaciones de la Coordinación de Humanidades, 1963.

León-Portilla, Miguel. "Iztcóatl, creador de una cosmovisión místico-guerrera." In *Siete ensayos sobre cultura náhuatl*, edited by Miguel León-Portilla, 117–44. Mexico City: Universidad Nacional Autónoma de México, Facultad de Filosofía y Letras, 1958.

León-Portilla, Miguel. *La filosofía náhuatl estudiada en sus fuentes*. Prologue by Ángel Ma. Garibay K. 3rd ed. Serie de Cultura Náhuatl, Monografías, 10. Mexico City: Universidad Nacional Autónoma de México, Instituto de Investigaciones Históricas, n.d.

León-Portilla, Miguel. *Quetzalcóatl*. Presencia de México, 1. Mexico: Fondo de Cultura Económica, 1968.

León-Portilla, Miguel. "Quetzalcóatl: Espiritualismo del México antiguo." *Cuadernos Americanos*, year 18, vol. 105, no. 4 (July 1, 1959): 127–39.
León-Portilla, Miguel. "Religión de los nicaraos." *Estudios de Cultura Náhuatl* 10 (1972): 11–112.
León y Gama, Antonio. "De la existencia de los gigantes y tiempo que habitaron la Nueva España." Manuscritos de León y Gama, no. 322. Paris: Biblioteca Nacional de París.
León y Gama, Antonio. *Descripción histórica y cronológica de las dos piedras que con ocasión del nuevo empedrado que se está formando en la Plaza principal de México, se hallaron en ella el año de 1790*. Introduction, biography, and notes by Carlos María de Bustamante. 2nd ed. Mexico City: Imprenta del Ciudadano Alejandro Valdés, 1832.
*Leyenda de los Soles*. In *Códice Chimalpopoca*. Translated by Primo Feliciano Velázquez. Primera Serie, 1. Mexico City: Universidad Nacional Autónoma de México, Instituto de Investigaciones Históricas, 1945.
Libro de Daniel. In *Biblia de Jerusalém*, 1275–98. Mexico City: Editorial Porrúa, 1985.
Linton, Ralph. *Estudio del hombre*. 6th ed. Translated by Daniel F. Rubin de la Borbolla. Sección de Obras de Sociología. Mexico City: Fondo de Cultura Económica, 1963.
Lizana, Fray Bernardo de. *Historia de Yucatán: Devocionario de Ntra. Sra. De Izmal y conquista espiritual*. 2nd ed. Mexico City: Imprenta del Museo Nacional, 1893.
López Austin, Alfredo. *Augurios y abusiones*. Introducción, versión, notas y comentarios de Alfredo López Austin. Fuentes indígenas de la cultura náhuatl. Textos de los informantes de Sahagún, 4. Mexico: Universidad Nacional Autónoma de Mexico, Instituto de Investigaciones Históricas, 1969.
López Austin, Alfredo. "Cuarenta clases de magos en el mundo náhuatl." *Estudios de Cultura Náhuatl* 7 (1967): 87–117.
López Austin, Alfredo. "La carga del destino en la tradición mesoamericana." Paper presented at "Temporalidades de los intercambios y de la apropiación cultural." Segundo Encuentro UBO-UNAM, Mexico City, Instituto de Investigaciones Históricas, UNAM, May 6, 2013.
López Austin, Alfredo. "Los señoríos de Azcapotzalco y Tezcoco." In *Historia prehispánica. Conferencias, 7*. Mexico City: Secretaría de Educación Pública/Instituto Nacional de Antropología e Historia/ Museo Nacional de Antropología.
López Austin, Alfredo. *Textos de medicina náhuatl*. SepSetenta, 6. Mexico City: Secretaría de Educación Pública, 1971.
López de Cogolludo, Fray Diego. *Historia de Yucatán*. Prologue by J. Ignacio Rubio Mañé. 5th ed. Colección de Grandes Crónicas Mexicanas, 3. Mexico City: Editorial Academia Literaria, 1957.
López de Gómara, Francisco. *Historia general de las Indias: "Hispania Vitrix," cuya segunda parte corresponde a la Conquista de Méjico*, edited by Pilar Guibelalde. With prefatory notes by Emilia M. Aguilera. 2 vols. Obras Maestras. Barcelona: Editorial Iberia, 1954.

Madsen, William. *The Virgin's Children: Life in an Aztec Village Today*. Austin: University of Texas Press, 1960.

*Mapa de Sigüenza: Pintura del Museo; Mapa de la peregrinación de los aztecas; Códice Ramírez*. Photographic image of the copy housed in the National Museum of Anthropology and History, published by John B. Glass. Catálogo de la Colección de Códices. Mexico City: Instituto Nacional de Antropología e Historia/Museo Nacional de Antropología, 1964.

Martínez Marín, Carlos. "La cultura de los mexicas durante la migración: Nuevas ideas." *Cuadernos Americanos* 22, no. 4 (July–August 1963): 175–83.

Mártir de Anglería. *Décadas del Nuevo Mundo*. Translated by Agustín Millares Carlo, with study and appendices by Edmundo O'Gorman. 2 vols. Biblioteca José Porrúa Estrada de Historia Mexicana, 6. Mexico: José Porrúa e Hijos, 1964.

Marx, Karl. *El capital: Crítica de la economía política*, translated by Wenceslao Roces. 2nd ed. 3 vols. Mexico: Fondo de Cultura Económica, 1959.

Marx, Karl. *Formas de propieded precapitalista*. Translated by W. Roces. Mexico: Ediciones Historia y Sociedad, n.d.

Mcafee, Byron, and R. H. Barlow. "La guerra entre Tlatelolco y Tenochtitlan, según el Códice Cozcatzin." In *Memorias de la Academia Mexicana de la Historia correspondiente de la Real de Madrid*, vol. 5. Tlatelolco a Través de los Tiempos, 7. Mexico City: Academia de la Historia, 1946.

*Memorial de Sololá: Anales de los cakchiqueles*. Translated, edited, and with introduction by Adrián Recinos. Biblioteca Americana, Serie de Literatura Indígena, 11. Published with Título de los señores de Totonicapán. Mexico City: Fondo de Cultura Económica, 1950.

*Memoriales con escolios*. In *Primeros memoriales*, in *Historia general de las cosas de Nueva España*, by fray Bernardino de Sahagún, 6: 177–205. 4 vols. [5, 6 (Cuaderno 2°.), 7 and 8]. Madrid: Fototipia de Hauser y Menet, 1905–1908.

Mendieta, Fray Gerónimo. *Historia eclesiástica indiana*. 4 vols. Mexico City: Editorial Salvador Chávez Hayhoe, 1945.

Mendizábal, Miguel Othón de. *El Lienzo de Jucutácato: Su verdadera significación*. Mexico City: Talleres Gráficos del Museo Nacional de Arqueología, Historia, y Etnografía, 1926.

Mendizábal, Miguel Othón de, and Enrique Juan Palacios. "El templo de Quetzalcóatl en Teotihuacán." In *Obras completas*, edited by Miguel Othón de Mendizábal, 2: 343–54. Prologue by Jesús Silva Herzog. 3 vols. Mexico City: Cooperativa de Trabajadores de los Talleres Gráficos de la Nación, 1946.

Mengin, Ernest. "Commentaire du Codex Mexicanus nos. 23–24 de la Bibliothèque Nationale De Paris." *Journal de la Société des Americanistes* 41, no. 2 (1952): 387–498. http://dx.doi.org/10.3406/jsa.1952.3743.

Metraux, Alfred. "El dios supremo, los creadores y héroes culturales en la mitología sudamericana." *America Indígena* 6, no. 1 (January 1946): 9–25.

Mier Noriega y Guerra, Fray Servando Teresa. *Historia de la revolución de Nueva España, antiguamente Anáhuac o Verdadero origen y causas de ella con la relación de sus progresos hasta el presente año de 1813*. 2nd ed. 2 vols. Mexico City: Imprenta de la Cámara de Diputados, 1922.

Molina, Fray Alonso. *Vocabulario en lengua castellana y mexicana: Colección de incunables americanos, siglo XVI, IV*. Madrid: Ediciones Cultura Hispánica, 1944.

Monzón, Arturo. *El calpulli en la organización social de los tenocha*. Primera Serie, 14. Mexico City: Universidad Nacional Autónoma de México, Instituto de Historia/ Instituto Nacional de Antropología e Historia, 1949.

Moreno de los Arcos, Roberto. "Los cinco soles cosmogónicos." *Estudios de Cultura Náhuatl* 7 (1967): 183–210.

Muñoz Camargo, Diego. *Historia de Tlaxcala*, published and annotated by Alfredo Chavero. Guadalajara: Edmundo Aviña Levy, 1966. Facsimile of the 1892 edition.

Nicholson, H. B. "Los principales dioses mesoamericanos." In *Esplendor del México antiguo*, edited by Raúl Noriega et al., 1: 161–78. 2 vols. Mexico City: Centro de Investigaciones Antropológicas de México, 1959.

Nicholson, H. B. "Pre-Hispanic Central Mexico Religion." August 1964. Photocopy of the essay published in the *Handbook of Middle American Indians*. New Orleans: Middle American Research Institute, Tulane University

Nicholson, H. B. "Topiltzin Quetzalcoatl of Tollan: A Problem in Mesoamerican Ethnohistory." PhD diss., Harvard University, Cambridge, MA, 1957.

Nicholson, H. B. *Topiltzin Quetzalcoatl: The Once and Future Lord of the Toltecs*. Boulder: University Press of Colorado, 2001.

Nowotny, Karl A. "Restos de especulaciones místicas de los indios prehispánicos." In *Summa Anthropologica en homenaje a Roberto J. Weitlaner*. Mexico: Instituto Nacional de Antropología e Historia, 1966.

Núñez de Haro y Peralta, Alonso, Arzobispo de México. "Edicto de 25 de marzo de 1795 en que condena el sermón de fray Servando Teresa de Mier." In *Bibliografía mexicana del siglo XVIII*, edited by Nicolás León, vol. 1: part 3, 182–187. 6 vols. Mexico City: Imprenta de la viuda de Francisco Díaz de León, 1906.

Olivé Negrete, Julio César. *Estructura y dinámica de Mesoamérica. Ensayo sobre sus problemas conceptuales, integrativos y evolutivos*. Acta Anthropologica, 2nd ed., vol. 1, no. 3. Mexico City: Escuela Nacional de Antropología e Historia, Sociedad de Alumnos, 1958.

Olivé Negrete, Julio César, and Beatriz Barba A. "Sobre la desintegración de las culturas clásicas." *Anales del Instituto Nacional de Antropología e Historia* 9 (1957): 57–71.

*Origen de los mexicanos*. In *Relaciones de Texcoco y de la Nueva España*, by Juan Bautista Pomar et al., 256–280. Introduction by Joaquín García Icazbalceta. Sección Historia, 2. Mexico City: Editorial Salvador Chávez Hayhoe, 1941.

Orozco y Berra, Manuel. *Historia antigua y de la conquista de México*. With a study by Ángel Ma. Garibay K., and a biographical and bibliographical contribution by Miguel León-Portilla. 4 vols. Biblioteca Porrúa, 17–20. Mexico City: Editorial Porrúa, 1960.

Palacio, Vincente Riva. *El virreinato: Historia de la dominación española en México desde 1521 a 1808*. Vol. 2 of *México a través de los siglos*. Mexico City: Publicaciones Herrería, n.d.

Palacios, Enrique Juan. "Teotihuacán, los toltecas y Tula." *Revista Mexicana de Estudios Antropológicos* 5, nos. 2–3: 113–134.

Palerm, Ángel. *Introducción a la teoría etnológica*. Colección del Estudiante de Ciencias Sociales, 1. Mexico: Universidad Iberoamericana, Instituto de Ciencias Sociales, 1967.

Parsons, Elsie Clews. *Mitla, Town of the Souls and other Zapoteco-speaking Pueblos of Oaxaca, México*. Publications in Anthropology. Ethnological Series. Chicago: University of Chicago Press, 1936.

Piña Chan, Román. *Arqueología y tradición histórica: Un testimonio de los informantes indígenas de Sahagún*. Mexico: Impresora de Pavía, 1970. Self-published, based on the author's PhD diss.

Pomar, Juan Bautista. "Relación de Tetzcoco." In *Relaciones de Texcoco y de la Nueva España*, by Juan Bautista Pomar, et al. Introduction by Joaquín García Icazbalceta. Sección de Historia, 2. Mexico City: Editorial Salvador Chávez Hayhoe, 1941.

*Popol Vuh*: *Las antiguas historias del Quiché*. Translated, with introduction and notes, by Adrián Recinos. 7th ed. Colección Popular, 11. Mexico City: Fondo de Cultura Económica, 1964.

Preuss, K. Th. "El concepto de la Estrella Matutina según textos recogidos entre los mexicanos del Estado de Durango, México." Translated by Carmen Leonard. *El México antiguo* 8 (December 1955): 375–96.

Ramírez, Ignacio. "El apóstol Santo Tomás en América." In *Obras*, ed. Ignacio Manuel Altamirano, vol. 1: 323–49. 2 vols. Mexico City: Editora Nacional, 1947.

Ramírez, José F. *El apóstol Santo Tomás en el Nuevo Mundo: Colección de noticias y memorias relativas a la predicación del Evangelio en América antes de su descubrimiento por los españoles, colectadas y ordenadas por*———. In *Bibliografía mexicana del siglo XVIII*, edited by Nicolás León, 3: 353–532. 6 vols. Mexico City: Imprenta de la viuda de Francisco Díaz de León, 1902–1908.

Redfield, Robert, and Alfonso Villa Rojas. *Chan Kom: A Maya Village*. 2nd ed. Chicago: University of Chicago Press, 1964.

"Relación de Chiepetlan, Gro. (1777)." Introduction and paleography by Robert H. Barlow. In *Memorias de la Academia Mexicana de la Historia correspondiente de la Real de Madrid*, 5: 239–56. Mexico City: Academia Mexicana, 1946.

*Relación de genealogía y linaje de los señores que han señoreado esta tierra de la Nueva España, después que se acuerdan haber gentes en estas partes: la cual procuramos de saber los religiosos infrascriptos, sacados de los libros de caracteres de que usaban estos naturales, y de los más* ancianos y que más noticia tienen de sus antepasados; Escrebimos por mandado de nuestro Prelado, a ruego e intercesión de Juan Cano, español, marido de doña Isabel, hija de Montezuma, el segundo deste nombre, Señor que era de la ciudad de México al tiempo que el Marqués D. Hernando Cortés vino a ella, en nombre y como capitán de S. M. In *Relaciones de Texcoco y de la Nueva España*, edited by Juan Bautista Pomar et al., 240–56. Introduction by Joaquín García Icazbalceta. Sección de Historia, 2. Mexico City: Editorial Salvador Chávez Hayhoe, 1941.

"Relación de Nuchistlán." In *Papeles de Nueva España*, edited by Francisco del Paso y Troncoso, segunda serie, 8, no. 1, 59–74. Mexico: Editor Vargas Rea, 1947.

*Relaciones de Yucatán*. 2 vols. Colección de documentos inéditos relativos al descubrimiento, conquista y organización de las antiguas posesiones españolas de ultramar, 2nd series, vols. 11 and 13. Madrid: Establecimiento Tipográfico Sucesores de Rivadeneyra, 1898–1900.

"Relaciones geográficas de la Diócesis de México." In *Papeles de la Nueva España*, published by Francisco del Paso y Troncoso, segunda serie, Geografía y Estadística, vol. 6. Madrid: Est. Tipográfico Sucesores de Rivadeneyra, 1905.

"Relaciones geográficas de la Diócesis de Oaxaca." In *Papeles de la Nueva España*, published by Francisco del Paso y Troncoso, segunda serie, Geografía y Estadística, vol. 4. Madrid: Est. Tipográfico Sucesores de Rivadeneyra, 1905.

"Relaciones geográficas de la Diócesis de Tlaxcala." In *Papeles de la Nueva España*, published by Francisco del Paso y Troncoso, segunda series, Geografía y Estadística, vol. 5. Madrid: Est. Tipográficos Sucesores de Rivadeneyra, 1905.

Reyes, Luis. "Los dioses tribales." *Religión, Mitología y Magia* (Mexico, Museo Nacional de Antropología) 2 (1970): 31–45.

Reyes, Luis. *Textos nawas de Veracruz y Puebla*. Unedited photocopy provided by author.

Rincón Montoya, Ana María. "Una justificación del señorío chichimeca: Estudio de los folios 60 Y 61r. de los Primeros memoriales de Sahagún." Thesis submitted to the Faculty of Philosophy and Letters, National Autonomous University of Mexico, Mexico City, 1971.

Rojas, Gabriel de. "Descripción de Cholula." *Revista Mexicana de Estudios Históricos* 1, no. 6 (November–December 1927): 158–69.

Román y Zamora, Fray Jerónimo. *Repúblicas de Indias: Idolatrías y gobierno en México y Perú antes de la conquista*. 2 vols. Colección de libros raros y curiosos que tratan de América, XIV and XV. Madrid: Victoriano Suárez Editor, 1897.

Ruiz de Alarcón, Hernando. "Tratado de las supersticiones y costumbres gentílicas que oy viuen entre los indios naturales de esta Nueua España, escrito en México, año de 1629." In *Tratado de las idolatrías, supersticiones, dioses, ritos, hechicerías y otras costumbres gentílicas de las razas aborígenes de México*, edited by Jacinto de la Serna et al., 2: 17–130. 2 vols. Mexico City: Ediciones Fuente Cultural, 1953.

Ruz Lhuillier, Alberto. *Guía arqueológica de Tula*. Introduction by Wigberto Jiménez Moreno. Mexico City: Ateneo Nacional de Ciencias y Artes de México, 1945.

Sachse, Úrsula. "Acerca del problema de la segunda división social del trabajo entre los aztecas (Fuentes históricas y análisis lingüístico)." Translated by Juan Brom O. In Traducciones Mesoamericanistas, 1: 73–146. Mexico City: Sociedad Mexicana de Antropología, 1966.

Sáenz, César A. *Quetzalcóatl*. Serie Historia, 8. Mexico City: Instituto Nacional de Antropología e Historia, 1962.

Sahagún, Fray Bernardino de. *Historia general de las cosas de Nueva España*, edited by Ángel Ma. Garibay K. Biblioteca Porrúa, 8–11. 4 vols. Mexico: Editorial Porrúa, 1956.

Sahagún, Fray Bernardino de. "Primeros memoriales." In *Historia general de las cosas de Nueva España*, 4, edited by Francisco del Paso y Troncoso. 4 vols., 1905–8. Madrid: Fototipia de Hauser y Menet, 1905–8 [5, 6 (Cuaderno 2°), 7 and 8].

Salas, Cristóval. "Descripción de Tetiquipa Río-Hondo, hecha por el señor————." *Revista Mexicana de Estudios Históricos* 2, no. 6 (November-December 1928): 114–7.

Saler, Benson. *Nagual, brujo y hechicero en un pueblo quiché*. Cuadernos del Seminario de Integración Social Guatemalteca, Cuarta serie, no. 20. Guatemala: Ministerio de Educación, 1969.

Séjourné, Laurette. "El mensaje de Quetzalcóatl." *Cuadernos Americanos*, year 13, vol. 77, no. 5 (September–October 1954): 159–72.

Séjourné, Laurette. *El universo de Quetzalcóatl*. Preface by Mircea Eliade. Translated by A. Orfila Reynal. Mexico City: Fondo de Cultura Económica, 1962.

Séjourné, Laurette. *Pensamiento y religión en el México antiguo*. Translated by A. Orfila Reynal. Breviarios, 128. Mexico City: Fondo de Cultura Económica, 1957.

Séjourné, Laurette. "Teotihuacan, la ciudad sagrada de Quetzalcóatl." *Cuadernos Americanos*, year 13, vol. 75, no. 3 (May–June 1954): 177–205.

Séjourné, Laurette. "Tula, la supuesta capital de los toltecas." *Cuadernos Americanos*, year 13, vol. 73, no. 1 (January–February 1953): 153–169.

Séjourné, Laurette. *Un palacio en la Ciudad de los Dioses (Teotihuacán): Exploraciones en Teotihuacán, 1955–1958*. Translated by A. Orfila Reynal, with drawings by Abel Mendoza H. Mexico City: Instituto Nacional de Antropología e Historia, 1959.

Seler, Eduardo. "Algo sobre los fundamentos naturales de los mitos mexicanos." In *Colección de disertaciones relativas a la filología y arqueología americana*. Gott, vol. 7, t. 3, primera parte, 284–327. 8 vols. Mexico: Archivo Histórico del Museo Nacional de Antropología e Historia, n.d. Photocopy of the work published in Berlin by A. Asher y Compañía, 1902.

Seler, Eduardo. "Aztlan, patria de los aztecas ¿en dónde estuvo?" In *Colección de disertaciones relativas a la filología y arqueología americana*, vol. 4, t. 2, primera parte, 34–48, 1902.

Seler, Eduardo. *Comentarios al Códice Borgia*. Translated by Mariana Frenk. 2 vols. Sección de Obras de Antropología. Mexico: Fondo de Cultura Económica, 1963.

Seler, Eduardo. "Periodo de Venus en los escritos hieroglíficos del grupo Códice Borgia." In *Colección de disertaciones relativas a la filología y arqueología americana*, vol. 3, t. 1, tercera parte, 112–45, 1902.

Seler, Eduardo. "Quetzalcóuatl-Kukulcán en Yucatán." In *Colección de disertaciones relativas a la filología y arqueología americana*, vol. 3, t. 1, tercera parte, 146–78, 1902.

Seler, Eduardo. "Uitzilopochtli, Dieu de la Guerre des Aztèques." In *Congrès International des Américanistes, Compterendu de la Huitième sesión tenue a Paris en 1890*, 387–400. Paris: Ernest Leroux Editeur, 1892.

Seler, Eduardo. "Wall Paintings of Mitla: A Mexican Picture Writing in Fresco." In *Mexican and Central American Antiquities, Calendar Systems, and History*, edited by Eduard Seler et al., 243–324. Translated under the supervision of Charles P. Bowditch. Smithsonian Institution. Bureau of American Ethnology, Bulletin 28. Washington, DC: Government Printing Office, 1904.

Serna, Jacinto de la. "Manual de ministros de indios para el conocimiento de sus idolatrías y extirpación de ellas." In *Tratado de las idolatrías, supersticiones, dioses, ritos, hechicerías y otras costumbres gentílicas de las razas aborígenes de México*, by Jacinto de la Serna et al., 1: 47–368. 2 vols. Edited, with critical notes, by Francisco del Paso y Troncoso. Mexico City: Ediciones Fuente Cultural, 1953.

Sigüenza y Góngora, Carlos. *Libra astronómica y filosófica*. Introduction by José Gaos. Nueva Biblioteca Mexicana, 2. Mexico City: Universidad Nacional Autónoma de México, Centro de Estudios filosóficos, 1959.

Siméon, Rémi. *Dictionnaire de la Langue Nahuatl ou Mexicaine*. Paris: Imprimerie Nationale, 1885.

Spence, Lewis. *The Gods of Mexico*. London: T. Fisher Unwin Ltd, 1923.

Spinden, Herbert J. *Ancient Civilizations of Mexico and Central America*. Handbook Series, no. 3. New York: American Museum of Natural History, 1928.

Spinden, Herbert J. "New Light on Quetzalcoatl." In *Actes du XXVIII Congrès International des Américanistes, Paris, 1947*, 505–12. Paris: Société des Américanistes, 1948.

Tapia, Andrés de. "Relación de———." In *Crónicas de la conquista, intro., selección y notas de Agustín Yáñez*, 25–78. 3rd ed. Biblioteca del Estudiante Universitario, 2. Mexico City: Universidad Nacional Autónoma de México, 1963.

Tello, Fray Antonio. *Crónica miscelánea de la sancta Provincia de Xalisco*. Critical study by Alfredo Corona Ibarra, with paleographic notes by José Luis Razo Zaragoza. Serie de Historia, 9. 4 vols. Guadalajara: Universidad de Guadalajara/Instituto Nacional de Antropología e Historia/Instituto Jalisciense de Antropología e Historia, 1968.

Thompson, J. Eric S. *Excavations at San José, British Honduras*. Washington, DC: Carnegie Institution of Washington, 1939.

Thompson, J. Eric. *Grandeza y decadencia de los mayas*. Translated by Lauro José Zavala. 2nd ed. Mexico City: Fondo de Cultura Económica, 1964.

Tibón, Gutierre. "El héroe Tepozteco." [Monterrey] *Humanitas*, no. 8 (1967): 449–59.

Tibón, Gutierre. "Mito y magia en la fundación de México." [Monterrey] *Humanitas* no. 11 (1970): 645–83.

*Título de los señores de Totonicapán*, trad. de Dionisio José Chonay, introd. y notas de Adrián Recinos. In [published with] *Memorial de Sololá. Anales de los cakchiqueles*, 209–42. Biblioteca Americana, Serie de Literatura Indígena, 11. Mexico City: Fondo de Cultura Económica, 1950.

Torquemada, Fray Juan de. *Los veinte i vn libros rituales i monarchía indiana, con el origen y guerras, de los indios occidentales, de sus poblaçones, descubrimiento, conquista, conversión y otras cosas marauillosas de la mesma tierra*. 3rd ed. 3 vols. Mexico City: Editorial Salvador Chávez Hayhoe, 1943–1944.

Tozzer, Alfred M. *Chichen Itza and Its Cenote of Sacrifice: A Comparative Study of Contemporaenous Maya and Toltec*. 2 vols. Memoirs of the Peabody Museum of Archaeology and Ethnology, Harvard University, vols. 11–12. Cambridge, MA: Peabody Museum, 1957.

Tozzer, Alfred M. *Landa's Relación de las cosas de Yucatán. A Translation*. Papers of the Peabody Museum, vol. 18. Cambridge, MA: Peabody Museum of American Arcaheology and Ethnology, 1941.

*Unos Annales Históricos de la Nación Mexicana*. Manuscrit Mexicain no. 222. Manuscrit Mexicain no. 22 bis. In *Corpus Codicum Americanorum Medii Aevi*, edited by Ernst Mengin, 2: xxiv–102. Havniae: Sumptibus Einar Munksgaard, 1945.

Vaillant, George C. *La civilización azteca*. Translated by Samuel Vasconcelos. 3rd ed. Mexico City: Fondo de Cultura Económica, 1960.

van Zantwijk, Rudolf. "Los seis barrios sirvientes de Huitzilopochtli." *Estudios de Cultura Náhuatl* 6 (1966): 177–86.

van Zantwijk, Rudolf. "Principios organizadores de los Mexicas: Una introducción al estudio del sistema interno del régimen Azteca." *Estudios de Cultura Náhuatl* 4 (1963): 187–222.

Ventancurt, Fray Agustín de. *Teatro mexicano: Descripción breve de los sucesos ejemplares de la Nueva España en el Nuevo Mundo Occidental de las Indias*. 4 vols. Madrid: José Porrúa Turanzas, 1960.

Veytia, Mariano. *Historia antigua de México, noticia sobre el autor, notas y apéndice de F. Ortega*. 2 vols. Mexico: Editorial Leyenda, 1944.

Villegas, Francisco de. "Relación de los pueblos de Tecuicuilco Atepeq. Coquiapa Xaltianguez." *Revista Mexicana de Estudios Históricos* 2, no. 6 (NovemberDecember 1928): 121–32.

Vogel, Virgil J. *American Indian Medicine*. The Civilization of the American Indian Series. Norman: University of Oklahoma Press, 1970.

Vogt, Evon Z. "H☐iloletik: The Organization and Function of Shamanism in Zinacantan." In *Summa Anthropologica en homenaje a Roberto J. Weitlaner*, 359–69. Mexico City: Instituto Nacional de Antropología e Historia, 1966.

Vogt, Evon Z. "Human Souls and Animal Spirits in Zinacantan." In *Échanges et Communications: Mélanges oferts à Claude Lévi-Strauss à l'occasion de son 60 ème anniversaire*, edited by Jean Pouillon and Pierre Maranda, 1148–67. Offprint, n.d.

Vogt, Evon Z., et al., ed. *Los zinacantecos: Un pueblo tzotzil de los Altos de Chiapas*. Colección de Antropología Social, 7. Mexico: Instituto Nacional Indigenista, 1966.

Weitlaner, Roberto, Pablo Velásquez, and Pedro Carrasco. "Huitziltépec." *Revista Mexicana de Estudios Antropológicos* 9, no. 1–2 (January–December 1947): 47–78.

Zurita, Alonso. "Breve y sumaria relación de los señores y maneras y diferencias que había de ellos en la Nueva España, y en otras poblaciones sus comarcanas, y de sus leyes, usos y costumbres, y de la forma que tenían en les tributar sus vasallos en tiempo de su gentilidad, y la que después de conquistados se ha tenido y tienen en los tributos que pagan a S.M., y a otros en su real nombre, y en el imponerles y repartirlos, y de la orden que se podría tener para cumplir con el precepto de los diezmos, sin que lo tengan por nueva imposición y carga los naturales de aquellas partes." In *Relaciones de Texcoco y de la Nueva España*, by Juan Bautista Pomar et al., 65–206. Introduction by Joaquín García Icazbalceta. Sección de Historia, 2. Mexico City: Editorial Chávez Hayhoe, 1941.

# Index

*Page numbers in italic indicate illustrations.*

Acamapichtli, 98, 179, 180, 185
Acatonale, 111, 139(n40)
Achitometl, 154
Achiutla, 54
Acolhuas, 96
Acopilco, 129
Acosta, Jorge R., 30, 32
Acosta Saignes, Miguel, 77–78, 87, 89
Acuecuexo, 129
Aculhua, 135
Aculmaitl, 77
Aculman, 77
Acuzamil, 9
Acxitl, 132
Acxotlan, 87
"águila y el nopal, El" (Caso), 98
Ah Nacxitl, 31
Ahpop, 4
*ahuehuete*, 90
Ahuitzotl, 128–29
albinos, as sacrifices, 130
alliances, Mexica, 177–78
Almaraz, Ramón, 30
*altépetl* (settlements), names for, 57
Alva Ixtlilxóchitl, Fernando de, 13–14, 49, 130, 131, 142(n112), 161, 186
Amantecas, 60, 62

Amaqueme, 152
Amimitl, 66
*Anales de Cuauhtitlán*, 35, 91, 111, 130
*anciennes villes du Nouveau Monde, Les* (Charnay), 28
Anderson, Arthur, 119
Ann, Saint, 70
Apantecuhtli, 117
*Apologética historia sumaria* (las Casas), 10
architects, Xochimilcas as, 62
Armillas, Pedro, 32, 108
artisans: ethnic groups, 61–62; families, 59, 60; heart power of, 122–23
astrology, 94
astronomy, 18, 25
Asturias, Miguel Ángel, "Culculcan," 41
*átlatl*, invention of, 92
autosacrifice, 8, 36, 152
avatars, 116, 117
Axcaxochitzin, 14
Axolohua, 83, 101–2
Ayauhtitlan, 79
Azcapotzalco, 25, 55, 127, 179, 180
Aztecs. *See* Mexicas
Aztlan, 47, 78, 79, 88, 96, 100, 131, 160; multiple locations of, 81–82
Aztlan Chicomóztoc, 79

Bacab, 10
Balam-Agab, 128
Balam-Quitzé, 89, 128, 138
Bandelier, Adolph, 27
Barrera Vásquez, Alfredo, 153, 158
Bartholomew, Saint, 14
Bartra, Agustí, "Quetzalcoatl," 41
bathing, childbirth and, 93
Batres, Leopoldo, 30
Beauvois, Eugène, 18
Becerra Tanco, Luis, *Felicidad de México*, 14
Benito Juárez (Veracruz), 52
Bernal, Ignacio, 36, 108
binding of years, 91, 96
birth. *See* childbirth
birthdates, 130
bloodletting, Ce Acatl Quetzalcoatl's, 8
Bochica, 17, 18
bodies, preservation of, 136–37
bones, as relics, 137
book burning, by Itzcoatl, 180–82
Boturini, Lorenzo, 15
Borunda, Ignacio, 16
Brackel-Welda, Othón de, 18
Brasseur de Bourbourg, Charles-Étienne, 17
Brendan, Saint, 18
Brinton, Daniel G., 23–24, 28, 55, 78, 79, 116, 148
Broda de Casas, Johanna, 118
Buddhists, 18
bundles. *See* sacred bundles
Burgoa, Francisco de, 14; *Geográfica descripción*, 157

Cahuy, 66
Cakchiquel, 59, 62, 78, 80, 86, 89, 135, 174, 191; deity incarnations, 117–18
calendars, calendrical cycle, 69, 89, 93; chronology in, 95–96; and founding of Mexico-Tenochtitlan, 98–99; migrations and, 99–100; ritual dates, 70, 96–97
*calmécac*, 66
*calpullis*, 44, 48, 95, 113, 115, 160, 171, 173, 177, 178, 181; Culhua, 179–80, 182; occupations and deities of, 45–47(table), 60–61, 69; as social collective, 59–60
Camaxtle, 53, 58, 86, 107, 150, 155
Camaxtli, 9, 27
Canpocolche, 77
captives, treatment of, 155

Caquy, 77
*cargadores* (carriers) of gods, 115
carpenters, Xochimilcas as, 62
Carrasco Pizana, Pedro, 4, 48, 78, 87, 108
Carrión, Jorge, "La ruta psicológica de Quetzalcóatl," 41–42
Casas, Bartolomé de las, *Apologética historia sumaria*, 10
Caso, Alfonso, 4, 30, 33, 184; "El águila y el nopal," 98; *El pueblo del Sol*, 81
Castillo, Cristóbal del, 108, 114, 118, 122, 184
Castillo F., Víctor M., 99
Catherine of Sienna, Pinopiaa as, 70
caves, 83, 135, 137; in creation myths, 51, 52, 80, 82. *See also* Chicomóztoc
Caxcane, 58, 153
Cazcana tribes, 31
*ce ácatl*, 97, 131; as birth year, 14, 24, 150
Ce Acatl, 31, 50, 187; biography of, 29–30; as historic figure, 27, 35, 36, 37; lineages of, 176–77
Ce Acatl Topiltzin, 69, 87
Ce Acatl Topiltzin Quetzalcoatl, 3, 37, 109, 116, 148
Ceballos Novelo, R. J., 30
ceiba trees, homeland and, 83
Cempoallan, 9
*cenotes*, sacrifices in, 83
center of world, Tollan as, 25
Centeutl, 178
ceramic arts, 34, 37
Cervantes de Salazar, Francisco, 78, 138, 189
*ce técpatl*, 98, 99, 131
*ce tochtli*, 94, 97, 98, 100
Chacaltongo, 136
Chadwick, Robert, on Toltec history, 37–38
*chalchihuite* (*chalchiuite*), 55, 137, 150
Chalchiuhtlatonac, 114, 184
Chalchiuhtlicue, 57, 66, 69, 152
Chan Kom, 60
Chapultepec, 97
Charency, Comte de (Charles Félix Hyacinthe Gouhier), 18
Charnay, Désiré, 27, 30; *Les anciennes villes du Nouveau Monde*, 28
Chavero, Alfredo, 13, 28; *Quetzalcóatl*, 41
Chay, 62
Chiauhtla, 11
Chibirias, 10
Chichén Itzá, 29, 31, 32

Chichilcuahuitl, 84
Chichimecas, 13, 14, 61, 62, 84, 126, 175, 177; creation of, 49, 51; migrations, 89, 96; protector gods, 44, 48
Chichitic, 178
*chicome ácatl*, 96, 97
Chicomecoatl, 107
Chicomóztoc, 51, 52, 78, 79, 80, 81, 88, 92, 96, 97, 99, 100, 120, 158
Chicomóztoc-Aztlan, 82
Chicomóztoc-Quinehuayan, 89
Chicomoztoques, 61
Chiconcóac, 83
Chilam Balam, 153, 158
Chilapa, 83
childbirth: death in, 123, 126; of men-gods, 127, 151; at Mixiuhcan, 92–93
children, 121, 123; sacrifices of, 128, 135
Chililico, 189
Chimalma, 3, 8, 9, 31, 51, 150
Chimáloc, 114
Chimalpahin, 91, 119
Chimalpopoca, 128, 135, 148, 180
Chochola, 77
Chololan, 13, 27, 53, 92, 102, 124, 186; Ce Acatl in, 176–77; in Postclassic period, 174, 175
Cholula, 65, 97
Cholultecas, 62
Christianity, 8, 17, 27, 70
Christopher of Chalma, Saint, 70
chronology, in histories, 95–96
Chuahtlequetzqui, 128
*cihuacóatl*, 147, 179
Cihuacoatl, 150
Cihuacoatl Quilaztli, 126
Cihuateteo, 123
Cincalco, 82, 136, 189
Cíncoc, 161
Cinteotl, 161
Cipactonal, 52, 69
cities, city-states, 63, 95, 171; founding of, 83–86, 98; and frontier peoples, 168–69; place names of, 80–81, 112(table)
Citlalatonac, Citlallatonac, 8, 51, 150
Citlalicue, 51
Classic period: "barbarian" peoples and, 168–71; end of, 172–73; religion, 171–72
Clavijero, Francisco Javier, 15
Coacueye, 126, 129–30, 159, 174

Coatemoc, 113
Coatépec, 11, 59, 81, 84, 86, 90, 92, 100, 102, 122, 160; and Huitzilopochtli, 111, 148
Coatépec-Chalco, 87, 137
Coatepec de los Costales (Guerrero), 4, 70, 87
*coatl*, 14, 15
Coatlán, 137
Coatlichan, 84
Coatlicue, 82, 90, 127, 132, 150
Coatzacoalco, 31
Cocolcan, 10
Cocom lords, skulls of, 137
Cocoxtli, 91
Codex/Códice Azcatitlan, 56, *57*, 84, *90*, 99
Codex/Códice Boturini, 75(n146), *85*, 89, *91*, 99, 110
Codex/Códice Carolino, 127
Codex/Códice Chimalpopoca, 38
Codex/Códice Magliabechiano, 43, 158
Codex/Códice Matritense de la Real Academia, 51
Codex/Códice Mexicanus, 99, 109
Codex/Códice Ramírez, 12
Codex/Códice Telleriano-Remensis, 52–53, 56, 94
Codex/Códice Vaticano Latino, 47, 51, 97, 150
codices, 12, 37; patron god guides and, 52–53
Cohuatl Icamatl, 79
Cohuatzontli, 127
Colhuacan, 92
Coltzin, 77
comic books, 42
commoners. See macehualtin
conception, 51; of hombres-dioses, 150–51
conch shells, 12
Condoy, 19
Con-Tici Viracocha, 18
Contzallan, 101, 127
co-optation, of population, 182–83
Copil, 83, 109, 120, 126–27, 128, 129
*copina*, meaning of, 119–20
Coquebezelao, 58
Cora, 25
Cortés, Hernán, as returning man-god, 133–34
cosmography, and place names, 87
cosmology, 147
cosmos, creation of, 49–50
Coyohuacan, 97, 128, 152
Coyohuaques, 156

Coyolxauhqui, 160
Coyotl Inahual, 60, 69
crafts, and ethnic groups, 34, 61–62
craft specialization: *calpulli*, 59–61; and ethnic groups, 61–62; and gods, 66–68; nobility, 63–64
creation, 32, 80, 83, 86; of ethnic groups, 48–49; gods and, 49–50; of humans, 51–52; myths of, 78–79
*Crónica mexicana*, 128
crosses, symbolism of, 7, 17, 18
Cuauhcoatl, 114, 120
Cuauhitzatzin, 83, 152
Cuauhnene, 111
Cuauhquechollan, 9
Cuauhtemoc, 8, 113
Cuauhtitla, 152
Cuauhtitlanecas, 44
Cuauhtlequetzqui, 101, 111, 114, 120, 127, 128, 178, 180, 184
Cuauhtli, 174
Cuchulcan, 37
Cuecuex, 48, 127, 128, 129, 180
Cuecuéxatl, 129
Cuetlaxtlan, 129
Cuextecatl Ichocayan, 79
Cuitlatépec, 83
Cuitlatetelco, 83
Cuitzeo, 127
"Culculcan" (Asturias), 41
Culhua, 65, 83, 97, 154, 179–80, 182
Culhuacan, 65, 77, 78, 81, 82, 91, 99, 131; hombres-dioses in, 150, 154
Culhuacan-Chicomóztoc, 51
Culhuacatépec, 134
cults, Postclassic, 175
Curicaueri, 48

Dahlgren de Jordán, Barbro, 157
dates: favorable and unfavorable, 130; myth-history events, 98–99; and ritual events, 96–97
dawn, as miracle, 86
dead: dressing of, 121–22; preservation of, 136–37
deaths: of hombres-dioses, 124–25, 128–29, 136–37, 138; of leaders, 126–27; of Quetzalcoatl, 3, 29; transformation after, 134–35; violent ritual, 189–90. *See also* sacrifices
deities/gods, 10, 37, 92, 117, 123, 150; and *calpulli*, 60–61; creation and, 32, 48–51; as deified humans, 107–9; dress of, 121–22; and human counterparts, 113, 114–15; of light, 23–24; and occupations, 67–68(table); Postclassic, 176–77; protector, 43–44, 51–53, 58–59, 66; rabbit gods, 120–21; representatives of, 190–91; sacrifices to, 125, 154–56, 189–90. *See also* hombres-dioses; protector/patron gods
*dema*, 44, 160–61
demons, 13; association with, 11, 108; possession by, 119–20
Díaz Infante, Fernando, 41
Dibble, Charles, 119
districts: occupational, 63; names for, 77–78
divination, 70, 93
Domínguez, Berta, *Quetzalcóatl*, 41
dress, of deities and representatives, 121–22, 123, 127
drugs, and sacrifices, 156
duality, of rulership, 147
Duarte, Manuel, *Historia de Quetzalcoatl*, 15
Durán, Diego, 11–12, 43, 54, 70, 89, 110, 135, 189; on Mexico-Tenochtitlan, 84–85
dwarfs, sacrifice of, 130

eagles, 53, 84, 91, 101–2, 147
Echuac, 10
*econitlacapixoani, econime*, 51
ecstatic states, 125
Ehecatl, 31, 175
Ehecatlan, 175
Ehecatl Quetzalcoatl, 161
ejaculation, and loss of power, 124
Eliade, Mircea, 86, 93
El Peñón, 129
encampments, of nomadic bandits, 87–88
Eopuco, 10
Erbalam, 174
esoteric language, in Mayan ritual, 158–59
ethnic groups, 34; creation of, 48–49; occupations and deities of, 61–62; patron gods of, 43–47, 69
evangelists, footprints of, 14
Evening Star, 28, 32, 33, 158

families, 47, 48, 171; craft specialization, 59–60; cultural patrons, 43–44
farmers, Toltecs as, 65
feathered serpent, 87

*Felicidad de México en el principio y milagroso origen que tuvo el Santuario de la Virgen María nuestra Señora de Guadalupe* (Becerra Tanco), 14
*Fénix de Occidente* (Sigüenza y Góngora), 15
fertilization, semen and, 49, 50, 51
festivals, 69, 160; calendrical cycle and, 96–97; and gods, 189–90
fifty-two year cycle, 6, 161; and hombres-dioses, 131–32
fire, 53, 66, 132, 177; ceremonial lighting of, 29, 96, 132
first fathers, 115
fishermen, fishing, 62, 92, 182
floods, Tenochtitlan, 129
Florescano, Enrique, 37
Florentine Codex, 57
foreigners, 17; in Tollan, 12–13
frontier/barbarian peoples, 168–69; labor specialization and, 170–71; religion and, 169–70
Fuentes, Carlos, 42
Fuentes y Guzmán, Francisco, 14, 181

Gagavitz, 59, 135, 153
Galí, Ramón, 30
Gamio, Manuel, 29, 30
García, Gregorio, *Predicación del Santo Evangelio en el Nuevo Mundo*, 13
García Cubas, Antonio, 30
García de León, Antonio, 4
Garibay K., Ángel, 118, 119, 120
garments, of deities and representatives, 121–22, 123, 127
gender, of mountains, 58
*Geográfica descripción* (Burgoa), 157
geography, celestial worlds, 80
god/goddess representatives, 115, 190–91; sacrifice of, 125, 154–56, 189–90
gods. *See* deities/gods
*Gods of Mexico, The* (Spence), 25
González, Yólotl, 108, 111
González Casanova, Pablo, 135
good and evil, Christian concept of, 8
Gouhier, Charles Félix Hyacinthe (Comte de Charency), 18
green stones, 150
guards, gods', 115
Guatemala, 14, 29, 55, 181
Guatezuma, 4, 8, 150

Gucumatz, 19, 31, 37, 50–51, 129
guidance, of patron gods, 52–53
guides, 109, 110(table), 111, 115; protector gods as, 52–53
Guzmán, Nuño de, 127
Guzmán y Córdova, Sebastián, 15

Hacavitz, 134–35
heart, 55, 102; divine power of, 122–23
Hernández, Benito, 54
Hernández, Francisco, 10, 109
Hernández de Córdoba, Francisco, 7
heroes, as gods, 32, 109
Herrera y Pérez, Manuel, 18
Heyerdahl, Thor, 18–19
Hidalgo, as home of Tollan, 29, 33
*Historia de los mexicanos por sus pinturas*, 48, 150
*Historia de México*, 9
*Historia de Quetzalcoatl* (Duarte), 15
*Historia general* (Sahagún), 153
*Historia tolteca-chichimeca*, 129, 147, 150
historiography, 9–12; Bandelier's, 27
history, 89; as cyclical, 93, 94; Itzcoatl and, 183–84; and myth, 148–49, 162–63; time in, 95–96
Holland, William, 55–56, 134
Holmes, William Henry, 30
Holy Trinity (Father, Son, Holy Ghost), 10
hombres-dioses, 115–16, 167, 121, 122, 123; characteristics of, 129–30, 149–53; after death, 136–37, 138; deaths of, 160–61; and fifty-two year cycles, 131–32; final journeys of, 124–25; as leaders, 116–17; leaving and returning of, 132–35; in Mexico-Tenochtitlan, 187–88; miracles of, 128–29; possession and, 119–20; in Postclassic period, 174–76; rebellion by, 125–26; sacrifices of, 154–56; sexual relations of, 157–58; Spaniards and, 13–34, 190–91; succession of, 127–28; *tlatoani* as, 188–89; women as, 126–27
homeland, 82; identifying, 83–84, 178–79; Mexica, 79–80
Hopi, 25
Huactli, 126, 174
Hueiculhuacan, 78
Hueimac, 11
Hueipochtla, 78
Huemac, 13, 14, 15, 31, 107, 108, 116, 126, 142(n132), 150, 152, 154, 174; deaths of, 129,

135, 157, 161; as hombre-dios, 159–60; as ruler, 34, 35, 37–38, 111
Huemac Tezcatlipoca, 24
Huetzin, 29
Huichol, 25
Huiecolhuacan, 124
Huitzilihuitl, 151, 180
Huitzilmoyahual, 127
Huitzilopochtli, 8, 53, 69, 82, 107, 114, 111, 117, 120, 122, 150, 154, 160, 178, 179, 180, 184; birth of, 90, 148; dates associated with, 98, 130, 131; death of, 124, 134, 161; equivalents of, 59, 77; and Mexica, 78, 83, 132–33, 185, 186, 187; and Mexico-Tenochtitlan, 84, 102; myth-history of, 148–49; as patron god, 47, 48, 56; representatives of, 189, 190; transformation of, 108, 118
Huitzilopochtli-Mexi, 47
Huitzilopochtli-Pochtlan, 78
Huitziltépec, 83, 134
Huitznáhuac, 160
Huixtocihuatl, 59
Huixtotin, 62
human remains, preservation of, 136–37
humans, 49, 92, 118, 120; creation of, 51–52; deification of, 107–8, 116; divinization of, 107–8; lives of, 56, 113–14; names of, 114–15. *See also* hombres-dioses
Humboldt, Alexander von, 17
hummingbirds, 108
Hunac Ceel Cauich, 31
hunters, hunting, 24, 62, 66, 92
hurricanes, 135
Hvidtfeldt, Arild, 118, 121

Icelandic missionary, 18
Icxitlan, 135
identity, 60; community, 156–57; and patron/protector gods, 54–55
Ihuitimal, 29
Ilancueitl, 150, 179, 180
Ilhuicatitlan, 186
illness, protector gods, 56
indigenous sources, 3–4
inheritance, of rulership, 111
intoxication, 120–21, 153, 157
Ipalnemohuani, 49–50
Iqi-Balam, 117
Itzamna, 19, 23

Itzcoatl, 113; book burning, 180–82; centralizing history, 183–84
itzlacozauhques amaquemes, 152
Itzmat, 108, 138
Itzpapalotl, 48, 126, 152
Iximché (Guatemala), 29
Ixtlilton, 155
Ixtliltzin, 189
Izcoaclt, 113
Izona, 10
Iztacchalchiuhtlicue, 51
Iztaccihuatl, 69
Iztaccinteutl, 130
Iztacmixcoatl (Iztac Mixcoatl), 2, 44, 69, 79, 118, 150, 179
Iztacmixcohuatzin, 115
Iztactototl, 152
Itztapaltetl, 109

jaguars, 91, 147
Jáltipan (Veracruz), 4
Jensen, Adolf, on *dema*, 160–61
Jesus, Saint, 70
Jesus Christ, Quetzalcoatl as, 19, 42
Jiménez Moreno, Wigberto, 30, 31, 32, 80, 108, 148; on place names, 100–101; on Quetzalcoatl as historic figure, 35, 36, 37
John the Baptist, 70
journeys, of dead men-gods, 124–25

Kabul, 138
Kelly, David H., 25–26, 148
king-priests, as deity incarnation, 116. *See also* rulers, rulership
kinship, 43, 60, 127; among protector gods, 68–69. *See also calpullis*; lineages
Kirchhoff, Paul, 30, 34, 35, 36, 87, 88, 95, 98, 147; on Aztlan, 81–82
Krickeberg, Walter, 35, 89, 92, 116, 121
Kukulcan (Kulkulkan), 4, 19, 30, 31, 37, 186; rise of, 175–76

labor, 60; specialized, 61–62, 170–71
Lafaye, Jacques, *Quetzalcoatl et Guadalupe*, 19
lakes, 92; homeland and, 83, 178–79
land, place on, 95
Landa, Diego de, 137
land ownership, 87
languages, in creation myths, 79

INDEX    223

Larráinzar, 134
leaders, leadership, 114; Postclassic period, 173–75; pueblo, 116–17
Lehmann, Walter, 119
León, Adrián, 127
León Portilla, Miguel, 36, 116, 132, 136, 184; on concept of "heart," 55, 122–23
León y Gama, Antonio, 16–17, 116, 181
lepers, sacrifices of, 130
*Leyenda de los Soles*, 150
lineages, 111, 128, 171, 185; Culhua, 179–80; Quetzalcoatl's, 176–77
López de Gómara, 60; history of Quetzalcoatl, 9–10
Luiseño, 25
Luke, Saint, 70

*macehualtin*, 63, 64, 95
Macuilocelotl, 60
Macuiltochtli, 60
maguey plants, 161
Mahucutah, 128
Malinaltecuhtli, death of, 135
Malinalxochitl, 69, 83, 109, 126, 128, 129, 178, 189
Mames, 130
Manco Capac, 17
*Manuscrito de la Biblioteca Nacional de México*, 80
Mariscal, Mario, 30
Marquina, Ignacio, 30
marriages, 69, 159
Martínez Hernández, Juan, 29
Martínez Marín, Carlos, 82, 89
Martyr, Peter, 7
Matilde Jesús, 24
Matla, 178
Matlalcueye, 58, 135
Matlatzincas, 156
Maxtla, 135, 148, 180
Maxtlaton, 128
Maxtlatzin, 127
Maya, 34, 52, 78, 79, 80, 137, 174; deification of men, 107–8; esoteric language in, 158–59; gods of light, 23, 24; on hombres-dioses, 121, 134–35; titles and surnames, 31–32
Mayahuel, 66, 161, 189
Meconetzin, 4, 135
Meliapor, St. Thomas in, 16, 17

*Memoriales con escolios*, 130
Mendieta, Gerónimo de, 12
Mendoza, Antonio de, 8
Mendoza, Diego de, 8
Mengin, Ernest, 99
men-gods. *See* hombres-dioses
merchants, 60, 62, 66; pueblo names and, 77–79
metal, 33
metates, and Xibalbá, 80
Meteuitli, 178
Mexi, 48, 77, 179
Mexicas, 47, 62, 101, 111, 135, 136, 154, 187; historical cycle, 95, 96, 132–33, 148; hombres-dioses, 117, 132–33; homeland, 79–80, 83; identity of, 54–55; migrations of, 83, 89, 92, 109, 113, 116; patron gods of, 48, 66, 78; power relations, 177–78, 185–86; rulership, 64–65, 184–85; *tlaquimilolli*, 53–54
Mexicatzinco, 100, 101, 113
Mexico, 77
Mexico, Valley of, 29
Mexico City, 78
Mexico la Vieja, 78
Mexico-Tenochtitlan, 61(table), 63, 81, 114, 133, 171, 190; founders of, 47, 111; founding of, 53, 83–86, 98–99, 100, 101–2, 178–79; god representatives in, 155–56; governmental structure of, 187–88; power, 185–86; rebuilding of, 184–85; rulers of, 147, 180–81; *tlatoani* in, 188–89; water and, 128–29
Mexico-Tlatelolco, founding of, 53, 102, 178
Mexitin, 48, 51, 90, *91*
Mexitli, 48, 77
Meztliapan, 81
Miahuaxihuitl, 151
Michabo the Algonquin, 23–24
Michoaqueños, 77
Mictlantecuhtli, 51, 135, 178
Mier, Servando Teresa de, 16
migrants, frontier, 168–69
migrations, 31, 49, 69, 80, 82, 147, 173; and calendrical dates, 99–100; and childbirth, 92–93; historical figures in, 109, 113–14; histories of, 95, 178; locating place, 178–79; Mexica, 83, 96, 111, 116, 148; nomadic hunters, 33, 87–88; and patron god guide, 52–53, 56; places in, 88–89; pueblos, 62–63; trees in, 90–91
militarism, Postclassic period, 173
military, 62, 64, 123, 129, 172, 184

Milky Way, gods of, 150
miracles, 86, 90; and city founding, 83–84; of conception, 150–51; of hombres-dioses, 128–29
mirror, Tezcatlipoca's, 54
missionaries, foreign, 18
Mitla (Yooba), 136
Mixcoas, 44, 49
Mixcoatépec, 135
Mixcoatl, 31, 32, 36, 135, 150, 152
Mixcoatl, Andrés, 117, 125–26, 128, 191
Mixcoatl Camaxtle, 150
Mixiuhcan, 92–93, 101, 127
Mixteca, 62
Mixteca Alta, dynasties of, 38
Mixtecatl, 150, 154, 177
Mixtecs, 34, 66, 84, 125, 135, 136, 188; codices, 37–38
Mixtitlan, 79
*mocexiuhtzauhqui*, 190
*mocihuaquetzqui*, 126
Mohedano, Hugo, 30
Molina, Alonso de, 118–19, 120
Moon, 18, 25
Moquihuix, 135, 148
Morning Star, 24, 29, 186; Quetzalcoatl as, 32, 158
Motecuhzoma, 8
Motecuhzoma Ilhuicamina, 82, 111, 129, 130, 132, 151, 184
Motecuhzoma Xocoyotzin, 63, 65, 65, 82, 121, 136, 171, 185, 187, 189, 190, 191; and Cortés, 133–34
Motolinía, 8, 64, 134
mountains, 57, 58; hombres-dioses and, 134–35; and protector gods, 58–59
*moyóhual/moyáhual*, in women's names, 126–27
*moyohualittoani*, 127
Muiscas, 24
Mújica Diez de Bonilla, Francisco, 30
mummies, 137
Muñoz Camargo, Diego, 12, 53, 80
mushrooms, 125
Mutul, 130
myths, 9, 153–54; biblical influence on, 89–90; creation, 48–49, 78–79; and history, 148–49, 162–63; time in, 93–94

Nacxit, 175, 176

Nacxitl, 4, 37, 123
*nahuales*, 82, 118, 125
*nahualistas*, 137
*nahualli*, 55, 118
Nahualpilli, 107
Nahuas, 4, 24, 52, 58, 64, 68, 72(n36), 86, 96, 121, 175; protector gods, 43, 56; transformation after death, 134–35
names, 4, 44, 111; of gods, 48, 109; of gods and humans, 113, 114–15; of hombres-dioses, 151–52; of homelands, 79–80; of pueblos, 57, 77–78, 92; of women leaders, 126–27
Nanahuatzin, 90
Nappatecuhtli, 55, 56, 107, 155
Nauhyotl, 135
Navarrete, Carlos, 87
Nayarit, 137
necromancer, Quetzalcoatl as, 13, 18
Nerthus, 19
Nestorians, 18
new fire ceremonies, 29, 91, 96, 132
*neyomaxitliztli*, 156
Nezahualcoyotl, 14, 129, 135, 148, 186, 188
Nezahualpilli, 135, 148, 151, 161, 181, 189
Nicarao, 109, 188
Nicholson, H. B., 36, 41, 44
Njordr, 19
nobility: Culhua, 182–84; schools for, 65, 66; specialized tasks of, 63–64
nomadic hunters, 33; encampments of, 87–88
Nonoalcos, 31
Nonohualcos, 37, 129
nopal and eagle, 84, 101–2
Nopaltzin, 14
Nowotny, Karl, 122
nudity, invention of, 92
numbers, numerology, 98, 147
Núñez de la Vega, Francisco, 137

Oaxaca, 177
Obregón, Jorge, 30
occupations, 72(n36); and deities, 59–61, 67–68(table); and ethnic groups, 61–62; nobility, 63–64; Toltec, 65–66
Ocelotl, Martín, 126, 191
Ocosingo, 78
Ocotecuhtli, 48
Ocuituco, 11
Ojedo, Juan de, 14

Olivé, Julio, 170
Olmec, 62, 89, 97
*ome ácatl*, 100
Ometochtli, 48, 191
Ome Tochtzin, 190
Opochtli, 107
orators, 62
Orchilobos, 8, 150
*Origen de los mexicanos*, 135
Orozco y Berra, Manuel, 13, 18
Ortiz Rubio, Pascual, 42
Othón de Mendizábal, Miguel, 29
Otomís, 31, 44, 48, 83
Otomitl, 150
Otontecuhtli, 48, 108
Oxomoco, 52, 69
Oztoteotl, 70

Pa Civán, 52, 80
Pahtecatl, 66
painters, ethnic groups, 61–62
Palacios, Enrique Juan, 29, 30–31
Palerm, Ángel, 168
Panoayans, 92
Panocos, 92
Pánuco, 12
Panutlans, 92
Papa, 11, 89
Papago, 25
Paroxoné, 135
patron gods. *See* protector/patron gods
patrons, cultural, 43–44
patron saints, protector gods as, 70–71
Pa Tulán, 52, 80
penitence, of hombres-dioses and priests, 152–53
personages, multiplicity of, 111; names of, 112(table). *See also* hombres-dioses
Petela, 137
Petlatzinco, 84
pilgrimages. *See* migrations
Piltzintecuhtli, 178
Piña Chan, Román, 36, 37, 116, 125
Pinopiaa, 70, 137
Pipil, 31
*pipiltin*, 64, 65, 66
*Pirámide del Adivino* (Pyramid of the Magician; Uxmal), 3
place names, 33, 87, 100–101, 109, 110, 111–12; for childbirth, 92–93; and cities, 80–81, 86; gods and occupations in, 77–78; for homelands, 79–80
Place of the Sun. *See* Tollan
Plancarte y Navarrete, Francisco, 29
plays, 41
Pleistocene mammals, burials of, 137
*Pluma rica, nuevo fénix de América*, (Ramírez), 15
Pochotl, 14
Pochteca, 62, 83
Pochtlan, 87
Pochtlantzinco, 78
poetry, 41
polytheism, 169–70
Pomar, Juan Bautista, 176–77
Popocatepetl, 68
possession, hombre-dios, 119–20
Postclassic period, 171; leadership in, 173–74
potters, pottery, 62, 80
power, 118, 124, 125, 138; divine, 126, 129; of heart, 122–23; Mexica, 177–78; origins of, 116–17; political, 128, 171
Poyauhtécatl, 129
Pozonaltépetl, 92
*Predicación del Santo Evangelio en el Nuevo Mundo, viviendo los apóstoles* (García), 13
pregnancy, Chimalma's, 51
Preuss, Konrad Theodor von, 24, 148
priests, 32, 127, 173, 188; and Mexica homelands, 178–79; penitence of, 152–53; ritual behavior of, 155, 156; sacrifices made by, 83–84; sexual relations of, 157, 158
priest-rulers, 44, 116
priest-warrior-guides, 44
primal couples, and pueblos, 52
*Primeros memoriales* (Sahagún), 109
prisoners, treatment of, 155
prisoners of war, sacrifice of, 189
progenitors, of hombres-dioses, 150, 151(table)
protector/patron gods, 78, 87, 109, 115, 178, 179; appropriation of, 183–84; bundles of, 53–54; of ethnic groups and cities, 43–47; as guides, 52–53, 110; kinship relationships of, 68–69; as patron saints, 70–71; in Postclassic period, 173–74; of pueblos, 51–52, 55–56; and rulers, 58–59; warfare and, 54–55
proverbs, Nahua, 4
*pueblo del Sol, El* (Caso), 81
pueblos, 44, 50, 58, 167, 170; founding of, 85–86;

leadership, 116–17, 173–74; locations of, 85–86; migrations of, 52–53, 62–63; names for, 57, 77–78, 79–80, 92; patron/protector gods of, 45–47(table), 48, 51–52, 54–56, 69, 115; spatial distribution of, 87–88
pulque, 66, 92, 156; production of, 170–71
Pyramid of the Magician (Uxmal), 3

Qhuav, 66
Qotuha, 117
Quechua, 24
Quequetzalcoah, 130, 158
Quetzalcoatl, 23, 27, 31, 35, 50, 51, 107, 111, 116, 117, 135, 137, 154, 160, 167, 174, 175, 178, 183, 185, 187; biography of, 150, 151, 152, 153; after death, 136, 137; death of, 29, 161, 186; and fifty-two year cycle, 131–32; final journey of, 124–25; as foreigner, 12–13; as historical figure, 8, 28, 36–38; lineages of, 176–77; as patron/protector god, 66, 87; in representatives of, 155, 189; sexual relations of, 157–58; whiteness of, 130–31
"Quetzalcoatl" (Bartra), 41
*Quetzalcóatl* (Chavero), 41
*Quetzalcóatl* (Domínguez), 41
Quetzalcoatl Chalchihuitl, 17–18
*Quetzalcoatl et Guadalupe: Eschatologie et histoire au Mexique (1521–1821)* (Lafaye), 19
Quetzalcoatl Huemac, 13–14
Quetzalmoyohuatzin, 101, 127
Quetzalpetlatl, 28–29, 152
Quiché, 58, 6, 78, 79, 80, 83, 86, 138, 181; deities, 37, 51; hombres-dioses, 129, 152, 153; incarnations of deities in, 117–18
Quilaztli, 189
Quinehuayan, 120

rabbit gods, 120–21
rains, 25, 56, 57
Ramírez, José Fernando, 161; *Pluma rica, nuevo fénix de América*, 15
rattlesnakes, images of, 56, 57
Rea, Alonso de la, 77
rebellion, 172, 182, 191
Recinos, Adrián, 59, 78
Red Tezcatlipoca, 48
*Relación de Coatepec-Chalco*, 153
*Relación de Mexicaltzinco*, 101
*Relación de Tilantongo*, 157
*Relaciones de Yucatán*, 77, 108–9, 130

*Relaciones geográficas*, 47
relics, 122, 137; in sacred bundles, 53–54
religion, 43, 48; Classic period, 171–72; collapse of Mesoamerican, 69–70; polytheistic, 169–70; Postclassic period, 175–76
Renaissance, 9
resistance, to Spanish domination, 125–26
Reyes, Luis, 44, 108, 161
riddles, in sacred language, 158–59
Ríos, Pedro de Los, 8
ritual dates, 70, 96–97
rituals, 86; city founding, 83–84; esoteric language and, 158–59; god representatives, 155–56, 189–90. *See also* sacrifices
Román y Zamora, Jerónimo, 12
Ruiz, Marcos, 130
Ruiz de Alarcón, Hernando, 59
rulers, rulership, 108, 110(table), 122, 161; bodies of, 136–37; Culhua, 179–80, 182; after death, 134–35, 136–37; lineages of, 111, 128; as men-gods, 116–17; Mexica, 64–65, 184–85; Mexico-Tenochtitlan, 98, 147, 148, 180–81, 187–88; protector gods and, 58–59; Tollan, 31, 34–35
Ru Ralcan, 4, 186
"ruta psicológica de Quetzalcóatl, La" (Carrión), 41–42
Ruz, Alberto, 30, 32

sacred bundles (*tlaquimilolli*), 115, 131, 137–38, 117; divine power of, 122, 123–24; in migrations, 56, 57, 114; of protector gods, 44, 53–54
sacred places, 82
sacrifices, 91, 96, 130, 131, 152, 160–61, 175, 186; of children, 128, 135; city founding and, 83–84, 85, 102; of god/goddess representatives, 125, 154–56, 189–90; Mexica, 185, 187; Yucatecan Maya, 82–83
Sáenz, César, 36
Sahagún, Bernardino de, 11, 33, 55, 70, 92, 109, 120, 136, 151, 174; on *tlatoani*, 188–89
saints, 34; patron, 70–71
San Antonio Tula (San Luis Potosí), 78
San Juan Atitlán, 130
San Juan de Ulúa, 65
San Martín mountains, 153
San Mateo Pochtlan, 77–78
San Pedro Tula, 78
Santiago Poxtla, 78
Satan (Devil), 13; possession by, 119–20; and

Quetzalcoatl, 8, 12
schools, for nobility, 65, 66
Schultze-Jena, Leonard, 118
sea crossings, in Chichimec migration history, 89
seasons, struggle between Quetzalcoatl and Tezcatlipoca and, 25
Séjourné, Laurette, 33
Seler, Eduard, 24–25, 79, 81, 108, 148, 157
semen, descent of fertilizing, 49, 50, 51
semiprecious stones, worship of, 137
serpents, 56, 57, 84, 87
servants, god's, 115
services, specialized, 64
settlements. *See* pueblos
sexual relations, hombres-dioses and, 153, 157–58
shamans, 127. *See moyohualittoani; nahuales*
short stories, 41
sickness, and deities' power, 121, 122
Sigüenza y Góngora, Carlos, *Fénix de Occidente*, 15
Siméon, Rémi, 119
singers, 62
social system, families and, 59–60
Sololá, 191
space, and time, 95
Spaniards, 3, 4, 7, 14, 136; and god representatives, 190–91; as returning hombres-dioses, 133–34
Spence, Lewis, 122, 148; *The Gods of Mexico*, 25
Spinden, Herbert J., 29
spirit/soul (*tonalli*), 55, 56
springs, origin of, 129
stelae, from Tula, 30
stone carvings, images of Quetzalcoatl, 37
suicide, ritual, 161
Sun, 25, 37, 50, 86, 153
supreme creator, names of, 49–51
surnames, protector gods and, 44
Suyuá (Suiuá; Suivá), 158

Tacuba, 181
talking boxes (*cajas parlantes*), 53
Tamoanchan, 51, 80, 88, 90
Tarascans, patron god, 48
Tecpanecas Culhuaques, 96
Tecpanecatl Tecuhtli, Gonzalo, 130–31
Tecpatzin, 134, 161
Tecpayo, 134, 161
Tecuanipan-Amaquemecan-Chalco-Pochtlan, 78
Tecuhtli, 131
Tehuacanos, 188

Telpochtli Tezcatlipoca, John the Baptist as, 70
Temazcatitlan, 93
temples, 54, 142(n112)
Tenayuca Mountains, 16
Tenoch, 120, 178, 179
Tenochca, 60, 62, 179, 180, 186
Tenochtitlan. *See* Mexico-Tenochtitlan
tentzonteotl, 70
Tenuch, 150, 179
Teotihuacan, 25, 33, 58, 90, 92, 124, 136; as Tollan, 29, 30–31, 33–34
Teotlixcas, 156–57
Teotloquenahuaque, 49–50
Tepanecas, 54–55, 179, 187
Tepaneca Tezozomoc, 180
Tepantitla, 58
*tepeílhuitl* (feast of the mountains), 56
Tepemaxalco, 99, 100
Tepetecuhtli, 129, 148
Tepetícpac, 131
Tepetzinco, 120
Tepeuhqui, 4
Tepeyácac, 70
Tepoztecas, 48
Tepoztecatl, 48, 60, 135
Tepozteco, 150
Tepoztlán, 48, 135
Tetzahuitl, 107, 117, 122
Tetzahuitl-Huitzilopochtli, 108, 115
Tetzauhteotl, 84, 108, 114, 124, 184; after death of, 136–37
Tetzauhteotl Yaotequihua, 114
Tetzcocanos, 62, 89, 129, 186
Tetzcoco, 100, 129, 153, 181, 186
Tetzcozinco, 100
Tetzinco, 101
Teuculhuacan, 78
Teuhtli, 68
Texcalco, 51
Texcoco, Lake, 25, 178–79
Texpolcatl, 158
Tezcatlipoca, 9, 12, 13, 24, 31, 32, 33, 35, 50, 56, 58, 107, 156, 158, 178; objects related to, 53, 54; representative of, 153, 190–91; struggle with, 18, 25, 28
Tezcatlipoca-Camaxtli, 24
Tezozomoc, 128, 135, 148
Tezozómoc, Alvarado, 54, 96, 102, 141(n94)
Theotbilche, 109

Thomas, Saint, in the Americas, 13, 14, 15, 16–17
Thompson, J. Eric, 31, 111
Thunder, representative of, 191
Three Kings Day, 42
Tianquizmanalco, 70
Tibón, Gutierre, 81
Tilantongo, 38
Timal, 129
time, 98, 161; cycles of, 93, 94, 96, 132–33; in histories, 95–96
Tiquinbalón, 174
Titlacahuan, 107, 189; representatives of, 155–56
Tizahua, 60
Tlacaelel, 111, 129
Tlacahuepan, 155, 189
Tlacatecolotl Tetzauhteotl, 118
*tlacaxipehualiztli*, 189
Tlachihualtepetl, 174
Tlahuizcalpantecuhtli, 31, 32, 175
Tlailotlaques Toltecas, 62
Tlalcocomolco, 84
Tlaloc, 28, 57, 58, 59, 82, 102, 134, 135, 178, 186
Tlalocan, 57, 135
*tlaloque*, 58
Tlaltecuhtli, 50
Tlamacazqui, 31, 178
Tlapaltecatl Opochtli, 191
Tlapanecos, 48
Tlapco, 25
Tlappan, 25, 137, 156
*tlaquimilolli. See* sacred bundles
Tlateloa, 102
Tlatlauhqui Tezcatlipoca, 56, 158
Tlatlayan, 25
Tlatlelolca Mexica, 102, 179
*tlatoani*, 147, 179, 180, 185; as hombres-dioses, 188–89
*tlatoque*, 180, 183
Tlatzallan, 99, 100, 114
Tlaxcala, 70, 78, 133, 135, 191
Tlaxcalteca, 89
tlaxilacallis, 60
Tlillan Tlapallan, 36, 137
Tlohtepetl, 114, 127
Tlohtepetl Xiuhcoatl, 114
Tloque Nahuaque, 50
Tochtepec, 78
Toci, 70, 155
Tohil, 31, 37, 66, 152

Tollan, 4, 9, 12, 18, 24, 25, 28, 62, 78, 92, 97, 124, 131, 138, 158; hombres-dioses in, 150, 152; and Huemac, 159–60; as mythical place, 79, 80, 88; in Postclassic period, 174, 177; rulers of, 34–35, 36, 37; Teotihuacan as, 29, 30–31, 33–34
Tollan Chalco, 80
Tollan-Teotihuacan, 29, 30–31
Tollantzinco, 28, 101, 152
Tollan-Xicocotitlan, 29, 30, 101
Tolocan, 77
Toltecas, 13, 24, rulers, 34–35
Toltecs, 4, 14, 25, 28, 31, 33, 62, 79, 98, 101, 110, 111, 185, 186; home of, 29, 32, 83; occupations of, 65–66; rulers, 34–35, 36, 37–38
Tolutépetl, 77
Tolutzin, 77
Tomoanchan, 79, 83
*tonalámatl* (divinatory almanac), 25
*tonalli*, 55, 56
Tonantzin, 70
Topiltzin, 4, 11–12, 14, 25, 31, 36, 109, 120, 135, 186
Topiltzin Aacxitl Quetzalcoatl, 17–18
Topiltzin Meconetzin, 13–14, 132, 133, 158
Topiltzin Quetzalcoatl, 37, 50, 185
toponyms, 84, 87; for settlements, 77–78
Torquemada, Juan de, 8, 12–13, 62, 96
Totec Tlatlauhqui Tezcatlipoca, 48, 156, 183
Totepeuh, 111, 150, 152
Totolimpanecas, 48
Totollini, 48
Totomihuaques, 96
Totonac, Totonacas, 48, 152–53, 175
Toxcatl, 160, 191
Toyua Yoco, 66
Tozzer, Alfred, 4–5, 31
transformation, 118, 125, 137; of persons and gods, 108–9; of women, 126–27
trees, in migration stories, 90–91
tribal alliances, Mexica, 177–78
tribute system, Mexica, 64
Tula (Hidalgo), 29, 30–31, 78, 80
Tulán, 52, 78, 79, 80, 83, 89
Tula-Xicocotitlan, 31, 32, 33, 37, 138, 186
Tutul, 175
Tutulla, 175
Tzapotlatenan, 107
Tzatzitépetl, 87
Tzeltales, 37
Tzintzuntzan, 77

Tzinzuni, 77
*tzitzimime*, 161
Tzompantecuhtli, 185, 186
Tzotzil, protector gods, 58–59
Tzotziles, 51, 55–56, 71, 134
Tzotzompan, 161
Tzutzuma, 129
Tzutzumatzin, 128, 129, 135, 148
Tzutzumpa, 130

Ulmecatl, 150
underworld, 49, 82
upperworld, 49
urban centers, 63; Classic period, 171–73
Utatlán, 58
Uxmal, 3

Vaillant, George C., 25
vegetation, gods of, 37, 161
Velásquez, Pablo, 78
Venus, 18, 28, 32, 33, 37, 151
Vetancurt, Agustín de, 15
Veytia, Mariano, 15
villages: barbarian, 168–71; religion, 171–72
violence, Postclassic, 175–76
Virgin of Guadalupe, 16, 17, 70
Votan, 18, 19, 37
Vucub Pec, 52
Vucub Zíván, 52, 78

warfare: Culhua nobility and, 182, 183; Mexica and, 184–85, 187; and protector gods, 54–55
warriors, 16–17, 61, 62, 108, 127, 173
water, 89, 174; deities of, 56, 59, 66; in myth-histories, 128–29; and settlements, 57–58
water-mountains, settlements as, 58
Weitlaner, Roberto, 78
wind god, 12, 27, 32
women: death in chidlbirth, 123, 126; transformation of, 126–27
world order, 49

Xelahuh, 79

Xelhuan, 83, 150
Xelua, 150
Xibalba, 80, 83, *86*
Xicalanca, 89, 97
Xicalancatl, 150
*xicalcoliuhqui*, 34
Xicco, 135
Xicomoyahual, 126–27
Xilo, 60
Xilonen, 155
Ximoayan, 189
*xip*, *xipe*, 118–19
Xipe Totec, 47, 109, 189
Xippacoyan, 152
Xiues, 37
Xiuhtecuhtli, representatives of, 155
Xiuhtlacuilolxochitzin, 126, 152, 174
Xiuhtlati, 60
Xochicalco, 37
Xochilmilco, 78, 189
Xochimilcas, 62, 91, 111, 181
Xochiquetzal, 12, 158, 180
Xocotl, 48
Xolotl, 14, 51, 111
Xomoco, 178
Xomuco, 48
Xuchit, 31

Yiacatecuhtli, 69, 107
Yooba (Mitla), 136
Yucatán, 7, 29, 78; Kukulcan in, 175–76
Yucatecan Maya, 188; sacrifices, 82–83
Yutoazteca, Quetzalcoatl and, 26

Zaachiylla, 135
Zacatépec, 154
Zacmutul, 130
Zactecauh, 59
Zapotecs, 34, 58, 70, 130, 135, 136, 137, 157, 188
Zeetoba, 136
Zinacantan, Tzotzil in, 58–59

www.ingramcontent.com/pod-product-compliance
Ingram Content Group UK Ltd.
Pitfield, Milton Keynes, MK11 3LW, UK
UKHW042122200326
4879IPUK00002B/23